To my loving wife,

Love Cliff

The Joy of being a Woman

Compiled and Edited by

Duane S. Crowther

and

Jean D. Crowther

International Standard Book Number 88290-015-3
Library of Congress Catalog Card Number 72-88910

Ninth Printing . . . . . August, 1977

Printed in the
United States of America
by

Horizon Publishers
& Distributors
P.O. Box 490
50 South 500 West
Bountiful, Utah 84010

Who can find a virtuous woman? for her price is far above rubies.

The heart of her husband doth safely trust in her, so that he shall have no need of spoil.

She will do him good and not evil all the days of her life.

She seeketh wool, and flax, and worketh willingly with her hands. ...

She stretcheth out her hand to the poor; yea, she reacheth forth her hands to the needy. ...

She maketh herself coverings of tapestry; her clothing is silk and purple.

Her husband is known in the gates, when he sitteth among the elders of the land.

She maketh fine linen, and selleth it; and delivereth girdles unto the merchant.

Strength and honour are her clothing; and she shall rejoice in time to come.

She openeth her mouth with wisdom; and in her tongue is the law of kindness.

She looketh well to the ways of her household, and eateth not the bread of idleness.

Her children arise up, and call her blessed; her husband also, and he praiseth her. ...

Favour is deceitful, and beauty is vain: but a woman that feareth the Lord, she shall be praised.

Give her of the fruit of her hands; and let her own works praise her in the gates.

(Proverbs 31: 10-13, 20, 22-28, 30-31)

FROM VISION TO FULFILLMENT

How
The Joy of Being A Woman
Was Created

The idea was there for many months, prompting us and crying out to be heard: there is a need for careful presentation of the wisdom and values of outstanding Latter-day Saint women concerning woman's roles in the modern world.

Idea was translated into action! We searched, striving to identify those choice women who had real insights to share, who had achieved, whose words would be respected because of their background and accomplishments. We sought special women of all ages.

Our quest was to find exuberant, lovely young ladies who could reflect the joy of woman still in her youth, and young mothers to depict the challenges and rewards of today's family. The search also reached out for women who had achieved in the arts—music, literature, and drama—and the insights of women successful in professional life. The wisdom of mothers of grown and maturing families was desired. We looked, also, for the refinement and dignity of women more advanced in years, who could share the insights of the matriarch, the grandmother and the widow. Hundreds of LDS women had the potential for helping write this book, but we finally reduced the list to a select few.

Then came that day on the phone, when we reached out across the nation with invitations to participate. Would they accept? Would these busy people be willing to devote the time and labor necessary to write, even though some were not experienced in writing? The response was overwhelming! We were amazed at their interest, their willingness, their graciousness, their desire to do their very best.

Each of these lovely women was asked to submit four or five topics about which she felt qualified to write. As editors, we then selected the subjects and approaches which we felt would best harmonize with the rest of the book. Each author was asked to write a chapter which was useful, and really filled with their suggestions concerning things which had worked well for them. The book was intended to be a helpful and valuable guide to living and functioning effectively and meaningfully in the many roles of womanhood. We asked each author to reveal herself and her family by drawing from many personal experiences, including some background about the national contests in which they had been judged so outstanding. It was our desire, too, that they share their attitudes concerning womanhood and about many of the important things in their life. These sisters were asked to approach their subjects carefully and to prayerfully seek inspiration and guidance as they wrote. All this was to be done quickly, for the deadline was only a few short weeks ahead.

The phone kept ringing as we labored to coordinate the effort. Laraine Day wrote her chapter in Switzerland and we communicated via her secretary in California, Beverly Allen. Lenore Romney wrote a page a day, with interruptions to attend the funeral of President Joseph Fielding Smith and the Republican National Convention. Her efforts were coordinated with calls by her secretary, Linda Schwarton, from Washington. Leone Doxey was traveling in Europe when we first contacted the authors. Our letter was waiting for her when she returned. With her usual efficiency she went to work immediately and was one of the first to complete her chapter. Joan Fisher, like several others, called and read pages of her work to us over the phone, seeking advice and criticism. Sherri Zirker and Rene Morin both have husbands who are regional coordinators in the BYU Admissions Adviser program. They met with Duane, who holds the same calling, while the men attended an advisor's convention at Brigham Young University.

Some worked under extra pressures: Jo Oaks had a baby before she could complete her chapter. Charlotte Maxfield gave birth to a son the week after she finished. Stella Oaks finished her chapter as she worked her last days before retiring. Karen Herd sandwiched her efforts between world-wide travels as a Miss America representative. Jaynann Payne dropped her manuscript off on the way to the airport, as she flew to speak at a series of Church Education Weeks in the northwest. She had held a wedding reception in her home several weeks earlier, and did her writing in between all the preparations for the event. Rebecca Glade moved to Chile, where her husband is a new mission president, and finished her chapter as she met the new challenges of becoming a mission mother. Every one of the authors of this book is a busy woman with many demands on her time.

As we talked to the authors, two things impressed us. First was their humility and respect for the other participants. Each seemed thrilled to be associated with the others, yet determined that her work would meet a high standard so as to be of the same quality as she felt the others were producing. We were impressed, too, with the spiritual approach they made to the task. Many sought special blessings from their husbands, for instance, to obtain strength and insight for the task.

The chapters arrived and the labor of editing began. We each went through every chapter with care, performing the many little tasks which are the lot of the editor. It was then that we began to fully grasp the scope of this book. We saw wisdom and models for meaningful living in each chapter and found idea after idea that could be applied in our own marriage and family to add richness and joy to our life. These concepts, we feel, are of universal value and can be applied in every home.

Various titles were suggested by the authors and others. We listed over fifty, wrestled with the possible choices, conducted several informal opinion surveys, and finally selected *The Joy of Being A Woman*. It was adapted from one of the title suggestions made by Elaine Cannon. We feel it's an excellent title which emphasizes the vitality of the authors and their chapters.

The book is organized in a chronological fashion, with an introductory chapter, then chapters by our two youngest contributing authors. Their words are directed to the younger woman who has yet to be wed. Then comes a series of chapters concerned with the young, growing family. The middle section contains chapters which help to define and enhance various aspects of woman's femininity, creativity and charm. The final chapters treat the numerous roles which today's woman must play and reveal the challenges and rewards of those entering the full maturity of life.

When typesetting began we searched for a new type face which would reflect the vitality and charm of the active, modern woman. We chose *Theme*, a contemporary type noted for its simplicity and clarity.

As our role changed from editor to publishers we conferred with artists, engravers, printers, and binders. Each one, as he learned of the nature and authors of the book, and as he became acquainted with the contents in greater detail, commented that the book was useful, vital, relevant, and one that will be widely read by women of all ages.

We feel that way too. Our association with these lovely women, and our intimate acquaintance with the words they have written, have brought pleasure and growth to us. It is evident, too, that their wisdom has broad application for all women. There is much in this book, with its variety of points of view, from which everyone can profit. Above all, the guidance for meaningful living by these outstanding LDS women clearly depicts *The Joy of Being A Woman*.

Jean D. Crowther
Duane S. Crowther
(compilers and editors)

TABLE OF CONTENTS

INTRODUCING — ELAINE A. CANNON

Elaine is a choice example of a woman who has combined the roles of wife and homemaker with a professional life and extensive community service.

She and her husband, D. James Cannon, have together raised six children. But during these busy family years she has also published over 3,000 columns, books, articles, and manuals. She has been a daily columnist and editor for newspapers in Salt Lake City for thirty years, has been a reporter of Seventeen *and* Better Homes and Gardens *magazines and an associate editor of the* Improvement Era *and the* New Era.

Civic work has occupied much of her time also. Elaine has been a delegate to the White House Conference on children and youth and has served on the advisory board of Utah Boys' Ranch, and the Third District Juvenile Court in Utah.

Honors have come easily to this popular example of womanhood. Even before she graduated from the University of Utah in Sociology in 1943, she had served as president of the Associated Women Students and had been named to several honorary societies. Since that time she has been listed in Who's Who in American Women, *been named* Woman of the Year *at three different universities and awarded the first-place* Writing-for-Youth Award *by the National Press Women. She is one of those special women in Mormondom to be named an all-Church Honorary Golden Gleaner and has also received an all-Church Special Service to Youth diamond award.*

How pleased we were to discover her willingness, in spite of the many responsibilities she was carrying, to write a chapter for this book. Indeed, the title for the whole volume came from what she had written. Surely no one is better qualified than Elaine A. Cannon to introduce our readers to the writings of these choice women.

JDC & DSC

1

THE JOY IN WOMANHOOD
by
Elaine A. Cannon

There she goes, the misty-eyed bride enveloped in her veils of romance, hope, fancy, practicality, modesty, allure and nest-building. Her cup runneth over with love. With her hand in the Lord's and her heart in her husband, she moves forward to the adventure of life. Ideally, it will bring her to the point where her hand will be in her husband's and her heart in the Lord.

This, of course, is what life is all about.

There are two important days in a woman's life—the day she is born and the day she finds out why. Then, with but one chance to live she must put into play her every strength, wile, talent and idea.

The Gospel Shapes Perspectives of Life

A woman with her life sweetened by gospel experiences, enlightened by religious training, strengthened by the ordinances and directions of the holy priesthood of God, is bound to have a different view of why she was born—no matter how liberal or emancipated or sophisticated she may think she is. Deep down she knows she is a cherished child of God and the recipient, with others of his children both male and female, of all the blessings of a plan of eternal life. The day she comes to understand her role, to be comfortable in God's will for her, is the day of her giant step.

To the man it has been given to lead and to protect. To the woman it has been given to love and to bear children. As a man shares in the joy of children, so woman shares in the elevation priesthood gives to life, for "...neither is the man without the woman, neither the woman without the man, in the Lord." (1 Cor. 11:11)

To the girl who marries later rather than sooner in this life, the promises and plan still hold. Her timetable before the Lord may be different. The lessons she has to learn, the tests she must meet for exaltation seemingly may delay the day of her "fulfill-

2

ment." But each woman in the Church who lives her life according to the commandments will know eternal exaltation in its fullest meaning—marriage with increase! Living to claim this promise is every woman's business, whether she has taken vows yet or not.

Women probably aren't to be without a certain restlessness in all of today's commotion about their role. Social change is ever with us. However, any new idea or attitude thrust upon us by the world should be carefully weighed against the eternal scheme of things. Actually, today's women have more "rights" and more status than they have ever had before, and yet a large segment of today's young women don't seem to be any happier because of it. It seems obvious that women need more encouragement to understand their roles as mothers, homemakers, and influencers. They need to learn to find the happiness God has promised to those who do His will. To listen and follow the distorted ideas of the world is to toss away our birthright—and for a mess of pottage, too.

The gospel of Jesus Christ provides freedom of spirit and choice vastly more meaningful than anything the cries of the radical world could demand. In addition, the gospel gives special guidance to woman's role and strength to help her keep her commitments. And in the keeping come the blessings.

Returning the Gift of Womanhood Tenfold

The Savior lifted women. He carefully helped those who would listen in a world gone sour to understand the worth of each soul, male and female. He taught women their important place through the events and teachings of His ministry. We are insulting the Savior, it seems to me, if we refuse to accept fully the gift of our role as a woman. It is tantamount to burying the proverbial talent, being ungrateful stewards. We must take the gift of being born women and return it to the giver increased tenfold.

On one occasion the Savior went to visit in the home of two beloved women friends and as the scriptures say, "Mary...sat at Jesus' feet and heard his word. But Martha was cumbered about much serving, and came to him, and said, Lord dost thou not care that my sister hath left me to serve alone? bid her therefore that she help me.

"And Jesus answered and said unto her, Martha, Martha, thou art careful and troubled about many things: but one thing is need-

3

ful: and Mary hath chosen that good part, which shall not be taken away from her." (Lk. 10:39-42)

Though Martha was careful about many things there was only one thing needful and Mary had chosen that.

To be a Mary is to be at the Savior's feet, learning those truths important to life, now and forever. This is the good part that cannot be taken away. It can be used in bringing Christ into the lives of others.

Mary wasn't cumbered about much serving. Some women wear motherhood, wifehood, servicehood like a flag draped about their shoulders in a Martha's or martyr's guise. They are cumbered about much serving. Others follow their role with happiness and joy, with grace and thanksgiving. They follow the word of the Lord and conform their lives to his teachings. There is balance in their pursuits.

Skill in One's Role Brings Fulfillment

To learn and grow as a human being is important. To become skilled in one's particular role is the avenue to fulfillment and success. Perhaps one of the good things to come out of women's rights movements over the years is the intellectual awakening that has come to women themselves. This kind of catharsis gets them thinking seriously about what it is to be a female as well as a human being. They have stopped to consider blessings and responsibilities, realities and the unchangeables, frameworks and possibilities.

It takes more know-how and courage to be a proper woman these days. Her intuitive, sensitive, caring qualities should be cultivated. To be a woman is to shape lives and thus truly change the world. Life for one who influences children—as a mother or a teacher—is more than reading gentle stories. It is preparing children to meet the social pressures of the day and to meet God later on.

Women Influence the Lives of Others

Margaret Mead tells of ways a woman can influence: "Through the ages, human beings have remained human because there were women whose duty it was to provide continuity to life—to be there when they go to sleep and when they wake up; to listen to tales of broken hearts, to soothe, support, sustain, and to stimu-

4

late husbands and sons as they face the vicissitudes of the hard outside world."

In a stirring address delivered at the tenth National Woman's Right Convention in New York in 1860 Mrs. Elizabeth Stanton stated the case for women beautifully. "If in marriage either party claims the right to stand supreme, to woman, the mother of the race, belongs the scepter and the crown. Her life is one long sacrifice for man. You tell us that among womankind there is no Moses, Christ or Paul—no Michelangelo, Beethoven, Shakespeare— no Columbus or Galileo—no Locke or Bacon. Behold those mighty minds so grand, so comprehensive—they themselves are *our* great works! Into you, O sons of earth, goes all of us that is immortal. In you center our very life, our hopes, our intensest love. For you we gladly pour out our heart's blood and die, knowing that from our suffering comes forth a new and more glorious resurrection of thought and life."

Great gifts in woman do not usually take the form that bring her recognition or wealth. Yet what rare satisfaction! The world is full of women who with happiness testify that their role in life is completely rewarding and that they are honored by men in the most beautiful sense of the word.

A woman's significant role, it seems to me, is that of being an influence wherever she is. She is God's special helper in giving life, but also in shaping the course of life. Consider the story of the 2000 sons of Helaman as recorded in Alma 56 of the Book of Mormon. It says, "They had been taught by their mothers, that if they did not doubt, God would deliver them. And they rehearsed unto me the words of their mothers, saying: We do not doubt our mothers knew it." (Al. 56:47-48) In the face of battle the influence of mothers is felt.

In II Kings is the report of the little captive maid who dared to suggest to her master, the proud captain of the hosts, that if he would visit her prophet he would be healed from his leprosy. This he did. The lesson about false pride is often preached. Seldom do we hear mentioned the "little captive maid" who played her important role.

If a captive maid can have such an influence, think of the great good today's women can have in all their circles. President

David O. McKay often counseled that "no other success can compensate for failure in the home." I would add to that powerful truth the teaching that "no amount of success can compensate for failure as a human being." Whether a woman marries sooner or later in life, she should work to be a successful human being, contributing comfort, peace, order, love and the wisdom of God to those around her. Brigham Young reminded women that her business was to qualify "for the part which may be allotted you to perform in the kingdom of God."

Sarah of old lived in a day when women were seldom seen in public and even in their homes were little more than slave—by law! The Bible reveals an ideal person-to-person relationship enjoyed by Sarah and Abraham. She earned his love and trust as he earned his from her by sharing his dreams, his knowledge of God and his faith. Sarah is the first recorded woman in the Bible to entertain strangers in her home (strangers who turned out to be angels who blessed her that she might have a child!) She is the first to be given management over her husband's flock and fields and servants when Abraham leaves to rescue Lot's family.

A woman relating to a man should think in terms of giving with a capital *G*. Give of her mind—ideas, creative approach, principles. Give of her heart—life, warm, welcome, love. Give of her time—listen, comfort, suggest, labor. A woman should move a man to goodness, foster faith, create an atmosphere of love and reminders of God. In counseling with man as he counsels with God a woman *permits* man to be strengthened in his leadership role. With singleness of purpose she should do what only woman can do—make a home and fill it with happiness.

Caring in a Womanly Way

What is the key? It is a matter of quality and goodness, of aliveness and fidelity. It is caring in a womanly way. To love a child you've never known, to reach beyond the corners of her own selfish interests, to play the supporting role to man, makes a woman womanly.

Surely to understand the general role of woman as a humanitarian and partner with God is not hard in the face of the facts. But to know the fine details of how to implement the ideal in our own life is something else. Each of us needs to go to the mountain

6

to find her own way. Bride or bachelor girl, teenager or grand-mother, woman should look for direction for each stage of life. This means keeping close to Heavenly Father through prayer and living His principles so He can operate in our lives. A patriarchal blessing is a great help. "Thy will for me" becomes a secret of success and insures freedom of spirit when one puts faith in God and leans not on her own wisdom or the dictates of the world.

In my home I have a poster that a special friend shared with me that was painted by Sister Mary Corita: "To believe in God is to know that all the rules will be fair and there will be wonderful surprises!" This I believe.

"Unfulfilled at home" the radical feminists declare. Never! Tired, maybe, when you've done the day's work, but when your child nuzzles you with a goodnight kiss or your husband suddenly drops his paper to smile at you, or a student drops a warm fan letter on the desk, this is all the joy a woman really needs. You feel your heart telling you things your mind just hasn't caught on to yet—you feel it is good to be a woman.

And your cup runneth over with love.

INTRODUCING – JANENE FORSYTH

How can so much activity be packed into the life of one so young? Janene first saw the light of day in 1954 when she was born in Provo, Utah. Her parents, Gordon and Nadene Forsyth, were active in musical and dance band activities in Provo during that era and some of their talent surely passed on to their daughter.

When Janene was five her family left Utah and moved to Arlington, Virginia. She lived the active life of a typical Mormon youth there (it's a good place to live—that's where Duane was raised!) and used her musical abilities for four years serving as Junior Sunday School organist. Hard work was a part of her life from an early age. By the time she had finished high school she had been a secretary, an instructoress at a health spa, had modeled professionally for three years and taught modeling for two.

In 1971 she won the coveted "Miss Ingenue" title in New York City. This modeling competition involved girls from across the country and from Mexico and Canada. The same month she was chosen second runner-up in the "Miss Metropolitan Washington, D.C." competition and was named "Miss Photogenic." In August, 1971, she was selected as "Miss Virginia Teenager" and enjoyed the honor of being voted "Miss Congeniality" by the other contestants. A month later she won the national "Miss American Teenager" title for 1971-72 in the contest at Palisades Park, New Jersey. This success has led to personal, radio and television appearances throughout the United States during the past year. Her notoriety has brought invitations to Janene to speak to LDS youth groups in various parts of the United States. She is now entering as a freshman at BYU.

Our desire, when we invited Janene to write this chapter, was that she reflect the values and attitudes of young women in the Church. We feel she has met this challenge admirably and that she reflects a maturity beyond her years. JDC & DSC

8

LIFE IS A LADDER
by
Janene Forsyth

Did you ever climb the winding staircase inside a high monument or tower? At intervals, as you ascended, you came to a window which let in light and through which, as you looked out, you glimpsed a lovely world outside the dark tower. You saw green fields and gardens, picturesque landscapes, streams flashing like silver in the sunshine, perhaps the blue sea yonder, and far away, the shadowy forms of great mountains.

How small, how dark and cheerless seemed the narrow limits of your staircase as you looked out upon the view that stretched from your window!

Life is like the ascent of such a column. While we are climbing up its dark stairway, there lies outside its walls a glorious world, reaching away into eternity, beautiful, and filled with the rarest things of God's love. When thoughts of immortality and knowledge of the gospel come to us, they are like little windows through which we have glimpses of the infinite sweep of life beyond this hampered existence of earth.

Eternal Prospects Influence Present Living

No one can ponder the theme of immortality without feeling the stir and glow of a better life within him. It is one of the most powerful motives for righteous living. Fortunately we have a marvelous plan, through which this righteous living can become a reality. It is a plan of *action*, a blueprint by which we can chart our lives. It is the Plan of Salvation whereby all gifts granted to us can be used, and used to the utmost. It leads us to accept the responsibilities which a loving Father has laid at our feet. If we use the doctrines of the gospel as the rungs on the ladder upon which we climb this staircase of life, then our ascent will be enlightened, and all of our duties and responsibilities will be relevant to the goal ahead—that of eternal life. We will realize the highest achievements and most satisfying joys.

Climbing the Ladder Requires Effort

A poet has written,
> Tis God gives skill,
> But not without men's hands.
> He would not make Antonio Stradivari's violin
> Without Antonio.

We cannot make it to the top of our ladder without effort on our part. One foot must be raised above the other in order to reach the summit. Joe Frazier, the boxing champion, said, "We have to do our own roadwork, whatever we choose to become in life." It may not be the most pleasant thing we would choose at that moment, but we should not permit today's convenience to outweigh tomorrow's development. Charles Kingsley said, "Thank God every morning when you get up that you have something to do that day which must be done whether you like it or not. Being forced to work, and forced to do your best will breed in you temperance and self control, diligence and strength of will, cheerfulness and content and a hundred virtues which the idle never know."

Latter-day Saints believe that these "work-induced virtues" are also rungs on the ladder to eternal life. We are known as busy people—but isn't it often said that if you want a task done well, give it to a busy person? In purchasing life, time is the medium of exchange. Time is the one thing we all possess. Our success in life depends on the way we make use of it. The advantage of leisure time is mainly that we have the opportunity to choose our own tasks. It is not time to be spent in idleness.

I have been taught that work is a blessing, but there have been times in my life when it failed to fulfill that purpose. I remember scrubbing the kitchen floor when I was young and not being able to perceive any blessing there. When there is no upward looking joy, no romance in one's effort, then work becomes drudgery and is no longer a power for good. The attitude with which we approach a task makes it either drudgery or a sacrament under our hands. To feel each day that we are developing strength and power, that we are living up to the fulness of our best possibilities—this is high romance—this is real living. To make, to create, to produce something necessary or beautiful, at once lifts us closer to companionship with our Heavenly Father.

My mother, who is an excellent seamstress, has sewn all of

my wardrobe during my reign as Miss American Teenager. Many times she has worked until three or four o'clock in the morning to finish a gown or some other creation for me. At one of my appearances in Washington D.C., a fashion designer from New York approached me and complimented me on the style and material and workmanship of my blouse. When I told him that my mother made it, he was astonished. He then suggested that if she should ever come to New York, she could work for his firm.

I told my mother of his offer, but she laughed and said that she would only work that hard for her loved ones, and that no money could pay the price she would ask—only words of love and gratitude. Her labors for me are truly a "sacrament under her hands."

Whether in work or leisure, it is important to keep our spiritual values uppermost in our lives, directing and determining our actions. Sometimes, when I must make an appearance pertaining to my title, I find that despite the excitement and glamour involved, a weariness of it all clouds my enjoyment. However, when I have an opportunity to appear for the Church, I feel joy and satisfaction in fulfilling my assignment. This is because my duties and responsibilities have suddenly become relevant to my goal of eternal life, and it makes all the difference in the world.

The Need for Spiritual Nourishment

This past year has been full of fantastic activity and opportunity for me, but there have been days when I found myself so involved with temporal obligations that when night fell, I was aware of a lack of spiritual nourishment. During periods of intense activity we should recognize the danger of neglecting our spiritual needs, and daily set aside a quiet time to converse with the Lord so that our spirits might be rejuvenated. Taking the time to pray at the beginning and the end of my busy day has truly uplifted me and given me the assurance that the Lord is there!

After participation in a Youth Conference or an Education Week for the Church, I feel a beautiful sense of peace and renewal. It is truly a rejuvenating experience. The joy of hearing a young girl say she's been inspired by something I may have said cannot be measured. Each time I speak to the youth of the Church I ask my Heavenly Father beforehand to bless me that I might be an

11

instrument in His hands and that I might do some good or speak the words that some young person needs to hear. More than once, when I have started my talk, I have set aside my notes and words have poured out of my mouth that I had not planned to say. It was as though I were not in complete control, that thoughts and ideas were issuing forth involuntarily, and sometimes I was surprised at what I heard. What a difference it has made in my life when I rely on the Lord and do and say what He wants. We all can establish a beautiful relationship with the Lord if we so desire and then we will be able to feel His inspiration and work and live for Him. This is an ultimate joy that can be a part of each of our lives. The moments of being lead by the Spirit are the thrilling and inspirational times when I marvel at Heavenly Father's goodness to me.

One such experience occurred in April, 1972 at a Girl's Life Conference in Huntsville, Alabama. The Spirit was strong and humbling and the testimony meeting afterwards was thrilling. Later our family received a letter from a lovely young girl from the stake, Andrea Morgan, who wrote: "...During the testimony meeting the girls expressed their love for the gospel and the hope and confidence that had been given them. It has made us feel beautiful, and we all want to strive for perfection, a temple marriage and a testimony of the gospel. One girl said 'I thought I had lost my testimony but when Janene gave her talk I wanted to run up to the front of the room and scream I've *found* my testimony!'...Thank you for letting her come to our conference...."

If we will dedicate our lives and mission to the service of the Lord, He will shower down blessings upon us and we can become an instrument in His hands for accomplishing His will among our associates in the Church. I have also had much opportunity to come in contact with many people who are not members and it is a joy to share the gospel with them. What a marvelous challenge the Lord has put before me. It has been remarkable to see His promises unfold into reality already in my life! Each experience has been an opportunity to grow and becomes another rung in my ladder of life.

Influencing Others with Gospel Teachings

Spreading the gospel, loving it and being proud of it is always an asset. The day before the final night of the contest, the contestants had the personality judging with the judges. Each girl had a certain time in which to go into the large room, sit around the big table, and answer the judges' questions. Right before I walked into that room I prayed to my Heavenly Father and asked for His Spirit to be with me. When I sat down with the judges, the first question that was given was "What is the Youth Council?" What a chance to spread the gospel! With excitement I told these people how wonderful the Latter-day Saint youth program was and all it had to offer. I also told of the strength and sincerity of the young people of the Church. In a roundabout way I bore my testimony to them, and they asked one question right after another on the Church until we realized my time was up. As I walked out of the room, I suddenly realized that I just talked about the Church and did not mention anything about me and my accomplishments. Seeing that they did not hear about *me*, I felt perhaps I didn't have a chance. Yet, when that exciting evening came, and after it was over, while pictures were being taken, one of the judges came to me, and with a sparkle in her eye she put her arm around me and told me they felt a spirit there when I spoke and were impressed with my testimony. Once more I learned never to be afraid of sharing your love for the gospel with others.

Before I won the title of Miss American Teenager, my family was very concerned and they prayed that I would not win unless I would use my new position as a tool in the Lord's hands to spread the gospel. On that final night of the contest, when they announced my name as the winner, I immediately looked upward and thanked the Lord, realizing that He had done His part and that it was now my turn to do mine. My eyes were beginning to be opened to the duty which lay before me.

Before long a real opportunity for missionary work presented itself. Cheryl Boswell, Miss Virginia Teenager 1971, who had gone to the Miss American Teenager pageant the previous year, phoned to congratulate me. In the course of our conversation she said, "Janene, I hear that you are a Mormon. What do you believe?" I was thrilled at this chance to bear my testimony and we talked on the phone for a long time. When she asked if I had had any spiritual experiences I invited her to our home and she came right over. We

13

shared these experiences and then we knelt in prayer. A seed of truth was planted that day and as the weeks and months passed it flourished and developed into a beautiful testimony. She was baptized on New Years Day, 1972.

This marked the beginning of those months when most of my leisure time was devoted to meetings with the missionaries and investigators in our home. It was a time of learning and understanding for me as well as my friends. It was a time of frustration and reward. How sad it was for me to see dear friends come so close to baptism and then for some reason decline to follow through. Some led lives which cried out for help, but as they floundered around in their troubled waters, they couldn't recognize the life preserver when it was thrown to them.

Such a one was Dave, who had all the missionary discussions plus many private ones with me. He even brought his friends to Church, but he couldn't accept the principle of tithing. The ability of a man to give of his income to the Church usually spells out the measure of his faith. It takes a lot of faith to accept that duty. In an old scrap book of my mother's I found a poem which her mother had given to her when she was my age. It is "Immortality," by Andrew M. Jackson, and has real meaning for me:

> I do not know why I came to You
> Called you "Good Master"
> And asked you the greatest of questions—
> How to obtain eternal life—
> As though You had the key.
> I wore silken garments,
> I had great possessions,
> Bore an aristocratic name,
> Kept the laws of the prophets scrupulously
> And never had been contaminated by the common herd.
> You had calloused hands,
> Your disciples, carrying with them
> The odor of fish and musty hovels,
> And your following of rabble from the streets
> Proclaimed You of the very common folk.
> Yet You are revered by millions
> Who breathe your name in prayer

While even the title that I bore is forgotten,
And all the immortality that I have
Came because I asked You that question,
And You gave me the ridiculous answer,
"Go, and sell what thou hast
And give it to the poor."
I went away sorrowful, for of course I could not do that—
It would have been very foolish.

Someday maybe Dave will come back, but for now, he has "gone away sorrowful." He is moving back down his ladder. The worst thing that can destroy us is our spiritual pride.

But not all was disappointment. During the time that Cheryl was meeting the missionaries downstairs in our home, my brother Karl was upstairs with his friend, Floyd Eckel, having the lessons with some other missionaries. For two weeks Floyd, Karl and the Elders met at our house every evening and had lively discussions. We always served refreshments and it became a real challenge to serve something different when it was happening every night. This was such a happy time for Karl. With each new meeting, as his own horizons in the gospel expanded, he loved his friend more. It was a joyous day when Karl baptized and then confirmed Floyd. Later, when he confirmed Cheryl, it was truly a time of rejoicing. We learned that it pays to speak out regarding our beliefs at the first opportunity, because there may not be a second one, and the reward can be so great!

"I must pray to God that somebody else may do whatever I leave undone. But I shall not have any right to that prayer unless I do my duty wherever I see it," wrote Edward Garrett.

I learned a valuable lesson by doing missionary work this year. It was this: it is the Spirit of the Lord which converts, not the individual. I learned that prayer and a genuine humility are essential. I learned that I could only do so much for my friends, and then they had to reach out in prayer to find for themselves whether or not the gospel was true. I learned that my burdens and frustrations could be alleviated by laying them before the Lord.

Hearing and Accepting the Answer to Prayer

The Lord has never disappointed me. He has always answered my prayers. Sometimes I do not receive the answer I would like,

15

but last year, April of 1971, I learned the importance of being willing to hear and accept the Lord's answer instead of what I wanted. I went to New York City concerning an international modeling convention, and much to my surprise I did well and received some very special offers. I came home on cloud nine thinking of all the money that had been promised me and expecting to move up to New York as soon as possible. During the following month I was thinking out the rest of my life and what I wanted. It was either going to be New York City or Brigham Young University and at the time it was like putting in front of a child a bowl of cherries and a bowl of carrots and telling him to choose which would be best. Then one night it dawned on me that the Lord had some say in the matter and that all I needed to do was ask Him. But then I realized I had to step out of my feelings and wants and be able to hear and accept His answer. So I prayed *very* hard that night. I believe I prayed harder and longer than I have ever prayed before. When I finally climbed into that bed, I felt a beautiful light spirit within my heart letting me know God had heard my prayer. The next day in school I was sitting in my history class just staring at a blank wall and thinking of nothing, when suddenly I felt that same sweet Spirit and, for the first time in my life, I actually heard a voice within me say—"Janene, you are *not* to go to New York. I have other plans for you and a special calling." I was so excited for finally knowing what my Father in Heaven wanted of me, I was floating on air! The thought of turning down all that money did not even enter my mind. None of that mattered any more. I knew I needed to get an education and prepare myself for the service of the Lord. I am now at Brigham Young University and loving it. I hate to think of where I could be now and my degree of happiness if I had decided not to turn to my God and seek His counsel and instead go to New York to live as a model. Turning to the Lord is an essential part of our eternal progression.

Tuned to the Same Pitch

Such a short span of my earthly life has elapsed, and I have a long way to go before I make it to the top of my tower—up my "ladder to eternal life." Whether my journey is plodding or sprightly depends, I guess, on how many little windows I can find

16

to brighten my way.

Since I don't really expect to travel this journey alone, I should examine my Plan of Action, my blueprint by which I am charting my life. This plan should lead me in the direction where I can meet the right companion who will marry me in the Temple of the Lord for time and all eternity. He will hold the priesthood, and be the spiritual and temporal leader in our home, able to bless me and our children. If we are worthy, it will be he who will lead us into the celestial kingdom.

I grew up in a home where there was much music. I learned that in order for two instruments to play together harmoniously, they must be tuned to one another. Marriage must be like the bringing together of two musical instruments. They must be tuned to the same pitch.

Tennyson wrote:

> In the long years, liker must they grow:
> The man be more of woman, she of man;
> He gain in sweetness and in moral height
> Nor lose the wrestling thews that throw the world.
> She mental breadth, nor fail in childward care;
> Move as the double natured poet each
> Till at last she sets herself to man
> Like perfect music unto noble words.

A wonderful tuning agent is prayer. I want it to weave a roof of love over our home and to build walls of protection about it. I am preparing for this now by praying with the young men I date. What a difference this makes, when you can humbly include the Lord in all you do. If we will draw together at God's feet every day, we cannot get very far apart. Some of my most beautiful memories of our family are those where my father led us in family prayer—where Vaughn, Karl, Mark, Heather and I joined with our parents in a circle around the kitchen table.

We must be careful that we do not only pray in our distress and need, but that we pray also in the fulness of our joy and in our days of abundance. These are vocal prayers, but there is also the prayer of a good life, quietly led day by day, filled with little acts of devotion, duty, kindness and good example. This kind of prayer leaves the deepest mark in the world, and on other lives too.

17

Actions Have Far-Reaching Influence

Long centuries ago, a little fern leaf grew in a valley. Its veins and fibers were delicate and artistic. It was very beautiful, but it fell and perished. It seemed useless and lost, for surely it had made no history and made no impression in the world. But wait...the other day a thoughtful man searching Nature's secrets came with pick and hammer and broke off a piece of rock and there upon it his eye perceived

> Fairy pencillings, a quaint design,
> Leafage, veining, fibers clear and fine,
> And the fern's life lay in every line.
> So, I think God hides some souls away,
> Sweetly to surprise us at the last day.

I imagine we are all due for some surprises. The quiet simple devotion of humble parents in rearing a good family may have a strong, far-reaching influence on the lives of their children and, in turn, on their effect on the world. In contrast, I remember the story of the man, inactive in the Church, who before he died had fifty-four descendants, none of whom were spiritually enriched by a knowledge of the gospel.

We cannot know the results of our actions performed, we may think, in anonymity, but they could set in motion a course of events of which we may never be aware.

One night at a dinner at the Sheraton Park Hotel in Washington D.C. I was seated between Vice President Agnew and another gentleman. During the course of the evening I naturally turned my coffee cup over on the saucer to indicate that I didn't wish to have coffee. I had also turned over my cocktail glass, unaware that anyone was watching. A little later, a reporter for one of the Washington papers came up and asked if it was I who had turned my glass and coffee cup over. Before I could answer, the gentleman at my side said "You better believe it! She's a Mormon." I was surprised. There were over a thousand people there that night and one would not imagine that what I did would be noticed. It made me realize that we are usually observed by someone. Whether or not we are aware of it, someone may be using our actions as a yardstick, and it is our duty to set a good example. It just might help that someone to find the little windows in his tower. We can't know how

18

many may be stumbling in the darkness, needing to witness our act of faith or hear our testimony. The tower is so dark for some, and many of the rungs on their ladder are broken.

In the *Doctrine and Covenants*, Sections 15 and 16, the Lord told John and Peter Whitmer that the thing which would be of greatest worth in their lives would be to declare repentance unto the people and to bring souls unto Him. I know that this is true for my life also.

I am thankful for the duties and responsibilities that have been placed before me by those who have been instrumental in shaping my life. In the fulfillment of these tasks I have grown, and moved a part of the distance up my ladder. We are always moving on this ladder of life—whether up or down. Each new thought and act is a step. And the more I grow the more I will realize I still have to progress:

> I reach a duty, yet I do it not
> And therefore climb no higher, but if done
> My view is brightened and another spot
> Seen on my mortal sun;
> For be that duty high as angels' flight,
> Fulfill it and a higher will arise
> Even from its ashes.
> Duty is our ladder to the skies,
> And, climbing not, we fall.
> -Author Unknown

May we always open our eyes and be aware of our progression here on earth. Keep your spiritual values uppermost in your mind and number one in your lives. Love the Church and your brothers and sisters, keep the commandments, and strive to be like our oldest brother, Jesus Christ. This is a challenge I not only give to you, but to myself as well. If we meet it, we will find continual joy as we climb the ladder of life.

19

INTRODUCING — KAREN HERD

We first saw Karen as Miss Idaho on TV during those breathless moments when they were about to announce the new Miss America for 1971. She emerged as first runner-up, and as lovely and charming as any other young lady there. This triumph marked the culmination of a series of victories in beauty competitions.

Karen was raised in Idaho Falls, the daughter of William and Iva Low Herd and the third of six children. High school years included the thrills of being a homecoming queen, a cheerleader, and membership in concert choir and other musical groups. She is an accomplished performer on piano and organ, and has served as a church organist and chorister. She has also been an MIA teacher and during the two years she has attended the BYU, has been a counselor in the MIA presidency.

Her travels have taken her to many states of the union and almost around the world. She hurried to complete this chapter before leaving on a USO tour entertaining servicemen in Japan and Korea. During the coming year her study at BYU in business education will be resumed.

Karen has been the official hostess for the State of Idaho this past year and has also been youth chairman for the Easter Seals and National Library Week. United Press International named her Idaho's "Woman of the Year" — the youngest ever to receive this award.

During the past year Karen has talked to literally thousands of young people across the country. We feel she has been a real influence for good, both within and without the Church. Our invitation to her was a specific assignment: she was asked to convey her standards and beliefs concerning courtship and marriage. Her example is one that many young women will emulate.

JDC & DSC

MARRIAGE—IT'S FOR ETERNITY!
by
Karen Herd

One fall evening four new college coeds sat around the kitchen table of their apartment excitedly exchanging ideas. They were expounding on the new-found knowledge gained from their vast experiences in the four weeks of their college careers.

"One thing for sure girls," remarked the willowy brunette as she flipped her long hair back off her shoulders, "we're not getting married this year. How ghastly! We're too young!" "Oh, for sure," agreed the others—"no way." "I know," said Linda, the cute short blonde, anxious to share her idea, "we'll find our 'one and only' in the fall of our junior year, get engaged at Christmas, and get married that following June and live happily ever after."

Everyone at the table thought that was a splendid plan, and having decided on their futures for the next three years, the four most practical and knowledgeable freshman girls on BYU campus scattered to their various beds for a contented night's sleep.

For a while this plan marked the course of their lives, but as time went on, things changed. Winter snow had come and gone twice since that evening, and the four coeds had now completed their sophomore year.

That spring, as the last hugs and tears of happiness were shared by those four girls at the wedding reception of their pal Linda, now departing from the group, they all realized that an eternal marriage takes a lot more preparation and planning than a few minutes out of a fall evening.

The Right Person, Right Time and Right Place

I was one of those young girls involved in that discussion. Now, three years later and, hopefully, a wee bit wiser, I would like to explore my present feelings with you concerning one's preparation for an eternal marriage.

It has been said, "There is nothing more important that you'll do in this life than to marry the right person at the right time in the right place." For girls especially, the joy of married life is something that is anticipated for years. Everyone has dreams of the perfect marriage—one that is filled with happiness and love throughout life and beyond.

Certainly there is no marriage that doesn't have its problems some time or another, but by preparing ourselves for an eternal marriage the way the Church teaches, we, as LDS girls, can surely eliminate many of the problems and unhappy experiences found in many marriages today.

Preparation through Knowing and Living Gospel Teachings

The way we act and the things that occupy our time each day make us what we are. Thank goodness we are given counsel all of our lives that helps us develop into the type of individuals we should be. Clear, realistic standards have been set forth to guide us in our conduct, our conversation, our dress, and other areas where we must discern between right and wrong. These standards are good. They are valid. Many others who are not of our faith also know of their value and importance in helping us avoid temptation and situations which cause sorrow.

It was interesting to note, when I competed for Miss America, that modesty in dress was encouraged, and that the contestants were instructed not to smoke, drink, or do anything not becoming to a young lady. I felt every one of the girls were of a very high caliber, although, out of the 50 finalists, only two of us were Mormons.

One particular contestant that I especially liked was from the East coast. She was a religion major, and soon we began discussing religion. During the conversation she asked me, "What religion are you?" "I'm a Mormon," I said. "You are a Mormon!" she said, quite shocked. "Well, yes," I replied, "there are a lot of us in Idaho." "Wow, I've never met a Mormon before!"

"Since I'm a religion major," she said, "I'm really interested. Could you please tell me about your church?" I proceeded to tell her some of the things that we believe we must do in order to get to the celestial kingdom (which was heaven to her) such as baptism, living a clean life, paying an honest tithing, and eventually being married in the temple for not only time but through all eternity. I explained to her that we had been given a plan to follow

22

and principles to live by, and that we knew why we were here on this earth—our purpose being to prove ourselves and live in such a way that we can return to our Heavenly Father someday.

She looked at me just fascinated and then said, "You know, in all the religion classes I take, we spend hours tearing down different beliefs and principles. You get so confused you don't know what to believe. You are really lucky to have this strong conviction and a path like that to follow. That is really unusual, particularly among kids our age."

At that moment I think I realized even more how really fortunate we are to have the Church and the great leaders that we do to give us counsel and guidance throughout our lives.

It seems like we're constantly getting lectured on dress standards, but I guess it's because we need it. In this "anything goes" generation of which we are a part, we still can live our high standards.

Each time we walk out the door, we are painting a picture of a Latter-day Saint girl. That means we are not only speaking for ourselves and our families, but we're representing the whole Church. That is quite a responsibility!

Whether we like it or not, people judge the type of person we are by our appearance, particularly the first time they see us. President Hugh B. Brown expressed this very well when he said, "Clothes do not make a man or a woman, but it's better that they speak for you than against you."

As LDS girls we should keep in mind that clothes are an advertisement of what we want to attract. If we dress modestly we will attract the kind of young men that want to treat us like a lady, but if we dress immodestly, we will attract the kind of guys that think they can get away with treating us otherwise.

When a girl feels she has to dress immodestly to get attention from guys, then she really has problems. There is never a time when a real man won't appreciate a clean, wholesome-looking girl.

Boys may kid and joke about such things, but when it comes to looking for a girl who they can take to the temple and that will be the mother of their children, who do you think they'll go after?

Preparation through Dating

Keeping ourselves morally clean in both thought and actions

is mandatory if we expect to be worthy of a temple marriage. The dating years are filled with new and exciting experiences, most of which will be remembered for a lifetime. We can either make these memories pleasant ones to recall or torture ourselves with guilt later on for not-so-pleasant experiences; it's totally up to us.

It takes courage a lot of times to do what we know is right in a given situation. The pressure can seem almost too great to withstand. But the pain and anguish one may go through to make the decision he knows is right cannot compare to the torment and sick, empty feeling that comes from lowering one's standards to escape temporary embarrassment or criticism.

When I was a senior in high school there was a boy that I had really been wanting to date for a long time. He finally asked me out for a Saturday night movie.

That Saturday afternoon he called to tell me the show we were going to see. He also said we would be doubling with another couple I knew, and that he would be by to pick me up at about eight o'clock. I hung up the phone and started towards my room to get ready. I wanted to be sure to look my best; after all, I just had to make a good first impression.

Just then Mom came into the room and asked, (as she always did) "What show are you going to tonight?" I told her and without hesitating she said, "I can't let you go to that show!" "What do you mean, not let me go?" I asked, immediately on the defensive. "I've heard that that is not the kind of show you should be going to," she replied. "Well Mom, I can't just call my date up now and say, my mother won't let me go to that show. Besides that, we're doubling with another couple. I'll wreck the whole evening!"

She still insisted that I not go. I cried. It still didn't do any good. Dad even got into the act and still insisted no.

"I'll shut my eyes, anything! Just this once, couldn't I go?" I pleaded. Both parents still insisted no.

Finally I decided I was losing the battle and called the girl we would be doubling with and told her my situation. "I've got a problem," I said. "What?" "Well, my parents won't let me go to that show." "You're kidding," she said. "No," I sheepishly confessed. "Well," she said, "my date and I have been wanting to see that show for a long time, so we're going to that one whether you

24

can or not." As you can imagine, I felt even worse.

When my date finally knocked at the door, I ducked into a nearby room where I could listen and let Mom answer it. After the usual "Hello" and "How are you this evening?" she said to him, "What show are you taking Karen to tonight?" He told her, and she said, "I really don't think that is a very good show for you kids to be seeing, and I would rather you take Karen to a different one. If the other couple wants to go to that one, you are welcome to take one of our cars and go to another one." "That's okay," he replied, "we'll go to a different one."

I then appeared out of the woodwork, just dying!! I didn't see how I could possibly recover from this experience. We went out to the car where the other couple was, and after a moment of silence, my date said, "Her Mom won't let her go to that show, so we'll go to a different one."

I could feel the heat under my collar as I turned red with embarrassment and tried to melt the icy stares I was getting from the back seat with a pleasant grin.

We ended up going to a Walt Disney special! I was never more happy for an evening to end. I kept thinking over and over to myself, I will never live this down! No way can I go to school Monday morning and face the teasing I was sure to get.

Surprisingly enough, however, when I got to school I discovered that no one knew about the situation as I had imagined, and I made it through Monday to the following Wednesday without any problem at all. That evening I received a telephone call from the boy with whom we had doubled. "Karen," he said, "we went to see that show tonight that we didn't see Saturday. It was so bad! I was really embarrassed that I even had a girl with me. I just want you to know that I really respect you for doing what your parents had told you to do."

It's been three years now since I've seen either of those two boys, but as a result of the Miss America pageant they both sent me a letter of congratulations. Both of them said, "Karen, I don't know if I ever told you this or not, but if there's anything I ever had for you, it was respect." If they had said, I remember you were a good cheerleader or played the piano well or something like that, it wouldn't have meant nearly as much to me.

25

You may not ever receive a phone call or a letter such as this; it was the only time it happened to me. But you will have the satisfaction of knowing that you did what you knew you should have done.

As LDS girls we expect to receive respect from the young men we date, and respect is something that must be earned. It isn't something that comes about overnight.

It's much easier to say "no" the first time than explain why you can't do something again.

My mother has given our family of five girls and one boy three rules on dating that have always helped me, and I'd like to pass these on to you.

1. Don't do anything you would be ashamed to have your mother see you do.

You might feel silly, but would you be ashamed? This sounds a little stiff, but if you really think about it, it isn't all that bad.

2. When you get home from a date, do you have a good or a bad feeling inside?

A good time to test this is when you wake up in the morning. Do you say to yourself, oh, I wish I hadn't stayed out that late, or I wish I hadn't done this or that; or do you have the kind of comforting feeling that comes from knowing you have done what you know is right and acted like a lady?

3. Can you face the person you have dated the next day or years later and look him straight in the eye, not having to feel guilty over whatever you did together or said to each other?

I think if we try to keep these rules in mind while dating, that when we find the one we want to marry in the temple, we'll be able to feel worthy to do so.

One of my best friends, who was just recently married in the temple, said to me, "I am so glad that I waited and didn't get physically involved with anyone else. I never thought anything could be so special as the relationship that the two of us have. It is so worth waiting for and keeping yourself worthy.

Why settle for anything less than this? A few moments of pleasure aren't worth destroying possibly a lifetime of joy and happiness.

26

Preparation through Being Close to Our Heavenly Father

Can you think of a more vital time in our lives to have our Heavenly Father's help than when we make the decision of who we will marry? What other decision of our lives will have more to do with our success or failure than this one? How very important it is that we are living the way we should so we can be in tune with our Heavenly Father and seek guidance as to the decisions we have to make.

A young couple whom I knew very well (let's call them Carol and Bob) thought themselves to be very much in love and were excitedly discussing their plans for the future. Included in their plans was a temple marriage, for although there was a time in Bob's life when he drank a little, that was all over, and he and Carol often attended Church together.

Carol was a bright, bubbly girl who had always followed the teachings of her parents and the Church. Because of this she hesitated a bit when Bob first asked her out. She wasn't exactly sure how much truth there was to the rumor about his drinking. Being mature and level-headed, however, she decided to be open-minded and try to help him.

Imagine her pride when Bob confessed that he had done some drinking, but because of her example, he was willing to give it up, ask for his Father in Heaven's forgiveness, and prepare to go on a mission.

It would be a long wait for Carol while Bob was on his mission, but she would study the scriptures too and be a perfect wife for him upon his return. No couple would be happier than they!

Carol's parents and family liked Bob because he was a well-mannered and personable young man. Being very perceptive and concerned for Carol's well-being, however, her parents couldn't help but wonder about the sincerity of Bob's intentions to go on a mission and become an active member of the Church.

Was he truly interested in making such abrupt changes in his life, or was he doing it only to please Carol? If so, would he stick with the changes?

When Carol's parents approached her about this, her first response was to rebel and accuse her parents of not trusting her judgment.

Meanwhile, the weeks passed as they curiously awaited Bob's mission call. Some of the other boys in the ward had already received their calls, but still the weeks slipped by with no response.

This gave Carol some time to think and prompted her to follow her parents suggestion to pray about Bob. Always in the past she had avoided actually asking the Lord if Bob was the one for her because she felt so sure that he was.

As Carol continued to pray, though, doubts began to arise, and when she found out that Bob had never even sent in his papers to go on a mission, she too wondered if he was becoming active only because of her.

Carol would lay awake nights torturing herself with the problem while her stomach seemed to produce huge, painful knots. Surely no one had ever had to cope with such terrific pressures.

When she talked to Bob about the possibility of their not being meant for each other, he would cry. Carol would cry, and finally their love for each other provided a cushion for the problem to be softened...momentarily! But very few days would pass befor Carol would begin to feel her doubts again.

Finally in desperation, she spent most of one night conversing with her Father in Heaven. By morning, she had no real answer as to why they weren't meant for each other, but one thing was for sure, they *weren't!* Never had Carol experienced such a strong feeling.

This time when she went to tell Bob about her apprehensions, she had the Lord with her, and it was surprisingly easy to simply explain that she didn't know why, but they were not supposed to be married. She told him she loved him, but she couldn't go against her Father in Heaven's promptings. They were too strong.

The next year-and-a-half were by no means easy for Carol. None of the boys she dated even compared to Bob. None of them seemed fun. None of them made her feel as important as Bob did. Many, many times Carol was confronted with the temptation to give it all up and run back to Bob. Surely nothing in their marriage could be as painful as the anguish she was presently experiencing.

At a time when she thought she could surely take no more, she was once again driven to her knees to solicit her Father in Heaven's help. The tears streamed down her cheeks as she pleaded for relief and poured out her heart.

Gradually Carol was comforted, and the rest of the night was peaceful. Two days later she met a handsome, recently returned missionary...her future husband!

Today Carol is married, has a happy little girl, and she and her husband are experiencing joy that far exceeds the intensity of any sorrow Carol previously knew. She will tell you herself that she thanks the Lord every night for her darling, devoted husband and for guiding her to make the right choice.

When Bob no longer had Carol as a crutch, he reverted back to his drinking, took up smoking, and married a girl of similar caliber.

Isn't it comforting to know that we can receive divine guidance in making our decisions? Our Heavenly Father has told us that he will help us if we only ask, and he will!

Probably the most important preparation we could ever make in planning our marriage is to constantly consult with our Father in Heaven. If we keep the doors of communication open, we may know the joy of making the right decision and can confidently say "I do" on our special day.

Why Marry in the Temple?

In my travels this past year, I have had the wonderful opportunity of speaking to and conversing with thousands of LDS youth. I find that the majority want a temple marriage and have strong convictions of their own. They feel that marrying in the temple is a privilege and a blessing, not an obligation.

As Church members, we are taught from the time we are small that we should be married in the temple. Of course, it goes without saying that to reach the highest degree of glory in the celestial kingdom we must be married in the temple.

What are, then, the most obvious advantages of a temple marriage?

1. *This is the way our Heavenly Father has commanded us to marry.* Marriage is such an important step in our lives that it should begin the right way. With all the problems of life, what

a comforting feeling it would be to know that we had pleased the Lord and now had a special claim upon his guidance, blessings, and protection.

2. *It is a most sacred and special ceremony.* Couples want the "perfect ceremony," especially girls who are perhaps a little more romantic and see their future husbands as "Prince Charmings." The physical surroundings in the temple are beautiful—an ideal setting for a marriage ceremony.

The one officiating in the temple takes time to create an atmosphere of happiness. The bride and groom are given special counsel and encouragement. They are reminded of the sacredness of their marriage vows and the obligations of trust and loyalty to each other.

The effects of different types of wedding ceremonies upon young people are very important. My mother told me that during World War II, when there were so many hasty marriages, that often the brides would come from a civil marriage and burst into tears. What should have been a happy experience had turned out to be a dark shadow—something they didn't even want to talk about in years to come.

3. *We are married for time and all eternity.* In spite of the trend in the world today to regard marriage as merely a social arrangement, to the young people of the Church, marriage is still regarded as a sacred and permanent institution. After all, a temple marriage isn't something you can just hurry into. Any girl or boy with the proper outlook on life will be more careful in his decision when the vows he takes are not only for this lifetime, but forever!

They agree that whom they really love, they want for always. The most important difference between temple weddings and all other marriages is this blessing: On this earth and beyond, we may be together with our companion and children. Where else can we be married for time and eternity?

4. *We will have the protection of the power of the priesthood.* A couple of years ago both of my older sisters were married in the temple to two fine young men. Now Pam and Anita both have the cutest little baby girls you've ever seen.

Anita's baby was the first grandchild in the family, and being the little sister, one of the first questions I asked was,

"Well, Anita, what was it like having a baby? Was it really as bad as they say it is?"

"Yes," she explained, "it's hard on you, and frightening! But Karen, I was so glad that I had a husband that held and honored the priesthood. Just before I went to the hospital, Steve gave me a blessing that I would be safe and well and that everything would go smoothly. Even during my pregnancy when I would get really sick, Steve would bless me. I can't tell you how important the priesthood is in a home and how comforting it was for me, particularly at that time."

Both couples are so excited and anxious to raise these special little spirits that are their very own forever in homes blessed with the priesthood and gospel of Jesus Christ. That's what life is really all about, isn't it?

One thing I can say from experience is this. I've traveled almost all over the world, been entertained royally, tasted the best food, stayed in the best places, and met famous people, but there is no thrill that can compare to a happy home where the spirit of the gospel is present. No amount of material pleasure can give the real joy that comes through living the gospel and having contentment in the home. That's why I will prepare myself to the best of my ability to be married to the right young man, in the temple, for all eternity.

31

INTRODUCING—VIRGINIA F. CUTLER

How do you summarize the accomplishments of a woman when her list of achievements is ten pages long? And they are no small successes, either—they're "one-liners" like: BS degree, University of Utah; MA degree, Stanford University; PhD degree, Cornell University, 1946; other training at Wharton School, University of Pennsylvania, and at Vassar College.

Work experience? Virginia was a high school home economics teacher for many years, a home demonstration agent in California for six years, a professor and head of the Home Economics Department at the University of Utah for eight years, a technical advisor in Southeast Asia for seven years, the Dean of the College of Family living at BYU for five years and Chairman of the Department of Family Economics and Home Management there for another two. A variety of other jobs and assignments are also on the list.

Honors? They include scholarships to five universities, a Fulbright professorship for teaching abroad and being named a delegate to the World Forum of Women in Brussels in 1962. That same year she received the BYU Distinguished Service Award, an honor she has also garnered from the University of Utah and Cornell University. In 1972 she was chosen as Utah's "Mother of the Year" and was also singled out as a national merit mother. She's listed in the various "Who's Who" volumes, holds membership in numerous honorary and service organizations.

Publications? There are many, primarily pamphlets and articles, with a combined distribution of over a million.

Virginia is the mother of two children whom she raised after being left a widow during the third year of her marriage. She still has found time for extensive Church service, including fourteen years on the YWMIA General Board. The rewards of diligence and perseverance have been hers, and she has truly tasted the fruits of joyous womanhood.

JDC & DSC

DECISIONS THAT MAKE A DIFFERENCE
by
Virginia F. Cutler

There is a tide in the affairs of men,
Which, taken at the flood, leads on to fortune;
Omitted, all the voyage of their life
Is bound in shallows and in miseries.
On such a full sea are we now afloat,
We must take the current when it serves
Or lose our ventures.

Shakespeare (Julius Caesar, Act IV, Scene 3)

Each Era of Life Requires Choices

Important decisions made during the several major tides of life must be timed for the period when most applicable, for each phase of development in life is dependent upon what has preceded it.

During the first twenty years of one's life, three very basic decisions need to be made to guide life's course. If good judgment and wisdom are exercised in making these decisions, the foundation for future growth and happiness is laid. The three basic decisions are:

1. A decision about one's religion or ethical beliefs and the part they should play in all of life's activities.
2. A decision about the development of talents and abilities in order to earn a living and be a productive citizen.
3. A decision about values and attributes essential in a marriage mate.

Preparation for making these decisions begins in the cradle. If by the mid teens they are made, so much the better—but at least by age twenty some firm answers should be forthcoming.

The tide for the second twenty years (20-39) requires a concentration on family, home and profession. Decisions will relate to the marriage partnership and to the method of acquiring and managing resources, to the establishment of a home and the place

33

of children in it, to the type and location of the home and its suitability for optimum growth and development of the family. The educational and professional advancement of marriage partners requires careful thought and planning. While it is certain that one can learn and adjust and continue to do so throughout life, it is easier to work intensively in expanding one's knowledge during this period than it will be later on. Thus this phase of life for both husband and wife must not be neglected.

The third score of years (40-59) might be labeled the "launching years." At this time decisions must be made about the children's missions, advanced schooling and marriages. There may be a need to gently shove children out of the nest as they become adequate and competent to carry forward on their own. Parents' greatest obligation during this period is to make sure that the offspring are given the best possible background for establishing homes and carrying forward the family ideals and traditions. Wise discussion can make this possible.

The fourth score of years (60-79) are the "recovering years" or the empty nest period. At age 60 the U.S. Dept. of Health reports that women may expect to live 16½ more years and men may expect to live 12½ more years. It is very likely that one mate will survive the other during this period. Discussion must be made about how to use diminishing resources and abilities to the best advantage and how to make these golden years a productive and happy period of life.

The last twenty years (80-100) could be the most creative years of life if adequate planning and preparation have been made for them. At this stage one might still be actively engaged in the world's work or be resigned to rocking oneself to death. It all depends on decisions made earlier in life, on the strength of character that has resulted and on the degree of motivation to continue to strive toward making the world a bit better for having lived in it. Our General Authorities are remarkable examples of how the active and productive life can continue and reach high levels of accomplishment at the later stages of life.

"Two Roads," the poem by Robert Frost, reminds us that a decision once made leads one in a certain direction and that it is difficult and unlikely that one will retrace his steps and go back to another route. A decision made in haste with a myopic view may take one to what may seem to be rosy, easy path—whereas, a thoughtful decision made with a hyperopic or far-sighted view may take one to a more difficult route with thorns and thistles to combat. But in the final measure of the worth of a life the decision that requires the greatest effort may perhaps bring the greatest development and happiness and make all the difference.

Important Decisions for the Teens

It is well for young people in their teens to look down life's highway and try to visualize what they hope to be and hope to accomplish ten—twenty—fifty years hence. If they develop the maturity to see that road sharply and clearly and at the same time acquire the ability to be flexible in adjusting to changed situations while moving toward their goals, they will bring to pass their own predictions. It must be remembered, however, that no two lives are the same. Every person is unique in potential and special abilities. What is right for one may be disaster for another. But it never hurts to aim high. In fact, it brings out the best one has to offer.

A patriarchal blessing can be a tremendous asset in charting the path for spiritual perspective to the future. It can serve as a guide and can be used for constant reference. To illustrate:

A young girl, age 16, obtained a patriarchal blessing. Three great promises were given:

1. That she should obtain a goodly education and that the way would be opened up for her to achieve it.
2. That she should become a teacher of young and old, friends and strangers, at home and abroad.
3. That she should become an honored mother in Israel and her teachings by precept and example should live in long remembrance among her posterity.

She believed implicitly in those promises. She realized, however, that she must complete high school requirements and go to the university. No other member of her family had gone to a university and she did not know how this objective would affect her family nor what the financial drain might be on the family affairs. She made the decision that she must support herself.

35

When high school day was announced at the university she decided to attend and to enter one of the contests. She won first prize, which was a four year scholarship to the university. The way was indeed opened up for attaining the educational promise given. With this excellent beginning she was able to obtain part-time jobs to pay for every day expenses. She worked in a laundry, as a maid, as a typist, as a clerk in a store, a waitress, and as a switch board operator before completing her degree.

She concentrated on preparing herself to be a teacher and, since she planned also to be a wife, mother and homemaker, she majored in home and family studies. This preparation, she decided, could be used two ways: at home and to earn a living. She knew she must test her abilities as a teacher before she could think about marriage, so she taught school for three years and then was married to a very choice person who answered the criteria she had set up for a marriage mate.

They built a home and planned for the future, intending to rear a large family. They set the goal to make their home a heaven on earth. All seemed like "moonlight and roses" for two years. There was one baby and another on the way when suddenly her husband died.

Decisions at a Time of Crisis

At this critical point a new decision had to be made. Should she accept her parents' invitation to live with them? Or should she quickly try to get work and go it alone? After reading her patriarchal blessing she decided on the latter course. She knew that no two women can run the same household—that one must always be subordinate to the other. She knew, after analyzing the situation, that she loved being independent and mistress of her own affairs. She also wanted her family to have some special identity and not be integrated within another family unit. So within two weeks she had a position and has since then carried forward as homemaker, mother, grandmother, and teacher for more than forty years.

As had been promised, the way was opened up for her to obtain higher degrees to improve her knowledge. She can relate some miraculous experiences in connection with this promise. She taught friends and strangers—old and young—at home and abroad.

Both children grew up and served on missions. Both achieved the doctoral level in education. Both chose remarkable marriage mates and established homes of honor and integrity.

Decisions for Sunset Years

Even though she is past retirement age she has decided never to retire. She continues to serve as a Church and community worker in her state and in the nation. She expects to live to be a centenarian and to take care of herself all the way. She has said many times that she didn't have the opportunity to "pay her way in" when she was home but that she certainly intends to "pay her way out" with something to spare when she leaves. She has already established scholarship funds totaling about $100,000 at a number of universities which are helping other students with financial problems to attain a goodly education.

Here are questions which have been asked about the foregoing illustration:

Question: How could the mother described spend enough time with her children to really have an influence on them when most of her time was required to be the businesswoman?

Answer: She concentrated on quality of time spent with them rather than on quantity of time. They worked closely together as a family unit. They remodeled houses, painted and improved them. There were rock collections and model airplane projects. There were animals and chickens and gardens to care for. A branch of the Church was started and meetings were held in their home. Many groups came for meals and special events.

She made a decision about overall direction. A passage from Deuteronomy (6:5-9) was her guide:

> Thou shalt love the Lord thy God with all thine heart, and with all thy soul, and with all thy might.

> And these words, which I command thee this day, shall be in thine heart:

> And thou shalt teach them diligently unto thy children, and shalt talk of them when thou sittest in thine house, and when thou walkest by the way, and when thou liest down, and when thou risest up.

And thou shalt bind them for a sign upon thine hand, and they shall be as frontlets between thine eyes.

And thou shalt write them upon the posts of thy house, and on thy gates.

To follow this directive she had to teach by the language of the feelings as well as by the language of words, and by example and reminders.

Question: What do you mean language of the feelings and reminders?

Answer: One can never teach anything which one does not fully believe. What is in the heart can be communicated faster than what is said through speech. A babe in arms is extremely sensitive to the language of the feelings. Everyone can retain and develop this sensitivity and can learn to measure the quality of a person through this language.

Reminders refer to standards of dress, choice of foods for the family diet, the care and love of the home and surroundings, carrying forward family traditions, standards of behavior, what is done on the Sabbath Day and at tithing settlement.

Question: It must have been difficult to refrain from having too strong a mother influence on the children when there was no father present. How was this problem overcome?

Answer: She realized this danger and deliberately planned to have families come for Sunday dinners so that strong male persons could become known to the children. This led to hikes, skiing and many other activities with their fathers. One of the fathers was a chemist and gave the children some cast off equipment that they used to set up their own laboratory in their bedroom. Several of the men became heroes to the children and they idolized them and tried to be like them.

Question: There must have been some lonely hours and periods of discouragement. Was there any special remedy to combat such feelings?

Answer: Yes—She kept her Bible handy. Her favorite remedy for any negative feeling was the 23rd psalm:

The Lord is my shepherd; I shall not want.

(She never had any serious need that was not provided for)

38

He maketh me to lie down in green pastures:
> *(Every place where she lived was made into a green pasture)*

He leadeth me beside the still waters.
He restoreth my soul:
> *(She never used tranquilizers or pills, belief was all that was needed)*

He leadeth me in the paths of righteousness for his name's sake.
> *(This applied to the children also)*

Yea, though I walk through the valley of the shadow of death, I will fear no evil: for thou art with me; thy rod and thy staff they comfort me.
> *(This dispelled fear)*

Thou preparest a table before me in the presence of mine enemies:
> *(She knew that whatever was needed to combat evil forces would be provided and it was)*

Thou anointest my head with oil; my cup runneth over.
> *(Yes it did—with much to spare for friends and neighbors)*

Surely goodness and mercy shall follow me all the days of my life: and I will dwell in the house of the Lord forever.
> *(She believed this implicitly)*

Formulas for Decision-Making

Question: I can see how the patriarchal blessing provided a guide for spiritual perception and for making decisions, but aren't there some scientific formulas that can also be used?

Answer: Yes indeed, and she used these devices, but she always felt that the motivation for follow-through on decisions was stronger because of the spiritual insight. Here is the decision making formula—**PACT:**

P=Problem: Define the problem—be specific:

Young widow with one child and one yet to be born has $3000 insurance money. She must pay $1000 for burial expenses, $300 tithing and owes $3500 on her home. What should she do about the support and care of her family?

A=Alternatives: List all possible alternatives:

    1. Settle bills, sell house, live with parents

    2. Same except take turns living with parents, then with

39

husband's parents

3. Start looking for another husband to support family
4. Pay bills and apply what is left on mortgage, apply for teaching position, pay own way, hire someone to care for children

C=Consequences: List consequences in reference to A:

1. Lose family identity and personal independence
2. Same as No. 1
3. Irreconcilable with basic beliefs
4. Keeps identity of family. Be independent, support self and family

T=Tactics: Make decisions and steps needed to begin:

1. No. 4 decided upon
2. Apply for position
3. Arrange for interviews
4. Arrange for someone to care for home and child
5. Plan home and work schedule and tentative budget for one year

Question: The **PACT** formula makes sense and is easy to remember. Did she have any other formulas for follow ups?

Answer: Yes, she devised two other formulas that were very helpful to her and which have helped thousands of others. Here they are:

KIES (pronounced keys) The keys to success in decision-making are:

*K=Knowledge—*Acquire all possible facts and knowledge about the problem.

*I=Internalize—*Understand all the facts and see their personal application.

*E=Eternalize—*Examine the facts in terms of their long-time effort.

*S=Share—*Share knowledge with rest of family and with others. Get reaction and suggestions.

This last formula is essential to provide the step-by-step procedures to accomplish a goal. The acronym is used to make it easy to remember—even though the letters do not follow in exact order.

COPE—One can cope with any problem by following these three formulas and by having in addition—the spiritual perspective.

P=Plan—List objectives, work and detailed targets.

O=Organize—List all resources available (human and nonhuman) and put them to work.

C=Control—Keep objectives clearly in mind and see to it that action takes place in the direction desired.

E=Evaluate—Make frequent checks on progress. Get rid of "bottle-necks," and improve the plan as is deemed necessary.

Basic to all the decisions we make must be a firm belief in God and belief in ourselves as children of God. In the example cited, this spiritual relationship motivated her to decide:

1. To obtain a patriarchal blessing
2. To do whatever was necessary to bring to pass the promises made
3. To enjoy life to the full and help others to do likewise

A prayer uttered by St. Francis of Assisi epitomizes her sense of mission. It offers an excellent guide for many of the choices we all must make:

> Lord, make me an instrument of your peace.
> Where there is hatred let me sow love;
> Where there is injury, pardon;
> Where there is doubt, faith;
> Where there is despair, hope;
> Where there is darkness, light; and
> Where there is sadness, joy.
> O divine Master,
> Grant that I may not so much
> Seek to be consoled as to console;
> To be understood as to understand;
> To be loved as to love;
> For it is in giving that we receive;
> It is in pardoning that we are pardoned; and
> It is in dying that we are born to eternal life.

41

INTRODUCING — ETTIE LEE

"I will provide family-type homes myself for boys with delinquent tendencies." This was Ettie's resolve in the late forties, after observing the failure of various other agencies to meet this important need. In 1950 she opened the first of her homes for boys. Today there are twenty-three homes functioning in Utah and California. Thousands of boys have felt the beneficial effects of her program since its inception.

Ettie had spent her life in the field of education before she ventured into social work. She graduated from Northern Arizona Teachers College in 1908 and taught in the schools of Arizona from 1902 to 1914. She then took Bachelors and Masters degrees from the University of Southern California in 1916 and 1920 and taught in Los Angeles junior high and high schools until 1927. She was an instructor at the University of Southern California and the superintendent of teacher training in the City Schools of Los Angeles until 1946. She is the author of three textbooks. Her work since beginning her homes for boys has been to create the kind of environment which makes it possible for neglected boys to grow into mature, conscientious citizens.

In 1959 she was named "Teacher of the Year" by the California Teachers Association and was also awarded a plaque for the Most Distinguished Service to Youth in the Los Angeles area. The title "Woman of the Year" was conferred on her by the Los Angeles Times. In 1966 she was named "Teacher of the Nation." Brigham Young University named her "Woman of the Year" in 1968 and she was recipient of the Alumni Achievement Award from Northern Arizona University in 1971.

Ettie Lee, perhaps more than any other author in this book, shows the far-reaching good that can be accomplished by the efforts of a single woman.

We salute her.

JDC & DSC

EVERY CHILD'S RIGHT: A GOOD HOME
by
Ettie Lee

I have been fortunate to have not just one family, but many. Each of my homes is a family unit—with a "Mom," a "Pop," and children. I am convinced that there is no substitute for the family experience. However, I also know that the closeness of living together can often produce conflicts and tensions, and that the success of the family relationship depends largely on how these conflicts and tensions are resolved. In deciding just which elements make up a good home, I have analyzed my own experiences to find some of the lessons we learned from the three thousand boys who have been in our homes in the last 22 years.

Parents Must Take Time to Show Love

I remember one of the first boys we accepted into our Ettie Lee Homes and the lesson he taught us. He had been accused of molesting women in the public park. They called him a sex maniac, and because of his record of leaping out of the dark to embrace women, the authorities were determined to put him in a psychopathic hospital. But the Judge asked me if we could help him. As I talked with this 12-year-old youngster, the true story began to emerge. He was the only boy and the oldest child of a very large family where his mother was kept busy tending to all of the younger children. She believed that showing affection to a boy would make him a weakling and she raised him by cold, scientific theories. At night he would sneak out of his room. He would go to the park, and when a motherly-looking woman would come along, he would run up and hug her, then disappear into the bushes. We placed this boy in one of our ranches where the plump, loving, middle-aged mother would put her arms around him often and let him know he was a loved and wanted member of the family. This boy was not a sex maniac. He was just a lonesome little boy who was desperately searching for the love that his own mother had not been able to give him. All children need to feel loved and wanted, and

43

as soon as he received this reassurance, his problem cleared up.

A Home Must Be a Haven from Cares of the World

I have seen so many children who continually run away from home or who spend most of their time in the streets because home is not a pleasant or happy place to be. Their parents are always arguing; the rest of the children are constantly fighting; and there is dirt, discord and confusion wherever they turn. No wonder they would rather be somewhere else. The physical surroundings of the home, together with the emotional atmosphere, are extremely important in providing a healthy family experience.

Each Child Must Be Listened To and Accepted

I recently had one of my former boys visit me for a Sunday afternoon. As we sat reminiscing over his experiences in the home and some of the boys we both knew, he said, "You know, Aunt Ettie, the thing I like to remember best from the time I lived in the Home is the way Mom and Pop always took time to listen to me when I had a problem. They didn't condemn me because I had problems. They accepted me and loved me anyway, and helped me to find solutions that worked."

His comment started me thinking. One of our boys had a father who was a very successful businessman. The boy said that he actually had to make appointments just to be able to talk with his own father, and even then they were constantly interrupted by secretaries, attorneys, vice-presidents and bankers demanding immediate decisions and advice. There was such a poor relationship between this father and his son that the boy had been on drugs for two years before his father ever became aware of it, and only then because the police brought it to his attention. The son told me that the only way he could get his father to listen to him or pay him any attention was by getting in trouble. When he finally got into enough really serious trouble the father at last was forced to pay attention, but by then it was too late for effective communication between them.

Parents must make the effort to listen to what their children have to say and must keep an open mind. Talking over problems honestly and openly is the best insurance against what is too often called the "generation gap" but in reality is merely a "communication gap."

44

Each Family Member Shares Planning Responsibilities

The Family Home Evening program has been a great help in our homes. Because most of our boys are not LDS, we don't call them family home evenings, but in each home we have a weekly meeting where all the boys sit down with Mom and Pop to discuss what is happening in the home. At this time, family differences are resolved and plans for the next week are formulated. Each boy is encouraged to take part, to air his grievances, and to suggest methods of improvement. Each boy has the right to speak without interruption, and is listened to by all other members of the family. After such meetings, the boys come away with a greater feeling of unity and an attitude of love and respect for each other and for their homeparents.

These weekly home meetings have convinced us all that family unity is built through involving each member of the family in the responsibility and planning that is essential to successful family operation.

Parents Must Make Necessary Decisions

Of course, all of our homeparents have not always had things run smoothly. Many have suffered from the same problems that have made the boys' original homes so ineffective: over-permissiveness, lack of structure, immaturity, etc. A few years ago, one such couple came to me with tears in their eyes because of their inability to handle the boys in their home. As we analyzed what they were doing, it became apparent that part of the problem was their failure to realize and accept fully their role as parents. The husband wanted to be a "buddy" to the boys and as a result was unable to mete out discipline when it was needed. The wife, as a result, felt that she had to compete for the boys' affection so she would give in to their every demand. This only added to the feelings of insecurity that the boys in the home already felt. As a result of this couple's inability to recognize their role as parents, the boys in this home weren't getting the discipline and training they needed.

This story, however, has a happy ending. The couple was able to see where they were making their mistake and correct it before any real damage had been done in the lives of their boys. Through solving this problem, the young couple grew in wisdom and maturity, and were thus able to meet the needs of their boys much more effectively.

Structure Is an Essential Part of Family Life

It is no wonder to me that our country is facing difficult times. We read daily of the increased drug problem, of lack of respect for authority, of riots and killings. Our young people are being left to run at will, to make their own decisions and think only of their own pleasures. We are seeing a great decline in family life here in this country. When people live together there must be boundaries on both personal property and personal liberty. Unless we return to this important concept, the concept of a secure family, I am sure our nation will continue to be beset with internal turmoil. The family was instituted by God for a purpose. Adam and Eve were commanded to multiply and replenish the earth. Their charge was to teach their children and bring them up in righteousness. Through the ages the penalties for parents who have failed at this task have been severe. There is absolutely no other place where children can obtain the training that is available to them in the home. If the family fails in its job, the children, and society, will be forever cheated.

I have seen these children as they come from unhappy families —no respect, no manners, no goals, unable to show love because they had never experienced it. I have watched them develop into loving, caring, well-adjusted personalities through the magic of family living.

Children must be made to understand that parents are human, too, and that they also have needs and feelings which must be considered. The well-structured family must provide a place for each member, and each must be allotted the responsibility of work suitable to his age and abilities, and recognition for work done. The dignity and self-respect which comes from participating in a successful family experience can be learned in no other way, and is the surest base upon which to build respect for others.

Children Not Only Need, but Want Discipline

A lack of proper, consistent discipline leaves a child wondering if he is really loved. One of the boys who came into our homes was from a family where the father and an older brother were in prison

46

for narcotics and the mother was in the women's prison for check forgery. This boy had been shuffled from relative to relative and had never found consistent guidance or discipline. He was constantly in trouble with the law and had eventually been arrested for his participation in a gang shooting episode. While he was held in jail, his parole officer asked him to examine his past life carefully, and then to write out just exactly what it was he wanted for his future. The following is his letter:

Dear Mr. Johnson: I am writing you this statement, concerning my situation. My intentions are to try and convince you that I am not lost in this world, but if given the chance, I will succeed. I need a proper home with parents who are willing and able to understand me. These parents must be willing to help me, when I ask for help, or really am in need of it. I want these parents to treat me like a person who is able to succeed. I want them to be encouraging. I don't want them to treat me like a kid, I want them to treat me like a young man.

I also want them to have faith in me, I want them to be someone who I can talk over my problems with. I want them to be someone who I can explain things to and get results, parents who will encourage me when I'm let down. I want some parents who I can ask, and will know why I ask. I don't want these parents to be forcing me to a goal they think is best, but I do want these parents to work with me, with understanding. I need these parents because they can change my way of life. They can put more realization into my life. They can help me plan and make me see things more clearly. I do want these parents to understand, that I am growing up and on my way to manhood. They must also understand that a boy of my age does not need the love and care that a younger boy would need. I don't need a place where I'll receive too much love, but a place to get started, to lead on in my education, to plan for my future. I need a place to make a man of myself. The trouble with me is that I really haven't had a good start in life. Someone would always interrupt my life. They would not let me keep going. I would get discouraged and would get out of line. I would feel like not trying, like quitting, stopping right here.

But my faith was too strong. I felt I had something ahead of me, and something worthwhile going after. Right at this moment I need help. I need these parents to help me succeed in life. It seems to me that there's a reason or a cause behind every person's

47

behavior. I'm young, but I'm very much concerned about my life. To me my life means more than anything else in the world. I've lived here in this world 16 years, and from 10 years of age to 16 years of age I've wondered about myself. I've wondered about other people, why they behave as they do, what makes them do what they do. And you know something, I haven't yet found out what there is to know. I think that there's something more to life than just living. There's more things to know than you understand, or want to know. I ask myself, why did I do wrong? I don't know, I was there.

Life is strange. There's a place for everyone, and where you grow up, and how you grow up, the environment you live in, your life, everything around you makes you what you are. There really isn't much cause to punish a person directly, without understanding that person. No one can really judge a person by his acts, what he does, or how many times he does it. The thing is to look into this person's life and understand why he does what he does. To see back to his life when he was young, how he grew up, and in every person a story will come out, why he is what he is. I can only say that I need this home very very much. To me this home is a light, a light that leads to more light. I think I can find happiness in this proper home. It's just understanding that I need, time to study and think deep into my life.

Please help me, help me to break this wrong doing, help me to set my feet on the ground. Help me to feel that I won't run off to another world, but that I'll remain fighting and building myself to success. Help me by giving me this home and these proper parents. Thank you.

Sincerely written,
Richard

This boy was placed in one of our homes with capable parents who were able to give him direction and kind but firm discipline. Since that time he has graduated from high school, joined the Church, fulfilled a mission, was president of his college class, married, and is now studying to be a teacher.

Having found the loving and consistent discipline and guidance he needed, this boy has now become a warm and loving parent in his own right. He sees clearly the importance of discipline, and uses it effectively in his work with his scout troop and with his own children.

I'm sure that the family experience obtained by this boy was the instrumental factor in salvaging his life. There can be no greater job for parents anywhere than to know they have helped prepare their children for a good life and for eternal rewards.

Parents Must Allow Children to Live Their Own Lives

There is yet another important aspect of family living and that is in the area of free agency. Parents are charged with teaching and preparing their children, but there comes a time when parents must let go and allow their children to live their own lives. Parents must not over-shadow the lives of their children. In all families, even good ones, there can be children who will not necessarily be affected by every aspect of parental teaching. Even God, the supreme Father of all, lost one of his sons, plus one-third of all of his children. Lehi lost two of his sons, and many other great men of the scriptures and of modern times have lost children to the temptations of Satan. With all of this, it was realized in the original plan that man must have the freedom to choose for himself. It is this way in each of our families also. The final test of growth within a family comes when the parents let go and the child stands by himself to make his own choices and to answer for them.

The key to this concept is in knowing just when to let go. It is a wise parent who understands the members of his family well enough to gauge their emotional maturity as well as their physical growth.

Parents Must Teach by Precept and Example

Children are extremely perceptive and are quick to notice inconsistencies. I think one of the most interesting things that I have observed in the lives of these boys who come into our homes is their sensitivity to hypocrisy. In their minds, all adults are hypocrites. I used to wonder at this but the more actual families I observed, the more I concluded that too often we really do say one thing with our mouths and another thing with our actions.

Let me tell you about another of our boys. The first time I saw him, he was a very bitter, angry young man. He was standing off by himself. The rest of the boys in the home were playing basketball or talking and laughing with Mom and Pop. He just didn't seem to fit in nor did he want to. After the boys had all gone to bed, I sat up with Mom and Pop and asked them about him. It was the same old story. He came from a good, solid family. They were well-respected in their community and no one seemed able to understand why the boy was the opposite of everything the family stood for. This puzzled me also, and the next day I asked this boy to sit down with me and tell me his story. (I have found very few children who won't respond to love and understanding from a sincerely interested adult.)

At first, he put on a tough front, but as his story progressed, tears began to appear in his eyes. He said his parents had taught him that he must be honest, yet when someone would call that they didn't want to talk to, they told him to say they weren't at home. He was taught not to judge or condemn others, yet gossiping and talking about their friends seemed to be his parents' favorite table conversation. He was taught to stand up for what he thought was right, but at the same time they put a premium on being popular and part of the in-crowd, even when it meant compromising their standards. As the tears welled up in his eyes, he said, "I was always confused and I decided never again to believe adults. They just can't be trusted." My eyes, too, filled with tears and my heart ached; not alone for this boy, but also for his parents who had failed to master a very elementary principle. They had failed to teach through example. It is all too easy to tell children how to live and to pour out idealistic platitudes that we feel obligated to pass on to our children. Yet when we fail to live by them ourselves, we begin to break down the bonds of trust that we should be establishing.

There is one of our hymns that I have always felt had particular meaning for me. It is often called "Love at Home."

There is beauty all around, when there's love at home;
There is joy in every sound, when there's love at home.
Peace and plenty here abide, smiling sweet on every side,
Time doth softly, sweetly glide, when there's love at home.

In the cottage there is joy, when there's love at home;
Hate and envy ne'er annoy, when there's love at home.
Roses bloom beneath our feet; all the earth's a garden sweet,
Making life a bliss complete, when there's love at home.

Kindly heaven smiles above when there's love at home;
All the world is filled with love, when there's love at home.

Sweeter sings the brooklet by; brighter beams the azure sky;
Oh, there's one who smiles on high, when there's love at home.

I can think of no greater joy than the peace and contentment
which comes to a home where the parents are kind and loving and
the children feel wanted and welcome. Home is not a building, it
is a spirit and a feeling. Unless our homes have this spirit and feeling our families will never enjoy the progression and unity that is
possible, and unless they experience these things in their own
homes, how will they ever be able to pass them on to their own
children? It is not the big things in a family experience which insure
continuity, it is the small things—the family traditions, the private
conversations, the quiet walks, the shared confidences. Family life
is made of love and understanding and only through good family
experiences can we find the cures for our ailing society.

INTRODUCING — JOSEPHINE C. OAKS

The year 1972 marked a pinnacle of success for Jo when she was chosen the national Young Mother of the Year. We feel her young family of seven children, from eleven-year-old Kathleen to newly-born Leticia, is representative of many family units in the Church today. Her husband, Merrill, an opthalmologist, is the son of Stella Oaks, another author in this volume.

Jo was raised in Payson, Utah, and attended the Brigham Young University, graduating in 1960 with a dual major in Child Development and Family Relationships and Elementary Education. Even before graduation she went east with her husband as he went through medical schools in Rochester, New York; Lexington, Kentucky; and St. Louis, Missouri. These moves opened the way for extensive Church service: she served as District Relief Society president, Stake Primary president, Ward organist, and Ward Primary president. One of her most interesting assignments was helping to coordinate the efforts of volunteers serving hundreds of meals to visitors to the Palmyra LDS Pageant. During this period she also worked as a teacher in a university experimental nursery school and as a substitute teacher in the public schools. Merrill spent three months doing eye surgery in El Salvador and Jo, and their three small children, went with him.

Since their return to Provo, Merrill has been called as Bishop of one of the student wards at the BYU and Jo finds herself as the "mother" for several hundred college students. Her work as president of the Young Mother's organization in the Provo area has given added opportunity for growth and has paved the way for distinction she has received.

Our invitation was for her to share her insights concerning the raising of a young family. We trust that you will find them useful and thought-provoking, as we did.

JDC & DSC

MOTHER OR MARTYR
by
Josephine C. Oaks

My husband called our home from the hospital room. The phone rang! Who would answer: Gregory, Amy Jo, Julianna, Kathleen, or the babysitter?

Then we could hear all of them jumping, clapping and talking at once. "It's a baby sister! Oh! A baby! Can we hold it? When will you be home?" Oh, to capture the excitement of that moment forever!

Then Gregory, four years old, exclaimed with excitement, "Mommy, do you have a baby puppy for me?" There was some disappointment for him, but only for a moment as we explained we had something even more special, something he could hold and help care for.

This was number seven. Number one would be nearly 11 years old. It doesn't seem so long ago that we were calling home from Rochester, New York, to inform my excited parents of their first grandchild and Merrill's mother of her sixth.

I remember how proud we were of every little motion she made; all the pictures we took could fill a drawer. She occupied all our time, went everywhere with us and filled our lives with joy. Whenever she cried I jumped. I remember someone saying to me: "There is no one busier than the mother of one."

Now our home is full of seven little busy ones, whose needs are ever present. I find myself pushed too near my limit of patience. I suppose I could begin to feel that I am a martyr, condemned to every-day drudgery, filling the needs of my family with no time for myself. At times such feelings do creep in. However, motherhood is my supreme fulfillment and I enjoy the challenge of this most exciting of all roles. I will share with you some of the attitudes and methods of child rearing which we use in our home in attempting to properly rear our children and make parenthood a satisfying experience.

Appropriate Expectations

The atmosphere of our home is based on freedom with limits. Whenever possible we give our children alternatives. They are free to make choices within limits we establish. This increases their self-confidence, gives more independence, and puts the responsibility for the outcome on their shoulders. It also gives them experience in choosing the right, and as they grow older, they are able to formulate their own choices with greater ease. As they gain experience in making choices they become more autonomous and begin to formulate their own limits with guidance as needed. Freedom of choice makes a democratic home, but limits are needed for security. The world is large and presents too many problems to the child if parents do not narrow the choices to those which the child is prepared to handle.

When giving choices, one must make sure he can follow through. One of our babysitters was asked to get our 2½-year-old ready for bed. He ran off, and as she stood watching him head for the outside door, she said, "Do you want to get ready for bed or not?" She expected him to say "Yes," but instead he voiced the inevitable "No." She stood there not knowing what to do, so we had a little discussion about giving choices. The decision for getting ready for bed had been made, but Marlo could be helped to make another choice, if asked, "Would you like to come by yourself or would you like me to help you come?" Here a two-year-old is quick to see one choice allows him his independence and the other does not. If he chooses not to come then I follow through and carry him to his room to get ready.

Other types of choices are also appropriate in this situation. "Would you like to play train and choo choo to your bed or would you like daddy to piggy-back-ride you...?" Be sure daddy has agreed previously to this choice or mommy will need to give the piggy ride.

Suppose however, he chooses not to take the choice of going to bed. He has already decided for some reason or another that bed isn't for him. Then is the time to firmly, but gently, carry him to his bed. Children need the security that comes from having parents follow through in a consistent manner.

Toilet Training

An area of frequent frustration for mother and child is toilet training. A child does not acquire bladder and bowel control until he is physically and emotionally ready, no matter what the parent feels. It is like walking. We can coax, prop him on a chair and cheer when he takes one or two steps, but he goes back to crawling which is more secure. Full development and utilization of the walking skill comes only after he is fully ready.

From a child's point of view, he doesn't have time to be involved in any project until he is ready. This rings a bell for me, as right now we have three in diapers. Our 2½-year-old boy and our 18-month girl will probably set aside their diapers at about the same time. Thank goodness for a washing machine!

But, what are some signs of readiness? Girls begin indicating signals around two years and boys around three years. That is the time I place a potty chair in the bathroom. The potty will be more acceptable than the toilet for the child, since his feet can rest on the floor, which reassures him against the fear of falling off or in. He can be independent in getting off and on without someone to lift him. Since the furniture is new and belongs to him he may spend a lot of time trying it out until the newness wears off. This is his first introduction and further usage is his prerogative.

One fine day he wakes up dry in the morning or from a nap and he likes the idea of sitting on his potty. He produces and we react with excitement. He notices our excitement and he feels rewarded. Perhaps he won't wake up dry or show any more interest in the potty for several days, weeks, or months, but our first step in training has been completed. In the interim, we ignore his failures and disinterest and praise his successes, few as they may be. As he begins to show more and more interest in the potty and wakes up frequently with dry diapers, we know he is training himself and we must allow him to proceed at his own pace without any outside pressure. When success is fairly regular, I can involve him in a special shopping trip. Just the child and I go alone to buy the training pants or underpants. This special trip where he participates in purchasing something for only his use, gives him a sense of accomplishment and further endears him to his new possessions.

If the panties are in the storage closet, a special time is planned when the two of us rearrange their placement to a space belonging to him where he can comfortably reach them.

Caring for Bed and Rooms

The smaller the child the more a parent needs to help him in caring for himself and his belongings. Our younger ones vacillate between wanting to make their own twin beds and feeling proud of their accomplishment, and wanting no part of pulling up the covers. Since I cannot expect them to function on an adult level, I give them a choice, "Amy, would you like me to help you make your bed or do you feel like making it yourself?" Amy is six years old and most of the time likes companionship when the bed is made, but sometimes she says, "I don't feel like helping today." Occasionally this is fine too, because I must admit to myself that sometimes I don't feel like making my bed either. Then I say, "Okay, I'll make it for you today and perhaps you will feel different tomorrow." She knows I've accepted her feelings and she can be safe to feel that way.

Our four-year-old boy occasionally makes his bed to surprise me and I always express delight in his accomplishment. Perhaps once a week I might suggest he make it or help me make it. If he runs off, I ignore him because there is plenty of time to teach responsibility for keeping one's room clean. Right now it is a fun game and we want to keep things on a positive level. As soon as I insist he make his bed, I have given it a negative connotation and I become vulnerable to engage in a power struggle. I don't expect more than behavior appropriate for his age.

Our older children, eight and eleven years, have an alternative about keeping their bedrooms clean. The limit that I feel comfortable about is that their rooms need to be cleaned once a week. They may keep their room up each day or clean it on Saturday when the vacuuming is done. If the room is ready to be vacuumed and they have not cleaned it then the responsibility to vacuum becomes theirs and both vacuuming and cleaning need to be done before they go off to play.

Since their idea of a "clean" room may differ from my idea, they were each given a list of things to be done which meet the standard of "clean." If they wish, they may check items off as they are accomplished in order to save themselves time.

56

If they choose to take off their dirty clothes and throw them on the floor each night for a week that is their problem because I only wash those things that are brought upstairs to the laundry hamper. Therefore, they assume the responsibility for their clothes. I will wash them if they arrive for my attention. Here the girls are setting their own limits and the responsibility for the outcome rests on their shoulders.

Yes, they've had to go to school in dirty socks once in awhile, but believe me, it does not happen again for a long time.

Training at Church

Taking little ones to church can be most unpleasant and frustrating, especially if the father sits on the stand each Sunday and is not available to help with the children. Here again, freedom with limits gives the children security and trains them to stay within an acceptable area, providing both parents work together consistently, and have jointly established the limits.

When our daddy first began to sit on the stand, several of the younger ones desired to join him. The limit was set that they could go from one end of the row to the other but not past that. Every time they started testing the limit by stepping out of bounds they were firmly but gently placed back within the boundaries and their attention was channeled to other areas such as a book or quiet toy.

On occasion they have gotten out of the boundary line before I could get them. Since both my husband and I realized this might happen, we both decided to let the child come to him and I would stay in my seat, rather than race the child to the stand, causing bigger commotion. He gives them no attention or recognition for their achievement, but firmly and gently takes them by the waist and faces them away from him and brings them back to me.

They find no punishment, no reward, acceptance or comfort. Their desire to sit on the stand is not reinforced in any way and we have no problem with this. They stay with me where they can play quietly or sit on my lap and receive the attention they desire.

When possible I ask someone to sit on the row and help me, but I always tell them, if I'm in the process of training a child, that their role is to help the wandering one stay within his boundary line.

Consistency of parents is a real key.

Parents Making Choices

Parents are also making choices constantly whether we are aware of it or not. Our choices make a pleasant or unpleasant atmosphere. In our living room is a lovely low glass table which sits in front of our long, gold and green-striped couch. I would love to place an art piece on it to accentuate the beauty and attractiveness of this table. But can I appropriately expect very small children to always avoid an interesting object which is down at their level? Here I find myself making a choice: to enjoy the living room and allow everyone else the same opportunity or be a slave to the glass table and art piece by guarding constantly with "No! No!" Since "No! No!" is eventually tuned out or ignored, or sometimes considered to be just a game, we have decided to leave the glass table bare. We are more relaxed and so are our children.

Whenever my husband arrives home from work and desires to sink himself into oblivion he grabs the newspaper out of the mail box and proceeds to the gold rocker in the living room. If dinner is ready, the paper accompanies him to the table. Now there is a problem which always exists with this choice of behavior—it's anti-social! The children have never heard "anti-social" verbalized in regards to this little matter but they all sense it and react. When the paper arrives at the dinner table, I react.

My husband and I have talked about his choice of behavior and the timing of it and it has taken him awhile to change, but the outcome of making the wrong choice is always inevitable. When the newspaper went to the front room, the patter of feet and a growing chorus of excited voices could be heard coming to greet their daddy whom they hadn't seen since the night before, but only to be met by a barricade of black and white print. What happened was the only natural thing: jump and crash the high wall down. There sat Dad, looking disgusted at having been interrupted. He firmly pressed out the wrinkles saying nothing and straightened the paper back up again. Crash! Down it fell again, this time with gales of laughter. Now the power struggle begins between Dad and the kids. Dad trying to finish the article he had started and the kids making sure he did not. Kids are smart and since they have more time to spend on outwitting us they will win a battle of wills every time. They always win, and smashing the newspaper is really fun!

If the children are not around when he arrives at the gold rocker, he reads until they come and since he shuts out all noise around him when he reads, he knows they have arrived when the first smash occurs. He sets down the paper and lays on the floor and they line up for a slide down Dad's knees and a lift over his head. When they have been given the attention they came for, we eat dinner and they go off to play, leaving Dad to read in peace.

The business of Dad reading the paper or letters at the table posed another type of problem. Everyone was hungry and the service for passing food was not efficient, even though Dad thought he was doing a good job. He was perfectly able to tune out the little voices anxious to tell about the day and it was confusing with everyone talking at once. His love for the paper was real and needed, but in everyone's estimation it was not needed at the table.

We talked about it and Dad would try and do better, but once in awhile he would forget. We decided the next time he brought his reading material with him, we would follow his example. Several reading books were placed at the end of the table near the older children who sat directly across from him. Sure enough, the time came when he forgot. Nothing was said, but the reading began. These books were the most interesting and involved we could find and so they were hard to put down. The progress of the meal ground to a halt and Dad soon laughingly agreed the paper must go.

Quarreling and Fighting

We have some quarreling and fighting; we wouldn't be normal if we didn't. Children have problems and need to work them out. Children's natural way of solving problems doesn't follow the Golden Rule. In order to minimize fighting we let them achieve their own solutions instead of running to their aid. Besides it wouldn't be possible or fair for me to play judge and jury since I seldom know all the evidence of provocation. If one of the children gets himself in a tangle and expects me to bail him out, I do not find he is less likely to repeat that behavior.

Quarreling at the dinner table isn't pleasant. Those involved are invited to leave the table and go outside. Since no one likes to leave a group, the children generally prefer to drop the argument and remain.

Emphasizing Personal Worth

Each child within the family unit needs to know how important he is and who he is. By having his efforts and achievements accepted and acknowledged by mother and father he is helped to see himself as a worthwhile person.

Some evenings when I retire I look back over the day's activities and evaluate my performance. Some days the quality of mothering could be improved, especially in helping one particular child to feel a greater worth. This profession of motherhood is the most challenging, humbling, and exciting blessing that the Lord bestows on women. We are partners with God in helping His children to return back into His presence. With His help I can solve any problem.

One day, I was concerned lest I had neglected one little gal, and as I pulled the covers back, there on my pillow was a note printed next to some creative pasting of sequins, ribbon, feathers, and colored paper which read: "Than you for beig my perents. Love, Julianna."

Tears rolled down my cheeks as I searched for paper to tell my love for her. Then I quietly laid it on her little table under her dolly figurine night light. She would read it first thing before getting out of bed in the morning.

Julianna had made my day, set an example for me, and I felt my worth more keenly. I will send little private notes more often.

One of the most valuable home evening activities we have done this year was having each write something good about another. The children had their own mail pockets pinned on the bulletin board in the kitchen and every day something positive was written and placed in the proper slot. Those who couldn't write were helped. Each day they wanted to know what had been written about them. At the next home evening everyones' paper was read to the family and each child glowed in the worth of himself and his contributions. Periodically they ask to do this activity again.

Another self-esteem activity is where everyone in the family takes a turn verbalizing some positive attribute to a designated family member, until all members have both received and given.

Parent-and-Child Times

In order to reinforce the worth of the children we feel each needs quality time alone with mother or daddy, as often as possible. Here are some things we do:

Story Time—Before they're tucked in bed at night they each choose one book to be read by a parent. The one whose book is read sits on one side of the parent and helps turn the pages or helps with the sound effects. If he chooses a flannel board story he may tell it to the others.

In the summer they have the option of story time or a little longer out-door play.

Older children love to hear stories also. They can choose a longer book with chapters and we read as many as time permits.

Outstanding children's literature is prized in our home. From the time our children are old enough to enjoy looking at a book and understanding simple words, usually around the age of two years, they start receiving "best books" for Christmas and birthdays that belong to them alone. Many of these books include the Caldecott and Newberry award winners. We distinguish between the inexpensive books and the better literature by calling the latter "best books." These books have "limits" on them so the children are taught responsibility in caring for them. Babysitters are also informed of the difference in care such as:

1. Best books are read, looked at, enjoyed and put back on the shelf so no one walks on them, throws them, or tears them.

2. Best books are kept in their special place when crayons are being used.

3. Best books may be read before bed time, but not taken to bed or napped with since they may get torn or their covers broken.

4. Best books must be replaced by the owner out of his allowance if they are damaged because of his carelessness.

Trips About Town—Each child takes his turn to go to the beauty shop with mom. They are given a dime to purchase a treat. While I'm under the dryer they can sit next to me and we'll read or look at magazines together. They also receive individual at-

61

tention from the beauty operators.

They also understand that mom sometimes gets a special time alone when no one comes along. This is time I need for studying a lesson or preparing a talk.

The boys, three and five-years-old, go with their dad to the barber shop and they have their turn for a grooming just like daddy. They get suckers from the barber as a special treat.

The children take turns going grocery shopping with me. The child may choose one package of something for the whole family but no more. Usually this consists of a bag of cookies or a box of "junk" cereal as I call it.

By taking only one child I keep scores of unwanted items from being tossed in the supermarket basket. The older ones learn about food prices, selection and the economics of quantity as well as quality purchasing.

A Day Off—In the June 1972 issue of the *Ensign,* p. 6, I ran across a clever idea by Elwood Peterson which we have tried and "We like it." Everyone who is old enough gets a "day off." We all consulted the calendar and everyone chose a day which appealed to him. I chose my husband's day off so we could spend our time together. On his day at home I like to visit with him and help him. I don't get much done on his day off anyway, besides follow him around talking about anything that has occurred or helping him fix the list of collected items and gadgets that need a masculine touch. We also may do some shopping together.

This special day means no responsibilities other than clearing off one's dirty dishes from the table after a meal. In the afternoon or evening that child receives special time and attention from a parent to help him do something he enjoys. It may be cooking or baking together, reading together, shopping for some wanted or needed item, going for a special ice cream treat or food goody, or just talking in a place where no one else is. If they choose a treat or toy they buy it with their own allowance. Each one feels like a king or queen on his special day. The result: They cooperate better the other days.

Birthdays—The child who is celebrating his birthday gets to choose where he would like the family to go for supper. He can choose any place in our area; of course, the menu must consist of something on the level of hamburgers and ice cream. He may also have a party with his friends if he desires.

Bedtime—Just sitting on the edge of a child's bed and visiting with him about a special problem or subject he chooses is rewarding to both parent and child. This is a marvelous time for training, a time when he can gain a better understanding of how he might solve a problem between him and others.

Just the other evening, one of the children voiced a desire. They love chocolate ice cream and I like to eat it, but honestly do not enjoy the stain and mess of its color, so I avoid it when possible. It had been a long time since I'd purchased any because when it is around I eat it. This posed a dilemma. The children wanted some and I didn't. How could I be fair to those who had been patient with me? Here was my solution: "How would you like to have all the chocolate ice cream you could eat?" The eyes grew big and you know the answer. "Okay, I'll take you four oldest ones to the store tomorrow and you can choose a half gallon of your favorite flavor of ice cream and eat it all yourself. You may use your own money. Then I will buy ice cream to be shared by the younger ones."

The next day the idea spread quickly so the rules were discussed and agreed upon by everyone.

1. Ice cream could only be eaten after the noon or evening meal.

2. Those with individual half gallons would keep theirs in the freezer downstairs and eat it downstairs at their table scaled to their size.

3. Each one would be responsible to return his spoon to the kitchen for washing.

4. Each would be allowed to finish his half gallon at his own pace.

I stayed out of the ice cream since it didn't belong to me and their need for chocolate ice cream, for a time, was satisfied. They, of course, realize this was a special treat to be indulged in rarely.

Parents' Love

Whenever Merrill comes home from the office, I'm usually in the kitchen putting the finishing touches on the evening meal. He always enters with a positive attitude, greeting the children who are helping me and those little ones who are hungry and pulling at my skirts. It's always noisy this time of day with everyone's needs showing. He never passes me by without a fond embrace and "I love you." "How was your day at the office, dear?" A few moments of adult sharing, family prayer, and then dinner. Observing us expressing our love for each other, our oldest daughter thoughtfully said, "Daddy, do you love mommy more than me?"

"Yes, I love your mother more than I do you," he replied, "but it is a different type of love. Your mother and I have been married for eternity and we will have each other forever, but someday you will fall in love, marry and leave us."

The children derive basic security from knowing the bond between us is of prime importance. Yet living at this time when divorce is so common they have found it necessary to seek reassurance by asking, "You're never going to get divorced are you?"

Our love keeps growing because we keep nourishing it. We too, just like our children, need special times together. Two or three times a month we go alone to dinner, a play, or a ball game. At least once a year and twice if possible we schedule a trip together and leave the children home with a young couple whom we can trust.

It isn't easy to find a young couple capable of caring for seven children, so sometimes we separate them and take the smaller ones not in school to Grandma's house.

The children like to have someone else come for a week since they are catered to in different ways.

Generally these trips are medical conventions; but there is usually ample time for recreation together. While he is in meetings I enjoy catching up on scrapbooks or histories needing blocks of time which are never otherwise available.

It is the closeness of our marriage which makes it possible for me to enjoy the children so much. I never feel that I have to solve important family problems alone.

When I have had a hard day and the problems of the family seem insurmountable, my husband comes home and helps me put the problems into perspective.

Serious problems we take to the Lord. With this support from my husband and the firm knowledge that the rearing of a good family is the most important accomplishment of this life, the feeling of being a martyr is rare and the feelings of joy and satisfaction are great.

INTRODUCING — VIRGINIA BLUMVE KUNZ

Virginia, better known as "Ginger" by her friends and acquaintances, is a California teacher with significant accomplishments to her credit. After graduating from high school in Pasadena she attended BYU, the University of California at Berkeley, and California State College at Los Angeles, finally graduating with a bachelors degree in education in 1961 with further graduate study following later. She worked her way through school with a variety of jobs including service as a Girl Scout Counselor and as a stewardess for United Air Lines.

When she entered teaching, Ginger found her contribution was to be made with the youngest children. In 1964 she introduced the Initial Teaching Alphabet reading program into the Laguna Beach schools with great success and saw the area's reading scores rocket to the top of the state and remain there. The Laguna News Post named her "Woman of the Year in Education," 1970. In 1971-72 she designed and implemented a differentiated-staffing teaching program in the same area.

It was 1971 when Ginger, together with her husband Monte (also an educator) and their four young daughters, were chosen the All-American Family from California. They participated in national competition and placed sixth nationally—no small attainment! The same year she placed second in the Tappan National Cooking Competition.

Ginger enjoys working with young people. She directed a teenage group on a six-week tour of Europe and the Mediterranean area in 1970. This past May she was fleet captain for a group of fourteen junior high students in a trip floating down the Colorado River. Quite a gal!

Her recommendations on school preparation and readiness have real merit and wide application for many mothers of young children. We commend them to you.

JDC & DSC

66

HELPING YOUR CHILD SUCCEED
by
Virginia Blumve Kunz

Awe, joy, a closeness to God, an overwhelming feeling of responsibility...haven't we all felt these emotions when looking into the precious faces of our newly-born children? How incredible to think that these sweet spirits, newly-arrived from God's presence, could be entrusted to us!

We immediately begin pondering on how to help these little people develop to their fullest potential. Research in the field of child development tells us that the period which encompasses the first six years of a child's life is the time we have the greatest influence.

As a mother and teacher for some fifteen years, I have been challenged to learn about the early intellectual and emotional development of children. This chapter first deals with the learning process of young children and then discusses ways to help your child through the preschool years and then, on to school.

Early Decisions

Children make basic decisions about themselves and the world around them at a young age. These decisions can greatly affect their later accomplishments and intelligence. As a teacher, I find many of these decisions already made and quite deeply instilled by the time children reach kindergarten. Some examples of decisions children make are:

Positive	Negative
It's fun to be me.	I'm not pretty.
Teachers are fair.	Nobody likes me.
I can do anything.	I can't.
I'm smart.	I'm dumb.
I'm good at counting.	It's too hard to count.

One major role as parents is to have an environment that will encourage our children to make positive decisions. Often, the negative decisions are irreversible or can only be changed by extensive counseling given with great insight and understanding.

If each of us gave some thought to our attitudes about ourselves and our surroundings, we would trace many of them to our early childhood decisions. A young Norwegian girl in her twenties came to live in our home for three years. Very early in her life she had made the decision that she wasn't pretty and, as a result, lacked self-confidence. But she was a lovely girl with large doe-shaped eyes, a perky tipped-up nose, a cute little size eight figure, and a special gift for fixing her hair so that she always looked as if she had just stepped from a bandbox. In our home, she was valued for what she really was and not because of any relationship to us. (When I tell my own daughter she is pretty she responds, "Of course you say that. You're my mother.") Our young Norwegian girl was finally able to accept our sincere admiration and realize her attractiveness. This acceptance made a major change in her personality. She truly blossomed. She married a brilliant and handsome man who, she admits herself, would not have noticed her when she was so shy and unsure of herself.

Work Is Child's Play...The Work of Learning

During the formative years when the young child is making so many basic decisions, he also has a strong drive to learn how to do things. His pleasure is in manipulating, handling, trying, repeating, and investigating. I was watching a baby on her mother's lap at Church. The mother gave the baby a small coin purse to keep the child amused. It was wonderful to watch the baby tasting and feeling the leather, mastering the tricky clasp, taking the contents in and out, etc. The little purse kept the baby happily occupied with a learning experience for the entire meeting. My youngest daughter thinks that nothing is more fun than helping to cook, do the dishes and other such tasks. It is all learning.

Learning is naturally enjoyable, and small children learn voluntarily when their efforts are not distorted by pressure, competition, unnecessary rewards, punishments, or fear.

You Can Raise a Brighter Child

You can help develop your young child's intelligence when he is very young. These are the years when he is first learning and making decisions which affect his whole life.

Research in the field of child-development has discovered many fascinating facts about the intelligence of children. Among these are:

1. Children do not have a fixed intelligence level for their entire life, nor does their intelligence grow at a predetermined rate. Intelligence can be changed—for better or worse—by a child's environment. This is especially true during the earliest years of his life.[1]

2. Heredity does put a limit on how high the child's intelligence can develop. But this ceiling is so high that many scientists believe no human has yet even approached it.[2]

3. Changes in mental capacity are greatest during the period when the brain is growing most rapidly. And the brain grows at a decelerating rate from birth on.[3]

Time spent in helping your child develop his mental capacity is time well spent.

The Preschool Years

I have developed guidelines that will help every parent understand his young child. These guidelines, when used for the preschooler, will help your child to reach his full potential.

1. Exploration

Allow your child to explore. Dr. Joseph McVicker Hunt, professor of psychology at the University of Illinois states, "Curtailing the explorations of toddlers between nine and eighteen months old may hamper the children's rate of development and even lower the final level of intelligence they can achieve."

Beware of the playpen and use it sparingly. Don't leave an infant alone and crying with boredom in his crib or playpen, in an attempt to train him to be "good" and undemanding. The child's drive to explore and investigate, seek excitement and novelty, and

---

[1] J. McV. Hunt, *Intelligence and Experience*, (New York: The Ronald Press Company, 1961).

[2] Joan Beck, *How to Raise a Brighter Child—The Case for Early Learning*, (New York: Trident Press, 1967).

[3] Benjamin S. Bloom, *Stability and Change in Human Characteristics*, (New York: John Wiley and Sons, Inc., 1964).

to learn by using all of his senses is as primary as hunger, thirst, and avoidance of pain. Of course, you must make sure the house is child safe.

2. Experiencing

Give your child as broad a background of experiences as possible. Every new thing a child learns is based on his previous experiences. I remember my nephew thanking his mother for having the shoe-repair shop put new "crusts" on his shoes. Lori, one of my kindergartners who watched her cat have kittens, told us excitedly how the kittens were born in "Baggies." These are wonderful definitions based on previous knowledge.

Provide many experiences for your child to learn through his senses: vision, hearing, touch, taste and smell. Try to keep in mind that this is the way a child learns and be patient. Remember to be patient even when he is experimenting with the different textures of the foods you serve him or when he empties out your kitchen cupboards to explore their contents. React gently when you discover that little fingers have experimented with all of your make-up. When your son is behind the fort with the little girl next door, finding out just what *is* different between girls and boys, you may not condone it, but be understanding and remember that this too is a learning experience.

Little children are so active physically and mentally that no formal plan can take advantage of the opportunities for learning that constantly occur. Your child will learn best if you set the stage for him to make discoveries rather than just drilling the alphabet and other such memory tasks. Any place can be his "classroom." For example, if you go grocery shopping there are many exciting things to see while going to and from the store. Look for different kinds of trucks and try to figure out what they carry. In the store, learn the names of the foods; guess foods by their smell; count out the number of potatoes you want; learn about money; think of ten foods that begin with "b." Learning opportunities are limitless!

Be aware and you'll discover the endless possibilities for learning in the child's everyday world.

3. Learning from Mistakes

Encourage your child to enter enthusiastically into new situa-

70

tions and to try new things. We learn from every experience we have, good or bad. The child whose mother told her: "Don't go in the water until you learn how to swim," never learned how to swim.

It is important that your child understands that we all make mistakes and that mistakes are only stepping stones to success. Teach him that fear of failure should never be used as a reason not to try a new experience. You might want to point out some of your little failures so that he will feel more comfortable about his own, such as the lawnmower daddy took apart and couldn't get back together again or the new dessert you made that tasted like rubber.

As parents we must be free to allow our children to experience life even though it may be painful for them.

A number of children come to school each year afraid to enter into kindergarten activities because "They don't know how" and might not do everything "right."

4. *Developing Language*

Give your child a good language model to copy. Be conscious of having a pleasant quality to your voice. Avoid being too loud. Try to speak in complete sentences. Avoid using slang.

Your child's success in school will be greatly affected by his language development. It is, of course, his main tool for communicating. It will depend to a great extent on language of the adults about him in his earliest years of life.

Don't be afraid to use words your child doesn't understand. As he hears you use them he will gradually begin to know what they mean. If your child butchers a word the first time he tries to use it, either by mispronouncing it or using it in the wrong way, be sure to keep a "straight face" and as soon as it can be done without being too obvious, find a way to use the word correctly in your own conversation. The child will notice and gradually correct himself. Do not discourage delightful experiments with new words by squelching early attempts.

We have enjoyed our own children's experimenting with words. Kimberly, our eldest, used to love going to the department store so that she could ride the "alligator." Jeanette, next in line, asked me if she had good "apostrophe" (posture). One day my Patti was very excited to wake up and look out the window at the magical "froggy" weather outside. And Diana wanted to taste the "battery" when her sister was making cookies.

Play games in which you see if your child can find just the right words to describe certain feelings, tastes, textures, or beauties. How exciting to see the child learn to put his emotions and intentions into language, to learn to compare and to differentiate and to express abstract ideas. I am reminded of when my daughter Kimberly awakened her little sister Diana who said, "Don't, I'm looking at pictures!" What a great way to describe a dream!

Encourage your child to tell you stories. If he likes to tell imaginative stories, enjoy them but help him to understand the difference between "real" and "pretend."

5. *Listening*

Take time to really listen seriously to your youngster. Look him in his eye and give him your complete attention. Avoid "uh-huhing." Value your child's ideas and make an effort to give his questions thoughtful answers.

Teach him to listen to directions. Play listening games such as giving him three consecutive tasks to do: walk over and touch the door, turn around three times and go sit in that chair or, you might say, "Take the pencil, paper, and book to your daddy." Learning how to follow directions will greatly influence your child's success in school.

6. *Reading*

Reading to your child is one of the most beneficial experiences you can give. All little children love stories. This can provide a marvelous opportunity to instill values by reading stories with a moral and by selecting appropriate stories from our Church books. Don't neglect good poetry. Include variety in his diet of books with both real-life and make-believe.

7. *Orientation*

It will stimulate your child's intelligence if you help him to become oriented as to who he is in relationship to his family, location and time.

Help your child to become oriented as to his place in the family. Often make reference to the relationship of aunts, uncles, grandparents, etc. such as, "Aunt Frances is mother's sister." or "You remember that Grandpa is Daddy's father."

Help your child to be oriented as to where he is. Teach him his address and help him to know where his home is located with regard to his friends' homes, the park, his church, his town, etc. Help him to learn the value of your familiar tall buildings, local mountains, and other landmarks in determining where he is.

Help your child to become time-oriented. Make him aware of devices that help us to know what time it is such as clocks and calendars. Use these devices to teach him to count how many hours until Andrew's party begins, or how many more days it will be until Christmas. Make reference to the months and especially to the seasons and their characteristics.

8. *Reinforcing Learning*

When a child is finally old enough to attend Primary and Sunday School, have fun with him when he arrives home and assist him in recalling the stories, games and songs. He will remember what he has learned this way. Also, it sometimes helps you to correct misunderstood concepts.

9. *Praise*

Encourage your child with praise when he succeeds, not with scolding when he fails. Don't worry too much about conceit because the child's friends usually keep that in check. A person usually is only about as good as he thinks he is. The person who thinks he is somebody special will be most likely to succeed.

Be honest with your praise. Do not give it when it is not deserved.

In teaching I have found that I can accomplish almost anything with a child by giving him sincere praise for the good he does and by minimizing the bad. All children love a word of praise and will quickly try to do what is right to earn your notice.

Some children crave any kind of attention and will thrive on scoldings, threats, reminders, just so that you will notice them. Keep this in mind and emphasize the positive. I remember Matthew, a kindergartner, who thrived on any kind of attention. I had spent a backbreaking, tedious day helping each of my sixty kindergarten children (in two sessions) make beautiful clay handprint plaques for their parents' Christmas. They were all carefully

73

laid on the tables to dry. While I was busy for a moment, Matthew carefully poked his finger into the center of each handprint. It was so awful I could only laugh!

10. *Labeling*

Children can easily become "labeled." Use this to your advantage. Look for the good in your child. Give him a "label" he will want to keep. For example: "You are the best listener." "I like the way you always clean up." "I am glad you are here to help me because you are so good at figuring out how things work." "You are such a good cook." "You always are so kind to animals."

Watch out for negative labels that a child might end up believing about himself such as: "You can't get along with anybody." "You'd forget your head if it weren't tied on." "You never finish anything." "You have disgusting manners!" "That was a stupid thing you did."

Beware of embarrassing nicknames which can sometimes be difficult to change later on.

11. *Adapting to Life*

Don't allow your child to tattle and be a whiner, blaming everyone else for what he can't work out for himself. Don't become involved in your child's squabbles unless absolutely necessary. Let him work them out. Mother can try to protect her child to the point where she requests his seat be changed if he can't get along with the child next to him, change his class if he doesn't like his teacher, change a job if it's not just "right" and even change his spouse. This child is apt to grow into an adult who is willing to change everything but himself.

12. *Accepting Responsibility for Actions*

Let your child accept the consequences for his own actions.

I was talking to a friend the other day who is the mother of teenagers. She said that if there was one lesson that she wishes she had more deeply instilled in her own children when they were younger it would be that every action has a consequence and that we are each responsible for our own actions. If Robert is always hitting his friends, the consequence will undoubtedly be that no one will want to play with him. If Alice doesn't remember to put her favorite game away when she is finished playing, her baby

74

sister might get into it and lose the pieces. On the other hand, if Robert is good to his friends, sharing and being interested in their good time, he undoubtedly will be very popular. If Alice takes good care of her game, it should last for a long time. This is as it should be and parents should not try to prevent their children from learning this important lesson by accepting the consequences for them. If your child has been warned not to play ball near the neighbor's window but he does anyway and breaks the window, let the child apologize and earn the money to pay for what has been broken.

When our daughter, Jeanette, was barely three years old she wore her long blonde hair in two ponytails. One day she came trotting in to me and she had taken a pair of scissors, sheared off one of the ponytails and cut all of the hair off her sister's favorite doll. Later that evening I noticed that even our poor cat was missing all of his whiskers. Jeanette stood in front of our large mirror. She took one look at herself and she cried until her little heart would break. Action equals consequence. She learned a lesson. She hasn't cut a hair since!

At each stage of his life, under your guidance, your child should be allowed to bite off and chew up as much life as he can digest to prepare him for the responsibilities of adulthood.

13. *Loyalty*

Be loyal to your children. Don't betray confidences and don't talk about their personal shortcomings with family and neighbors, most especially within the child's hearing. Everyone doesn't need to know that John has a beautiful voice, but that Mary's dreadful voice is just like her Aunt Agnes!

14. *Example*

Always remember that your example is the child's greatest teacher. The way that you spend your time will have a great effect on your child's values. Do you love books and study and take classes to increase your knowledge? Do you enjoy good music, appreciate and share your joy in a magnificent sunset or delicate flower? What kind of activities does your child see you doing when you have time for yourself?

15. *Learning for Learning's Sake*

The motive for learning should be experience and knowledge.

Your child should not do his daily learning tasks to please someone else but for the pleasure he, himself, receives. Avoid statements like: "Please do it for mother." Or, "It will make grandpa so happy."

Using bribes should be discouraged except on a special occasion. Your child might come to feel he has to be "paid" each time he accomplishes something.

16. *Obedience*

Let your child know that your words must be respected and obeyed. If a child lacks obedience by the time he is two or three years of age, the chances are great that the mother will have trouble as the child grows older. God intended that we set standards for our children when they are too small to know what is in their best interests. Rules for your child's safety, health, developmental needs and general good manners need to be established. When these rules are broken, the child needs to be gently but firmly corrected. It is not a kindness to a child to be overly permissive and to make excuses for him when he is disobedient. For example: "I apologize for Johnny's rude behavior. He is so tired today," or "He didn't want to come," or "He's like that sometimes."

Many children equate discipline with love and will occasionally test you to see if you mean what you say. Your consistency represents security and love.

A child who has not learned obedience is apt to have great unhappiness during his school years and when he works for someone else.

17. *Self-Sufficiency*

Don't do a task for your child if he can do the task for himself.

Try to allow enough time so that he won't be rushed. Have you ever felt the frustration of being in a hurry and waiting for your child who tells you, "I want to do it myself!" Doing it himself is important. We need to recognize this and not lose patience. The time you may have saved by hurrying him may never be as valuable as the lesson he might have learned in those few spared moments.

76

18. *Learning to Make Choices*

Let the child have as much voice in making decisions involving him as he can handle. You want a thinking person, not a trained animal who obeys without question. There are many choices your child can make. Try to put him in a position where you can accept his choice. Choices might be: the kind of sandwich for lunch, the color of tennis shoes, or a playmate for the day.

I admire the mother who has the courage to let her kindergartner choose what he wants to wear to school and then dress himself. Hurrah for her for caring more about her son's development than her own ego. It can be embarrassing to see your child march off to school with navy-blue socks, brown-plaid pants and his favorite hot-pink shirt...backwards!

19. *Love*

It has been proven over and over again that the most nurturing factor in any home is wholehearted and enthusiastically-given love. Your child must know that although you may disapprove of his actions he can always feel secure in your love. If the child knows he has this kind of love it will be reflected in every area of his development.

School Years

Placement in School

Now that your child has spent his first golden years at home with you it is time to send him off to school. The kindergarten year is usually an exciting experience for both parent and child. Unhappily, this year is also the time that school problems begin to develop.

Is your child ready for first grade? My experience in working with elementary-age children has brought me to the realization that the decision you make with regard to this question may determine your child's success or failure in school. Therefore I have devoted the major part of my material to this section.

Would you force a child to walk at six months or to be potty-trained at eight months? Of course not! You realize he will master these tasks when "ready" and that this readiness age varies with the child. Do we exercise this same wisdom in placing our children in school?

Much research has been carried out in the last fifty years in the field of child development. A very substantial amount of this research has taken place at the Gesell Institute of Child Development, formerly affiliated with Yale University. The Gesell Institute feels that approximately 40% of our children have been placed in the incorrect grade. My own observation substantiates this.

Think about the child who, although very bright, cannot sit still for more than five or ten minutes at a time? What will he do when he can no longer sit still? Will he constantly be in trouble? What decisions will he make about school and, more importantly, about himself?

How does a child feel about himself when he is constantly confronted by impossible tasks?

Try to picture the kindergarten child at the end of the year still unable to write his name or use a pair of scissors well enough to finish a cutting project without the help of a classmate or the teacher. Should this child enter first grade the following year where major emphasis is put on writing letters and numbers?

What about the child who at the end of kindergarten cannot yet differentiate between simple designs but who will be expected to understand the complexities of reading when in first grade.

The child who is placed in first grade before he is "ready" is asked to perform beyond what his physical body, mind, and emotions can handle. He finds that no matter how hard he tries, he cannot do what is expected of him. He feels stupid, inadequate, and trapped. He knows that he is disappointing his parents, but he cannot do anything about it. This child can easily decide he hates school and develop a poor opinion of himself. A decision made at this grade level can be extremely difficult to correct later on.

The importance of the first years of school cannot be overemphasized. These first years are the foundation upon which all other education is built. It is the time when a child becomes accustomed to success or failure, which in turn, becomes a way of life for him. Success breeds success and failure breeds failure. This early failure often can influence his attitudes and self-concept for years to come, even for a lifetime.

What is Readiness?

Readiness is closely linked to maturity. Maturity is development which takes place without specific practice. Time is the most important ingredient of maturity. Maturation cannot be pushed. It must evolve naturally, in its own time.

Many children who are six when tested, are found to be the equivalent of five-year-olds in their development. This means their functioning and sustaining powers are at a five-year-old level. These children may be functioning at a six or even a seven-year-old level intellectually or in some other aspect of their development, but a composite of their whole development will place them at a five-year-old functioning age.

It is important to realize that protecting children from the effects of discouragement and frustration, which any person feels when asked to perform beyond his own working level, can pay off tremendously in terms of fulfillment and avoid the need for remedial measures at a later date. This can be so easily accomplished by giving your child an extra year of school if it is needed.

How does a parent know if his child is ready to begin kindergarten? If your son was born within the last six months before the cut-off date for admission I would automatically let him wait until the next school year except in a few extraordinary cases.

For the remainder of children whose age qualifies them to enter you should try to objectively evaluate your child to see if he seems to be less mature, more mature or just right in relationship to other children his age. You can be observing this in Primary and Sunday School.

If you are undecided, place your child in kindergarten and work closely with the teacher. Make her aware that if your child is doing mediocre work you would be open to the idea that he have another year in kindergarten to gain extra maturity before tackling first grade. It is important that you inform the teacher of your philosophy because some parents resist the suggestion of a second year with such vehemence that occasionally teachers lack the courage to mention it. I have had parents break into tears and run from the room. Others have their child tutored to try to make them more mature. I have even had parents take the suggestion so personally that they would not even speak to my husband!

79

You should be especially concerned over the very bright, developmentally young child. He may progress all the way through school because he can manage, barely, the academic work, but really he is too young to do his best. He is often a "C" or "B" student whose parents are consistently told through school, "He just doesn't work up to his potential." This child could probably be an "A" student, given the extra year of age. The teacher will rarely suggest retention for this kind of child. It usually has to come from the parent. It is easier for the school administrators to pass the children on.

A child who has been placed at his correct grade level should be able to understand all that is presented in the classroom, not just an average amount. School success may be defined as achievement without undue stress. A child should have enough spirit and energy left over after academics to develop into a well-integrated person. His life should not be narrowly limited to academics, but should reach out to all other aspects of life with confidence.

The ideal time to give children an extra year is at home, in preschool or in kindergarten instead of waiting until later in their schooling.

Often Asked Questions

The following are questions often asked by parents who are considering giving their child another year to mature at the kindergarten level:

Can a child who is developmentally less mature have as high an I.Q. as more mature children? Absolutely! This child just needs to gain a little age. EACH CHILD HAS HIS OWN DEVELOPMENTAL TIMETABLE. You are aware that the age a child enters puberty has no relationship to I.Q. nor does the age he loses and gains teeth.

Research has shown, however, that children's I.Q.'s have tested on the average of fifteen points higher when given an extra year of maturity to cope with their school work.

Is it true that boys and girls develop at different rates? Yes! At the age of six, boys are a half year less mature than girls. I am speaking of averages, of course. You can readily see how ridiculous it is to have an entrance age which is the same for both sexes. In

80

some Canadian Provinces, the law has been changed so that boys must be six months older than girls for school entrance.

If my child is borderline, that is, almost ready, but not quite, what should I do? When in doubt, give him the extra year. It cannot harm, but may be a life saver. Give him this bonus, this extra insurance.

If my child isn't ready, what does he do wrong? There is no "right" or "wrong" developmental behavior. A child is evaluated on his coordination, reactions, etc. to see if he exhibits four-and-one-half-year-old, five-year-old, or six-year-old behavior traits. These give the clues to his developmental age or his level of maturity.

Children, like water, tend to seek their own level. The child tells us by his behavior where he belongs.

What shall I tell my child who has been expecting to start first grade and now is going to a 2nd-year kindergarten? This is the question most often asked by parents.

Experience has shown us that children make this adjustment easily if the parents have a healthy attitude. You can tell your child you want him to be one of the older children in his class instead of one of the younger. He will undoubtedly enjoy every exciting, challenging minute of his second year. His extra age and "know-how" will give him status with his friends.

How come we are just hearing about all this now? They didn't worry about it when I was going to school. One good reason is that research and study in the field of child development have revealed much more to us as to how children grow and learn. Educators now recognize the pressures exerted on children by the increased amount of information that is now required to be learned and also the desire of parents to insure success for children through academic achievement. Young children need every advantage to cope with these pressures.

I know my child is "ready" because he has taught himself to read in kindergarten. Maybe yes...maybe no. Many children are ready to learn before they are ready to go to school. It takes a lot more maturity to go to school successfully than to just use the intellect. A child needs social, physical, emotional and neurological maturity as well as intellectual.

81

What happens to a child who starts first grade before he is ready? This differs greatly with the child and none of it is good. The most common outcome is academic failure. Sometimes, however, the very smart child does not protect himself by failing. Instead he becomes a "student," but he uses so much of himself doing it that he does not develop socially and becomes a failure as a person.

What about the child who is more mature than all of his classmates or who is very advanced in his schoolwork? It is usually best if a child can be placed according to his social, physical, emotional and neurological development. The teacher should then provide for the special intellectual needs of each child.

Each school district has its own way of providing for mentally gifted children. In our District they are kept in the regular classroom and the teachers plan carefully to provide for their special abilities.

If you find that the thought of your child waiting a year before entering school or having a second year of kindergarten before entering first grade is upsetting to you, examine your motives. Are you more concerned about your child's development or about what people might think or even the rearrangement of your schedule?

Think ahead to the high school years when your child is trying to be as sophisticated as his friends and is being confronted with early dating, drugs, and other such things that require maturity to handle well. What's your hurry?

I cannot overemphasize the importance of seeing that your child is placed properly in school. I have seen remarkable changes take place in children and their attitudes by being given an extra year when needed. Two years ago I had a shy, "slow" little boy who I was told would need to go into a special class for learning disabilities the next year. Instead I kept him for a second year of kindergarten and this year he was not only one of the most popular youngsters in his first grade class but was academically at the top of the class. I have personally witnessed these exciting changes in children over and over again. It is equally as exciting for the parents as for the children to see this kind of success and fulfillment.

82

Supporting Your Child's School Program

As in everything else, your child will sense how important you really think school and education is by your behavior toward his schooling experience.

I would like to make a few suggestions:

1. *Basic Philosophy*

Continue to keep in mind those points made in the introduction and preschool sections of this chapter. Most are not only important to the preschool child but continue to be valuable to the child's success in school.

2. *Volunteering*

Offer your help in the classroom. By helping in the classroom you can give very real assistance to the teacher. It will allow her to be freed from some of the routine busywork to better plan, prepare, and work with your child.

Being in the classroom in a working capacity also gives you the opportunity to watch your child functioning in his school setting. It helps you to see how he relates to other children, how he does his school work, and to see what and how the teacher is teaching so that you can better follow-up at home.

It is thrilling for the younger child to have his mother come to school. He is so proud and loves to show you his favorite activities and how well he can do. It, in a most meaningful way, lets him know how important you think school is.

Go to the teacher and offer your services on a monthly, bimonthly or weekly basis. You will enjoy getting to know the teacher and your child's friends in this way. Participating as a volunteer will also make it clear to you whether or not your child is in the grade where he belongs. You can see, first hand, just how he does.

3. *Grades*

Children and parents should not gear life to grades. It narrows the child's scope. It can easily teach him to learn for the wrong reasons. If the pressure at home for "good" grades is very strong the child often learns to cheat to get them. At the very least, the child learns to play the game of figuring out just what the teacher wants him to say and do. He sometimes doesn't feel free to express honest feelings or to report on those subjects that really interest him because it might lower his grade.

Always remember that a child's motive for learning should be for experience and knowledge.

4. Criticism

If you are unhappy with a teacher or the principal, be careful not to criticize either in front of your children. It can only result in insecurity and poor attitudes. It is not in anybody's best interest. Talk any problems over in private. Schedule an appointment with the educator involved and come to the appointment with a non-defensive attitude. Start the conference out with some sincere positive comments. Pleasantly express your concerns and then ask for opinions. This kind of communication will usually solve any problem with no hard feelings.

If you are still unhappy with the situation and you have done all you can about it, help your child to adapt to the situation in a positive, sunshiny way. We must all learn to do this occasionally.

5. Schoolwork

Treat the work that your child brings home respectfully. This can be difficult to do as it sometimes seems to be arriving by the ton...paintings, dittoed work papers, PTA notices, etc. Look through it carefully.

Display art work. The refrigerator is a great place; tape will not spoil the paint and it is in such a popular place in the house that it can be appreciated. A simple matted frame on any wall can be made to accommodate a standard-size easel painting and then change paintings from time to time. You can design a really eye-catching gallery wall of your child's work. Hallways are especially good for this.

Some people like to put up an entire wall of cork or bulletin-board material where all kinds of work can be displayed.

Have your child discuss his lesson papers with you, helping him with those concepts that he has found difficult.

When you throw school work away, (and you must or it will crowd you out of house and home) be discreet and don't let your child see it go.

6. *School Functions*

Make every effort to attend all of the school functions designed for parents. It is very sad to see a child work day after day preparing for Open House or a special musical program and then be one of the few whose mother "didn't care enough to come." This isn't always the case but it is hard to convince the child that there was another reason.

7. *Reading and Recitation*

It is most helpful to the beginning reader if his mother or someone else in the family can be his good listener. A child needs much more opportunity to be listened to individually than he can receive in the average class of 30 children. Find a cozy corner and let your child read you a good story...daily if possible. Older children enjoy this also.

Individual help is also especially beneficial in learning the rote arithmetic facts...addition, subtraction, multiplication tables and division tables. Flash cards are great learning aids.

8. *Own Work*

A mother can remind her child of school work that is due, help him to schedule his time and offer encouragement. But the child must learn to be responsible for seeing that his work is finished and turned in to the teacher. Mothers should not assume this responsibility and spend their time developing an ulcer because of a book report or science project that is due. I again stress that children need to learn that there is a consequence for each action and that if they don't assume the responsibility for turning in their schoolwork, they will have to pay the consequences. In this case, the consequences have probably already been clearly designated by either the teacher, parents or both.

When your child asks you for help with an assignment, be sure that you don't become over zealous and do the assignment. I realized that I had been doing this a couple of years ago. My daughter was assigned a report to do with a bibliography and a table of contents. I always had helped her with her reports but this time I was busy and could not. She started crying and became terribly upset. It was at this point that I realized that in trying to be helpful and loving, I actually had been doing too much on her reports for her. She felt she could not do her work without me.

85

What a great lesson I learned. It is better that your child's grade be a little lower and that he do the assignment by himself. Parents should give inspiration, encouragement, praise, suggestions, clarification, and assistance in finding material, but only those things that will assist the child and not make him dependent.

9. *Learning by Teaching*

He who teaches learns faster than he who listens. Let your child learn by teaching you. Anyone who has prepared a talk or taught a class in the Church will tell you that this is a true principle.

If a child tells his mother how to work an arithmetic problem, or names the fifty states, or tells her how to spell the words on his spelling list, he will be able to remember these things.

Also, help your child to find his own errors in problems. Guide him in thinking through the steps involved in finding the solution. This can be a real learning situation.

10. *Perception*

If your child is doing very poorly in school at the end of first grade or beyond then investigate the following:

A. Is he overplaced in school?

B. Has he been tested by a qualified person such as a school psychologist to see that his intelligence falls within the normal range?

C. Has he had a complete physical including vision and hearing?

D. Has he been thoroughly checked to see if he has perceptual problems, most especially visual-perception and auditory-perception? Unless your school has a very well-qualified person to do this testing, at the least a trained psychologist or psychometrist, try to take your child to a reading clinic which you will find in most large cities. Do not confuse this kind of testing with that an opthamologist or optometrist does.

Most problems can be helped if diagnosed early in the child's school career. You would be surprised at how often a serious problem goes undiscovered for years. The result can be failure for the child.

If your child has a perceptual problem he will usually need to have special help on a regular basis. Few school districts are able to provide this kind of help. I would recommend that you take your child to the specialists at a reputable reading clinic, recommended by your school if possible. They will prescribe a program just for your child. This treatment, if well done, will be worth the money and time involved.

After all is said and done, always remember that the best guidance in raising your child is turning to your Heavenly Father in prayer.

INTRODUCING—RENE MORIN

It was at breakfast in a Park City hotel that we first heard of Rene's experiences as mother of Utah's All-American Family. *BYU was holding a training session for regional coordinators in the Admissions Advisors program, and Art was there as chairman for the Franklin Region. We spent a pleasant time learning of their experiences in the 1971 national finals held in Florida shortly before the BYU conference.*

Rene and Art, with their eleven children, had placed in the top five families, had been first runners-up in the family talent contest (they all sang together), and had seen several of their children write winning essays in connection with the event. What impressed us most was their feeling of fellowship and love for all the participants. We know this same atitude characterizes their family and extends to all those with whom they associate.

Rene attended high school in Blanding, Utah, then graduated from Dixie Junior College, LDS Business College and Utah State University with a B.S. in education. She filled a mission to the Northern States Mission and then met Art, who was also a missionary. They were married in 1948 in the Salt Lake Temple. Their family, which is often admired as a "large, well-behaved" family, has four children in college, three in high school, two in jr. high, and two still in grade school. Art is a high school math teacher, while Rene teaches kindergarten.

Church service is a continual part of Rene's life. She has been a Relief Society president, an MIA counselor, a drama director, a teacher in all the organizations and ward music chairman. At present she teaches the 15-16 year-olds in Sunday School.

We wanted Rene to convey the values of a large, rural (Richmond, Utah), LDS family that is representative of many families in modern Mormondom. Those with small families can learn much concerning the happiness children bring from this lovely woman.

JDC & DSC

88

CREATING AN ATMOSPHERE OF LOVE
AND CONTENTMENT AT HOME
by
Rene Morin

The home where happiness securely dwells
Was never wrought by charms or magic spells.
A mother made it beautiful, but knew
No magic save what toiling hands can do.

Arthur Wallace Peach

The Home Must Be a Haven of Love and Acceptance

I would guess that John Ruskin grew up in a happy home: his definition would indicate so. He wrote, "This is the true nature of home—it is the place of Peace; the shelter, not only from all injury, but from all terror, doubt, and division."

Unless a home meets the needs for love and understanding of each member of the family, one may be justified in looking upon it only as a house, not as a home. The leaders of our Church have always been concerned about the quality of home life we have. They have given us counsel as to the type of homes we should provide for our families. They keep reminding us that it is possible to make our homes a bit of heaven on earth. I can't remember ever having heard President McKay speak without referring to the home, its sanctity, and how it could best fill its role. His statement, "No other success compensates for failure in the home," is a classic, and says in very definite terms what is of most importance in our lives. President Harold B. Lee also said: "The most important work you will do for the Church will be within the walls of your own home." The home exists for the family and the good it can do for them, not as a showplace, as some would believe.

A part of a mother's work is to make a home where children will want to be, where they are comfortable, and free from the problems that may plague them elsewhere. The family is secure because they know that someone cares for them. When they sense this love and security it is amazing what small things bring them a feeling of contentment—a clean home; a cheerful, pleasant mother; the smell of hot bread coming from the oven; a pan of cinnamon rolls shared with a friend to help them forget their differences.

Some years ago I had on my kitchen bulletin board a saying from President McKay that was a great help to me. He encouraged parents to let their children be children, to make mistakes without being made to feel that they were worthless. It is a natural process to err, but it is not too serious if we make of it a learning experience. How sad for a child to receive verbal or physical condemnation for every minor infraction or error.

As a child, visiting a cousin in another city, I went into a small grocery store one day. The store was adjacent to a house. One of the owner's small daughters had come into her father's store to get a bottle of iodine to put on an injury of a younger brother. As she opened the bottle, in her anxiety to comfort one she loved, she accidentally spilled it. The father, seeing his produce wasted, hastily tore a slab from a fruit crate close by and beat the child unmercifully, shouting at her all the time. He had no concern for anything but the iodine, completely unappreciative of the fact that she was in the act of giving comfort to another. I had never seen a parent beat a child before. I believe it was just as painful for me as it was for the poor child. I remember that for a day and a night I could not get this traumatic experience out of my mind—all over a little bottle of iodine, accidentally spilled.

Accidents will happen in the home, mistakes will be made. I think of President McKay's encouraging words each time milk is spilled at the table, a dish is broken, peanut butter and honey are found on the front room door knob, or the almost-new bottle of detergent is poured into the dishpan as a small helper tries to surprise me with clean dishes. Milk, detergent, and clean floors can be had again, but the crushed spirit of a child is something hard to restore, and much more valuable. It is a part of eternity. What chance do we give our children to grow and learn in love and understanding? What evidence do we offer them that they are more important to us than any mistake they could ever make?

Hopefully, criticism is seldom used in our homes as we try to develop the spirits He has entrusted to our care for a very short time. Joseph Joubert said: "Children have more need of models

90

than of critics. "If we thought more often of the love and wisdom in the Savior's reply: "He who is without sin among you, let him first cast a stone at her," we would be less critical of our own children and others around us. How much sweeter life would be if we could have it said truthfully of us: "He tolerated no failure in himself, yet judged others with tolerance unmeasured" (author unknown). How fortunate the child with parents who minimize his mistakes and weaknesses, but "accentuate the positive" and help him find his own strengths.

Home is a place where children feel important, where they have jobs to do. It is where someone has the time and patience to help them learn to sweep a floor, help them make cookies, make popcorn balls, use the sewing machine, make their bed. Children must be taught—they do not learn good work habits purely by instinct. As my daughter Julynn and I painted one of our front rooms this summer, we were petitioned by my daughter Carolyn, who is eight, to let her help. We did. She adores doing anything with her big sisters. She did a pretty good job, too. Any spots she may have missed are nothing compared to the satisfaction and importance she felt in helping. True there were lots of paint splatters on the old rug. But this gave us an excuse to redo the floor. So Charles, who is nine, and I bought large stacks of carpet samples and together we covered the floor with bright colored pieces. He dragged the 55-pound bucket of cement around the room while I cemented the pieces to the old rug. He even made a large M in the center of the floor. Now we have a beautiful new room, a bonus room because we did it. How proud the children are when someone mentions how they like our new room, how important they feel. How glad we were that we didn't say no when they asked to help us. Children like to hear "yes" whenever they can.

Mothers Set the Stage for Daily Living

Motherhood is serious business. It is very serious business when anywhere from six to fifteen people converge on the kitchen every morning just before breakfast is ready. People wanting breakfast—brown toast, white toast, oatmeal cereal, wheat cereal, hard eggs, soft eggs, boiled eggs, no eggs, peanut butter, honey, that jam we had yesterday, something that has no calories in it, something that will keep you from getting hungry by the end of 3rd

91

period. And that isn't all. Someone has the courage to ask for his clean purple socks at a time like this, a button on an orange striped shirt, the paper that someone brought home nine days ago, help with piano practicing, a couple of iron pills, help to find a lost contact lens, $14.00 to buy a new pair of boy's Converse shoes like the ones he lost. Oh yes, and a math book. Serious business?? No wonder she is wearing slightly graying locks. They will be grayer tomorrow.

Seriously, though, isn't it exciting being a mother? Who else can make so many people happy in so many different ways, so many times a day? Yes, I would have to say I love being a mother. A mother sets the stage for the performance that goes on every day in her home. The scenes and players may vary somewhat, but the mother's role is constant, continuous, and most vital. If she can accept her role in the home and feel good about it, her battle is almost won.

A mother learns to find her enjoyment in her home and family and in her services to them as she teaches and molds their lives. From them she gets her motivation, her purpose, and her "pay," so to speak. She needs no trophies, no medals, no banners—just appreciation and love. A mother learns to endure many things she didn't know she could endure. I recall when I was up almost all of one night with a sick baby. Morning came and I would love to have stayed in bed to rest longer but there was work to be done—children to clothe, a husband to get off to work, breakfast to be prepared. (Did you ever feel like a mother robin when all the hungry little mouths start opening for breakfast?) I felt like a nightmare, and the mirror told me that I looked like one. The children soon awoke and found me in the kitchen, beginning my day's work. They did not know what had transpired during the night. But one dear little boy, as he gave me his good morning greeting, looked at me and said in his sweet, innocent way: "Mom, you're just beautiful this morning." Since I always believe children when I can, I believed him. Suddenly I had new strength; strength which carried me through the long day and its many demands on an exhausted mother. It was all worthwhile and the load was much lighter because my children loved me and looked upon me as something special. My pay more than compensated for the long hours that day.

Last year we shared with our family a most delightful experience. We were chosen to represent Utah as her All-American Family at the national pageant in Florida. It was a very choice experience together, and we were really thrilled with the high caliber of families that represented all fifty states and the District of Columbia. If they were representative of family life in America, we have much to be proud of. We learned to love the families, 276 people, and they taught us many things.

As we participated in the pageant there were many forums and discussions by parents, in an effort to share wisdom and experience. One particular meeting was for mothers alone, and the subject had shifted to one of the popular topics of the day: Women's Lib. After hearing several mothers express themselves on the subject, one of the LDS mothers (of which there were five) said something like this: "I grew up on a very poor farm in Kentucky, with none of the conveniences or luxuries people have today. We were rather isolated, with no opportunity to enjoy the cultural advantages of the day. Now we have a comfortable home with a piano, which I have learned to play. My family has access to the opportunities of the day. I feel that I have been liberated." This was the reply of a loving, proud mother who found her joys in her family, in their togetherness, in making beautiful music with them. In fulfilling this great responsibility she had found her best self—she had been liberated.

Motherhood Requires Many Virtues

What is there about a mother that makes her part so vital and so special in creating a happy, contented atmosphere at home? The Lord must have known what it took to make home a bit of heaven on earth, so He planted the virtues in the hearts of mothers.

Patience is one of those virtues. It is a word that might have been coined especially for mothers. It has reference to things like being pleasant when you really feel like being otherwise; to keeping your voice always calm and sweet; washing and folding the same diapers every day for many months; doing the same dishes three times a day, week after week; feeding babies in the middle of the night; looking in the same places for shoes, books, and car keys day after day. It is helping a youngster with his school work when you could be looking at the newspaper; helping someone write a letter when you know that it is going to take at least an hour to write all he wants to say; it is looking for material for a Sunday School talk when you are really too tired. Patience is the box by the heat vent with the baby chicks in it who don't have a mother; it is turning your clean kitchen over to the kids and their friends to make cookies. Patience has reference to a lot of things a mother must do every day to let her family know that they are the most important things in her life. Without it, there would be no peace in the hearts of children in her home, only fear and apprehension.

Unselfishness is another word that is synonymous with motherhood. A good mother will often have to put the needs of her family before her own. She may give up something she wants for herself, or for her home, because the needs of another member of her family seem more important to her. A good mother truly learns to live for others. Unselfishness is being a good mother 24 hours a day, and staying sweet and pleasant through every minute of it. If a mother can exhibit these great qualities of patience and unselfishness before her children, and do it as though it were a privilege, she has said more to her children than if she wrote a whole book.

Most mothers are naturally compassionate—it is as instinctive with them as with a mother hen to mother her brood of chicks. Mothers usually think with their hearts, which helps make home a place where children, and adults, feel the security and contentment of love and companionship.

The mother must be prepared and able at all times to be compassionate, understanding, a listener who can forgive and soothe, no matter what the problem. A mother, no matter how efficient, how domestic, how well groomed, or how well informed—if she has not compassion, misses out on some of her most opportune moments to serve and to prove her love.

A father is a wonderful person to have around, particularly when he enjoys doing things with his family and is not ashamed to let them know that he loves them. Every child needs to know his father's love. I knew that my father loved me and it helped me through a lot of the difficulties of growing up. We love the father in our home, and he is not afraid or ashamed to put his arms around any one of us at any time and tell us that he loves us. It makes life meaningful and rich, and gives us all strength.

94

I shall always be grateful for a dear mother who exemplified great compassion for those around her, particularly those who were less fortunate, the sick, the handicapped. She made it easier for me to teach compassion to my own children. For months my children carried a Sunday dinner to a neighbor who lived alone, to bring a little comfort and happiness into her life. For many more months we invited a lonely widower to eat dinner or breakfast with us whenever he wanted to. Sometimes we carried it to his home, hoping that in some way the meal cooked and served with love would comfort the ache in his heart. My children say frequently: "Mom, can we take a loaf of your brown bread to _____. Their mother is ill." I think they really feel there are healing qualities in homemade bread, especially when it is shared with love and compassion. There may be, too.

I often tell my children how very proud I am of them because I never see them deliberately hurt anyone or anything. But sometimes we are almost overcome with compassion at our home. For instance, there are the two baby squirrels that have shared our house with us these past few weeks. The men in our family were logging in Idaho this summer with our daughter, Marilee, who cooked for them. They found the baby squirrels in an abandoned nest, with their eyes still closed. Marilee kept them alive with canned milk and brought them home for us to feed with medicine droppers. Soon they were eating fruits, nuts, drinking out of a lid, and eating jello out of a spoon at the table (which I tried not to see). They are such darling little pets, running up and down your clothing, sitting in your hand or on your shoulder, sleeping on your lap, running up and down the piano keyboard. They learned to climb up the old pine tree in our front yard, then come back to the house, scratch on the door and chatter to be let in. I am not sure just what you call it when four big boys take two small squirrels to the outdoor theater and allow them to sleep in their shirt tails or on their laps, but it all started from compassion for small creatures who had been deserted. Compassion for any of the Lord's creatures, large or small, is as He would have it.

Maintaining an Atmosphere of Spirituality

Homes are somewhat like people—they have a definite atmosphere or spirit about them. It is something you can feel, something very real. The size, the location, the purchase price of the home has nothing to do with the spirit of the home. I know of a home that existed first as a basement home, then as the family could afford they built on and finished the ground floor. The monetary value of the home may not be very great, but within the walls of that home exists a perfect spirit of harmony and love between all members of the family. I have been in it many, many times but all I have ever heard between parents, parents and children, and between children, is kindness, patience, love and understanding for one another. People may never be impressed with the exterior of the home, but the inside is beautiful, something you would never forget, because of the harmony and sweet spirit that exists there each day. As the children have grown up and moved away for college, I have heard others remark that they are the most thoughtful, considerate, unselfish children they have ever seen.

What makes the difference in homes? We could enumerate a lot of things that account for the spirit in a home. How do we create an attitude of respect and reverence for the values and the teachings of the home? Homes that become a bit of heaven on earth don't just happen—they are the result of planning, prayer, dedication on the part of parents, and a lot of other qualities mixed in. President McKay has said that the responsibility of creating a spiritual environment is primarily the mother's but the priesthood is to reinforce and strengthen her position and teachings. How much easier when there are two working towards such an important goal. Mothers should be teaching their daughters the importance of having the priesthood preside in their homes of the future. If we, as mothers, honor and sustain the priesthood, how much easier it will be for our daughters to do the same.

Love Must Be Shown

Probably the most important ingredient in any home would have to be love. This is what we speak of as brotherly love—where you consider the needs of others before your own. This is the type of love the Savior spoke of when He said: "Thou shalt love thy neighbor as thyself." Any other type of love wears thin when things do not run smoothly. Parents may not bring children into homes with every conceivable luxury. This is no tragedy. But chil-

96

dren are indeed wealthy who are born into homes where there exists a genuine bond of affection and love.

How can you be sure there is love in your homes? Not just by saying "I love you," but by proving it with your actions 24 hours a day. You cannot buy affection, you have to work for it. Perhaps the best answer to how you can get love in your home is to say simply: put it there yourself. Children are very perceptive. Never believe for a moment that they cannot tell when love is for real, or when it is only a pretense. Few things give children a greater feeling of security and emotional stability than to know that their parents really love each other. One author has said, "The most important thing a father can do for his children is to love their mother." Parents don't have to discuss their feelings for each other—children know. They can tell by the tones parents use when they speak to each other, by their thoughtfulness of one another, the little courtesies they extend one another, the respect they show, by the way they look at each other.

Sister McKay, in an excellent talk given in 1952, told of stopping at a service station in Los Angeles with President McKay. While she waited there a small boy approached her and said: "I guess that man over there loves you, doesn't he?" She assured the child that he did, that he was her husband. "Why do you ask?" she said. The boy replied: "Oh, cuz the way he smiled at you. Do you know I'd give anything in the world if my Pop would smile at my Mom that way." Then, with tears in his eyes, he told Sister McKay that his parents were going to get a divorce and how much he loved both of them. Sister McKay, with all her compassion and love, said that her heart bled for the sweet little child and all the other youngsters who suffered as he was suffering. Love is the healing influence that keeps homes happy and perpetuates them.

Children need also to know that they are loved by their parents. It is very easy to say: "I love you." But this may not be conclusive evidence. Our actions each day will be much more convincing—they will speak louder than what we are saying. Spending time with your child is one way to prove that you love him. Your time may be one of the most meaningful things you can give him. How easy to become involved in so many things that sometimes we think we have no time left for our families. Nothing is a worthy replacement for our time with our children. I heard of a father who wanted very much to prove his love to his children, so he told them very often that he loved them. One day as he said he loved them, one child said: "I know you do, you have told me a hundred times." The father sensed that his spoken word had not been too convincing so he decided that he needed to reinforce his claims by spending some time with his children. This was the proof that they needed, they were now convinced because their father gave of himself.

Each child may want a few minutes of your time alone each day. This takes real organization and planning but we find time to do the things we want to do most. Maybe what a child needs is just a listening ear—someone to hear him out. Maybe he needs the advantage of your experience and wisdom. Very often as a confused youth shares his problems with a willing listener, he is able to see through his problem and come up with his own solution. Then he feels good about himself and good about his relation with you because you were a part of it.

Music Brings Togetherness

One of the highlights at the Florida Pageant was the talent night, where each family would participate together. There were many clever numbers, a great variety of talents displayed, but when the judging was all over, three out of the top four winners were LDS families. In each case the whole family participated. This told LDS parents spend a lot of time with their families. Parents can never afford to get so busy that they cannot give their children the thing they most want, parents' time.

If you grew up in a home where there was lots of singing you know how it cements a family together. Somehow it pulls the bands of love and affection just a little tighter. I love the story about the two men who went to President Heber J. Grant to have him help settle their dispute. President Grant asked them to sing a song for him. After the first song he asked them to sing again. This they did. Still again he asked them to sing. By the time they finished they were both in tears. They threw their arms around each other in love, forgave one another and went their way in peace.

Yes, music hath charms, especially when it comes from those who are drawn together in love for the gospel. I get a warm, wonderful feeling as I think of the songs we sang at home when I was a child—the fun songs, the songs that told a story, and the songs about the gospel. One of my favorite songs that my father taught me in his beautiful bass voice was about Joseph who was sold into Egypt. I still love to play and sing it. I learned to love Joseph and the qualities that made him great in the sight of the Lord. Music is sometimes a means of touching a life when nothing else may be able to touch it.

One of the things I enjoy most of all is singing with my family, or with my four daughters as we sing together on different occasions. It affords us time together as we practice, plan and perform. It brings a special closeness to us, along with memories that will do much to enrich our lives. Children who learn to sing when they are small develop a love for singing that stays with them through their lives. Sing in your homes. It adds a new dimension and creates a feeling of harmony and contentment.

The Value of Family Night

About 1915 President Joseph F. Smith made the promise to the Church that if parents would hold Family Home Evening with their children once a week they would not lose one child. That promise has not been rescinded.

The Church could not make it easier for us to hold Family Night. They have closed the temples, had all Church meetings canceled on Monday night, and outlined and prepared beautiful lessons for us to use. Now all that is left for us is to gather our family around us, sing and pray, have the lesson, spend some time visiting or playing games, and have a special treat to finish the evening. Perhaps this will be the only time during the week some families spend together. How special it is!

I remember how eager I used to be about Family Night when I was a child. We loved the stories about the gospel our father would tell. We made honey candy, ate cold apples from our apple pit, sang songs, and played games together. But the nicest part about all of it was the good feeling it gave me to be with those I loved most in the world, and who loved me. It paid dividends of greater harmony between us, helped us feel closer to each other, and made us realize that our family unit was something special.

We started Family Night in our home when our first child was less than two. It was just a short time together, singing little songs, playing children's games, but it was very special because we were spending time with our daddy who was very busy going to school, working, and being Branch President. It was so special to our little son that several times during the day he would come and take our hands and beg to do it again. Now, of course, our Family Nights are different. With eight older children and three pre-teenagers, our programs have changed to fit our family. We take turns giving the lessons that fill a particular need in our family. We play "I'm Fresher Than You Are" together on our large lawn. We have Poetry Night. We make ice cream in our old-fashioned hand freezer and take it up the canyon on a picnic. We have scripture chases, bear testimonies to each other, discuss family situations that need discussing. We listen to the children's piano pieces and laugh together over pictures of the children taken when they were very small. All of these become very special activities because we are doing them together.

We had an insight into how our children feel about Family Night from a comment made by one of the children. On an afternoon when they were rather disagreeable with one another, I said: "What is the matter today?" One little boy said: "We need to have Family Night." Family Night is one of the things that help us create a spirit of harmony and peace in our home, because it brings us together in singleness of purpose. The Lord made us a promise—do we have the faith to receive the blessings?

Teaching the Gospel in the Home

The gospel is a great factor to bring love and contentment into our homes because it brings direction and purpose to our lives. How sad to see parents who decide to let their children grow up and then decide for themselves what to believe and what part religion will play in their lives. Do you ignore a garden and let it decide whether it will produce vegetables or weeds? Children are not capable of deciding these important things for themselves; they must be taught by someone wiser than they are. They must be taught when they are young and impressionable. The years before five are the most valuable years in their lives. As I put the sprinkler

100

on the lawn this morning, and set it to go where it would do the most good, I thought how like raising children it was. You can let children go and grow without your help and direction, but the result would not be what you wanted—just as the water running from the sprinkler would not go where it was needed, unless you gave it some direction or setting.

The time to teach children is when they are young. It is so easy to teach young children. All you need is the desire and the personal conviction of what you are trying to teach. Children respond to so many things: pictures on the wall, above their bed, on the bulletin board; verses attached to the fridge or above the sink; Articles of Faith cards placed where you can recite them during a meal or work period together; stories told at bed time with children around mother or daddy. You may find as we did that stories from the scriptures are the most exciting stories you can tell. Whenever we sent our children for a story book to have read, nearly always they returned with a book of Bible stories or Book of Mormon stories, or both.

Don't miss the delightful experience of teaching your little ones to pray. Prayers from the heart do much to bring a feeling of serenity and well-being to a home. When one of our children was very young and just learning to pray, he used to wake up in the middle of the night occasionally with his sweet little call: "Mommy, I didn't say my prayers." What a delightful lament to awaken to. I can say that I honestly didn't begrudge such an awakening. And the next few minutes we shared together were very choice, while he prayed to his Heavenly Father. These are among some of my dearest memories. I certainly never could ask for a better-paying job!

We talk often about some of the special prayers that have been offered in our home. Our boys believe that the special prayers and fasts they offered in behalf of BYU Coach Stan Watts had something to do with his recent recovery. I think the Lord must find it very easy to hear and answer the sweet, unselfish prayers of believing children. We received a letter from one of our missionary sons that he was somewhat discouraged over the lack of results they were having in their work. So, unbeknown to him, we held some special prayers and fasts, petitioning the Lord in his behalf. Within the week we had a letter from our missionary, filled with enthusiasm and success stories. He said it was the best week he had ever had. Still he knew nothing of our special efforts in his behalf, but we could account for his success and his new vigor in the work. What great peace and comfort come to those who learn to draw near to their Heavenly Father in sweet assurance that He will hear and answer their prayers. Even the little prayer that said: "Bless President Eisenhower and his cupboard (cabinet)," I'm sure did not go unheeded. Or the child's petition: "Bless this food and the hands that repaired it," was acceptable to the Lord because it was offered in faith.

One sure way to increase spirituality in the home is with family prayers, morning and night, with children participating. The fact that we invite our Heavenly Father to be with us through the day gives us a greater incentive to walk gently in His paths. How sad to know that in many homes children do not get to know their Heavenly Father through prayer, never develop faith in Him, and never come to know Jesus as their personal Savior. Such a little time and effort each day is required to give these experiences to our children, and yet how much different their lives can be when prayer becomes as natural and as regular to them as going to bed at night and getting up in the morning.

Putting First Things First

As we teach our children the gospel and help them arrange their values in life, what we are actually doing is helping them put first things first. The scriptures tell us: "Seek ye first the kingdom of God, and His righteousness; and all these things shall be added unto you." (Mt. 6:33) Sometimes that is easy, sometimes it is difficult, but it is always worth our best effort. Sometimes we forsake our plan for something easier, but hopefully not where the gospel is concerned. There can be no short cuts, no detours—just dedication and hard work.

What means most to us in our homes? What comes first, the TV or the Sunday School talk to prepare? The Fast Offering envelopes or the game of basketball in the back yard? The thing that is convenient for us or the needs of someone else? Do our children discern an attitude in us that says the cut of our clothing is more important than the intent of our hearts? Are we so busy trying to convince our children that service is the Savior's way that we neglect to care for a sick neighbor or comfort the widow? How will our children know what is of the most value in their lives—not from what they read or hear, but from what they see everyday in our lives. If parents can pick up the Sunday morning paper without reading the sports page or the funnies and put it carefully away until after Sunday School, I think the children will get the message that getting to Priesthood and Sunday School on time is even more important than finding out who won the football game last night. Children conform easily if they have a good pattern to follow.

Parents never cease being concerned about their children, but when they can see that they are putting first things first in their lives, it is a real source of satisfaction to parents. I think of our boy away at college, trying hard to get by on his meager funds. When his shoes were pretty shabby his parents sent him money to get new ones. The money was spent, but not on shoes. It went to buy tapes of the devotional talks at BYU; tapes that were used later all over Cache Valley, in priesthood quorums, Sunday School classes, firesides. Tapes that even went to New Zealand where they were shared on buses, in the Mission Home, and with investigators. Even one pair of shoes couldn't have gone that far. And somehow that young man must have procured another pair of shoes—I never saw him going barefooted.

Maintaining Order and Obedience

In the New Testament story where Martha came to the Savior to see if Mary shouldn't help prepare the food, the Savior indicated that Mary had chosen wisely. Somehow mothers must organize their homes to find time for a proper balance of spiritual and physical needs. Every mother needs to find time to teach her children spiritual truths as well as how to organize their time and lives. Everyone enjoys an orderly, clean home more than a home where disorder is overwhelming. Often a busy mother will feel she cannot afford the time to teach her children to work, that she can do it more quickly herself. This may make the difference later on between an orderly house because everyone helps, or a very disorderly, disorganized home because children have not learned to pick up after themselves.

Organization and order in a home let you feel comfortable

103

and soothes you from the troubled world. You can be at peace with yourself. Clutter and disorder cause tension and confusion. There is positive evidence to me in my own observations that children's moods and dispositions reflect the atmosphere of the home. It is worth the time and effort on mother's part to teach children to care for their personal belongings and their own rooms. It will pay great dividends later on, and how much more peace of mind she will have if children are helping to keep the home a place of order! There is no need to nag at them continually—teach them while young to put their belongings in special places, which are provided (and maybe even labeled). Patience and persistence are the key-words. Lots of encouragement and praise motivate children to try harder. And of course the mother's example in organizing and carrying out her duties is most effective as a teacher.

Benjamin Franklin wrote: "Let thy child's first lesson be obedience." What does obedience have to do with contentment and harmony in a home? Any parent who has made it one of his goals to have a happy, peaceful home would surely teach his children obedience. What is more disruptive than a child who doesn't mind? Answer: a houseful of children who don't mind. My mother knew that I was always searching for secrets to help me raise my children. She wrote once about a family who had visited her who had impressed her very much. She liked the way the children behaved, the pleasant relation between the mother and children, the sweet way the mother spoke and the way the children obeyed. Mother asked this successful young mother the secret of her success with her children. She received the answer: "I try to be sweet but firm." These two words have been most helpful to me in raising my children. They say a great deal to me.

These words, "sweet but firm," tell me I cannot afford to be cross or unpleasant, that my children will be more responsive to a pleasant tone of voice. They tell me also that I must be unrelenting in requiring obedience and whatever is best for my child. Children are not expected to know what is best for them. Adults, hopefully, will be able to tell them.

Children learn very young whether or not parents will demand obedience from them. When they find out they know exactly how

104

to react. If we consistently expect and require obedience from our children, we get it. The job of a parent is so much more fun, so much less terrifying, if children learn early that obedience is an important and necessary part of life. The most heartening thing about it is that children are also much happier and contented if they learn obedience.

A friend of ours, a counselor in a junior college in the east, relates well to young people and discusses freely with them the problems of youth. He says that youth wants desperately to have definite guidelines. They want to know that there are certain limitations, then they don't have to wonder where to stop. How needless to worry and wonder about what guidelines children will use because we have neglected to help point them out and we have not talked about the importance of them.

After a child learns to comply, do we let him know that we are proud of him, that we appreciate his obedience? Help him feel good about himself, he needs to take some credit for his performance. If he feels that you are pleased with him he will be pleased with himself. A little genuine praise goes a long way. Mothers may have to close their eyes to a few things children do, but be sure to catch all of the good things they do and let them know you think they are great. They can learn very young that obedience and conformity do much to create peace and harmony in themselves and in the home.

Giving Children Acceptance and Respect

A mother of a large family told me before I was married that one of the greatest challenges to her as a mother was being able to accept her children as they were, with all of their differences. Twenty-three years, and eleven children later, I have come to believe her. The scriptures tell us that the Lord created us in His own image. We are all His spirit children. But still we are endowed differently; we are blessed with different talents; we develop different dispositions, likes, interests, etc. As parents, our responsibility is not to develop our children all in the same mold, but to accept them as they come to us and work diligently and prayerfully to bring out the best that is in them. This has been a constant plea to my Heavenly Father as I have borne and taught my children.

105

Just as parents find individual differences in children, they should not expect or require the same thing from each child. Their job is to help each one reach his greatest potential. Each child must, however, receive the same degree of love, the same feeling of acceptance, regardless of talents, age, physical attributes, disposition, or social graces. There may be other children more talented, more handsome, more outgoing, but he can be at peace with himself knowing that he is accepted and loved as he is.

In my home when I was a child we were blessed with parents who loved to sing. They enriched our lives with the dear old songs they sang. One of the many songs I love to hear my mother sing was about a rich French lady with two little girls. One was "her darling, her pet"—the other was referred to in the song as "only me, only me." As the song told the story you knew exactly how lonely and sad the child felt who knew she was unloved and unaccepted by her mother. When the unloved child became ill and was dying, the mother felt great remorse and repentance. But her dying child comforted her by saying: "Don't you cry, Mama, it's only me." I tried to imagine the great pain she must have felt, knowing she was unloved and unaccepted by her mother.

If a child knows you accept him as he is, without any reservations, he finds it easy to accept himself, even if he has a few freckles, is shorter than he wants to be, and his hair is not the color he would have chosen. He will get the message from loving parents that these physical aspects are not what makes you love someone. My father always told me he loved my red hair and freckles. Then when I learned that as a boy he had them, I decided that only special people had red hair and freckles. He helped me accept myself. I didn't mind if my sister had beautiful black hair, my daddy loved me for myself.

Years ago when I was still searching for answers, a talk by a wise young mother was almost a revelation to me. She said that a child cannot love others until he loves himself. He cannot accept others until he accepts himself. This has been such a help to me, I have found it to be true. The main factor in his being able to accept himself is knowing that his parents accept him.

It is surprising and enlightening how much parents can learn from their children when they are willing to listen. I questioned one

106

of my teen-age daughters as to what suggestions she could make for me in writing this chapter. She made a timely suggestion. She said: "Talk about respect for children." As we discussed it briefly she made this observation: When children get older they show their parents the same respect that their parents gave them when they were young. I'm certain this would nearly always be true. Just because we are bigger than our children does not mean we can afford to treat them with less respect than we would treat our guests or friends we meet on the street. No one is more important in our lives than our families. They will believe this if we treat them with respect and kindness at all times, and this assurance in their lives will do much to bring a spirit of love and real contentment in our homes.

In the final analysis our homes are what we make them. We determine largely the spirit that prevails there, the quality of home life that goes on there, the strength of character that develops in each precious child. Our greatest effort will not be too much; our best will not be too good. Our pay-off comes when we find that our children have grown into warm, loving, understanding adults who will one day have happy, contented families of their own.

107

INTRODUCING—SHERRI ZIRKER

Talent, enthusiasm, and skills in many areas—they all add up to petite Sherri Zirker. Her philosophy: "I believe in filling our lives full to the brim with the 'can-do's' and being so very busy that there is simply no time for mischief. Involvement promotes unity and true growth."

She sews; bakes; paints; sings; dances; speaks; writes poetry, skits and a newspaper column; teaches, acts, and performs with her family at many functions.

Our acquaintance with Sherri reaches back to our days at BYU where interests in the Program Bureau brought us together. We watched her dramatic readings, dancing and singing on the talent circuit and saw her reign as "Belle of the Y" there also. She graduated with a major in human development & family relationships and a minor in speech.

Travel has played an important part in her life. She has lived in several communities in Arizona and Utah, in Alaska, Indiana, Mississippi, Peru, Mexico, and now resides in Warden, Washington with her husband and family. Ron is a school psychologist with ranching interests. Their five children range from 11-year-old Katherine Anne to Steven who has not yet reached one. Their family "Singing Strings" presentation placed right beside the Morin's talent rating in the national All-American Family finals. In that competition the Zirker family represented the state of Washington and were judged one of the top families.

Her current church service is on the Primary stake board, with past service in MIA and Primary presidencies and as a Relief Society teacher and work director.

Sherri has the desire to accomplish many things in life and to develop her talents fully. We feel her philosophy of personal education and development has real value and can be implemented with success in many families.

JDC & DSC

EDUCATION: PARENTS' SACRED OBLIGATION
by
Sherri Zirker

Where do you turn for a good education for your children? My husband (an educator by profession) and I gave serious thought to this question—especially as we observed the problems in the schools. We saw overcrowded classrooms, teachers threatening to strike, and controversial issues and teaching methods. We saw case after case of children who were incapable of learning anything due to disruptive conditions in the home. We saw friends raised in good homes lose their testimonies after coming in contact with the philosophies of men taught at major universities.

We finally knelt in prayer and asked the Lord to guide and direct us as we planned for the education of our children. Imagine our excitement when the answer presented itself. It was born within our minds and hearts as surely as though someone stood before us directly and spoke the words. *Parents hold the major responsibility for seeing that children receive a full and well-rounded education. Home is the proper place for children to receive much of it.* It required paying a price, but to us this worthwhile endeavor seemed paramount to all others.

President McKay taught this as he said:

Upon the proper education of youth depend the permanency and purity of home, the safety and perpetuity of the nation. The parent gives the child an opportunity to live; the teacher enables the child to live well. *That parent who gives life and teaches his child to live abundantly is the true parent-teacher.* However, today the customs and demands of society are such that the responsibility of training the child to live well is largely, and in too many instances, *shifted entirely from the parent to the teacher.*

In the ideal state, the teacher would be but the parents' ally. (Gospel Ideals, pp. 436-437)

What an obvious and simple answer, and yet, I had been led to believe that others were far better qualified than myself. That doesn't mean that we no longer value formal education. We need good "allies," experts in their fields from whom we can draw resources and supplemental help. We feel fortunate and blessed when our children have good teachers in school. But I have been "called and set apart" as the teacher responsible for the complete education of my child.

Sister Dixon, of the Primary General Board, once said, "Our life on earth was set up in a learn-by-doing experience." That, I believe, is the secret to success. If you don't know how to teach your children, still begin and try. You will discover strengths and talents you never knew existed, plus help all around to lend you wisdom and knowledge.

Home—The Ideal Classroom

When you really stop to think about it, where else can you find a more ideal classroom than the home:

The ratio of student to teacher is 2.5 students per adult (in our family, that is)

There is no teacher turnover

The Administrator (Dad) and the teacher (Mom) have a close-working relationship, with the same goals in view for the "students."

The school board? (Read our first Article of Faith)

Curriculum possibilities are unlimited

There are weekly teacher-administrator-student conferences where evaluations are made on the basis of individual abilities and personalities. Goals are set, precepts are taught, and love is expressed. (Family Home Evening)

Field trips have more value and can be far more extensive and imaginative than is possible in the typical classroom

The degree of "student involvement" is far greater than could be allowed elsewhere

At least eighteen years of schooling and apprenticeship is possible

Practical application opportunities are numerous

There is no legislation against prayer or against teaching eternal values

The salary is great: real joy in service and the privilege of seeing the fruit of your labors

110

We have extensive training available to help us do the job like a professional: the marvelous Teacher Development Program which has been instituted by the Church. Our Grand Coulee Stake President, Thurn Baker, impressed me with this statement he made to the teachers of our auxiliaries: "My greatest responsibility in using the Teacher Development Program is to carry out the program in my own family." Lorraine Simkins, an outstanding school teacher in my community, told me that the Teacher Development Program is better training than anything she ever took in college. In addition, she felt that the inservice lessons would be a real boon if adapted in the public school system. It would keep teachers abreast of new ideas, keep emphasizing values and motivate the teachers constantly to do their best. The Lord himself has provided the ideal classroom, an excellent training program, and a continuing source of truth.

Education: Responsibility of Parents

Our answer, then, was to assume the responsibility of educating our children ourselves, using every tool available to us after careful evaluation.

We began by becoming aware of the curriculum of each of our children in school and proceeded to get as thoroughly acquainted with the teachers and the administration as possible, while doing our best to create good working-relationships with them. We each accepted responsibility on the PTA Board, Ron as Legislative Chairman, and myself as Publicity Chairman. The insights into our children's school routine gave us the information we needed to begin at home. We learned the areas of study where we can assume responsibility.

We grew to understand the principles Elder Thomas Monson taught:

> We hear and we forget
> We see and we remember
> We *do* and we *learn!*

We also better understood Elder Paul H. Dunn as he quoted the following in one of his conference addresses:

> We can tell
> But never teach
> Unless we practice
> What we preach!

111

Encouraging Reading

It is important, we found, to read to our children from the time they were old enough to sit on our laps. It provides companionship, introduces them to the most basic skill they will ever use, and trains them from the beginning to value books as a source of learning. (We have been told that it takes school teachers only half as much time to teach reading to a child who is familiar with books and accustomed to having someone read to him.)

As our children learned to read, however, we knew they now had access to information both helpful and destructive. We felt our most important responsibility was to teach them a basis upon which to judge all ideas and philosophies. Rather than to try to set ourselves up as authorities on these matters, we felt it would be much to their advantage to guide them to the Standard Works of the Church for their source of truth. Then we tried to be a sounding board for their questions and answers. Our desire is that when teachers or friends confront our children with a contrary idea, they will have a "straight stick" by which to judge whether or not the thought is crooked.

Over the years we have tried several methods to help our children become acquainted with the scriptures as they learned to read. We think it's important to let them see us reading the scriptures frequently. Our children like to have the scriptures read to them too. (My husband and I read a little every night together before we go to bed. Right now we are reading the Doctrine & Covenants Commentary—and the stories that accompany the doctrine seem to interest our older children. Invariably when they will hear us, they get out of bed and come in to beg to listen just for a few minutes. How can you refuse *that?*)

Another method we have used is to learn to retell some of the stories and use them to fill in the time while we are traveling to or from a music lesson, or folding up towels together. (My mother did this constantly with us when we were growing up and we loved it. Our children respond just the same to it.)

When the children have questions about the gospel we take time to help them look up the answer in the scriptures. (You would be surprised how quickly *you* will learn how to do it.) We learned, too, to let them memorize a brief scripture that goes along with the Family Home Evening lesson and present it—or let them look it up on the spot rather than letting them read the scripture out of the manual. Other times we've let them read a story and re-tell it on some occasion.

We've tried other exercises to help them in their general reading. As you work with your children, you'll find it effective to encourage them to follow a recipe on their own. (One daughter somehow read ½ tsp. of salt to be ¼ cup of salt. She read recipes more carefully after she tasted the product!) We tried other things too, like writing down chores to be read accordion fashion so the children see only one chore at a time. (Intersperse it with a compliment or directions to eat a cookie—they'll love it!) And try pinning a thank you note to their dress, and posting the family's goal for the week on the bathroom mirror.

Writing

The excitement of learning to write begins when children discover that certain lines and squiggles on a piece of paper stand for their name! Let it be from *you* they experience that marvelous discovery. The rest can be given to the school teacher if you wish. You can provide them later with opportunities to experience the power of the pen such as

Writing letters to grandparents, homesick missionaries, friends, and shut-ins

Writing thank you notes for favors received

Recording their own histories

Making lesson plans and charts for Family Home Evening

Making work charts and keeping records

Writing stories and poems

One special delight our children experienced was sending a Valentine with a poem they originated to President David O. McKay. He surprised them by answering!

Another special experience is writing a weekly column in our community newspaper, The Warden Register, called *Family Forum*. It is a project we developed to increase family unity within our sphere of influence. The editor, Marge Owen, has kindly printed numerous articles our family has written and we have met many wonderful families through our effort.

Each child receives a Book of Remembrance at the age of

eight and is expected to keep it up to date.

Our eldest daughter, Kathy (age 11) recently commented to me that "It makes me feel happy to read something I've written and see that it is good."

Our children's grades in school seem to rise, too, as their ability to write well increases.

Arithmetic

The practical use of arithmetic never took on as much meaning as it did when my husband undertook the task of teaching finance to our children. He bought three dozen hens and a rooster and told them if they wanted to find their own customers, clean and box the eggs, distribute the goods and collect their bills, that the money was theirs to divide and spend. The hens reside two miles away at their Grandpa's. Since they are unable to get over and back to feed and water chickens, they hire Grandpa (a widower) to do that at the cost of cleaning his house once a week. This was agreeable to both parties and has worked out very well. A long story of tears and triumph can be told about this venture alone, but it is strictly a business. If either parent is called on to help (such as delivery) they must pay five cents a dozen to us. We were not to accept orders or money, but leave it entirely in their hands (so hard for Mom). Our children also have cherries and apples for sale in season. They agreed to pay us a percentage for use of the trees or arrange to buy the trees from us. They each have saving accounts. Ron agreed that for every dollar they earned that went into the bank, he would match it (for college and missions). If they spent it, however, there would be no match. It was interesting to watch the struggle between pleasure now and value later. (Once in the bank, this money isn't to be withdrawn until age 18.)

Government

We have found many ways to teach the value of good government and citizenship and also the results of bad government. As we encourage them to honor the "head-of-the-house" for the sake of order, so we encourage them to honor the "head-of-the-land." Changes can only be made through due process of law. We took our children to the voting booth and showed them how it worked.

114

Bedtime stories have been of great men and women in history.

We can afford to buy our clothes or bread—but deliberately make them wait at times *to show that worthwhile things take time.* In this day of "instant food," "instant hairdos," no-iron clothes, etc., sometimes people don't appreciate the time, effort, and training that have gone into the producing of such things. We feel this may be one reason why the youth are crying for peace *now!,* as though it can be brought about "instantly" like so many other things. When the children make a bad batch of cookies, we can show how training, following directions, and experience can help them produce a better product. When an outfit doesn't fit, it will take time and more effort to make something that will. When bad laws go into effect, it will take time, training, and experience to remove and replace them.

We formulated our own rule for good citizenry, and find it effective in our home:

Consider before committing an act what the result would be if everyone did it, and how you would feel if someone else did it to you.

We have tried to follow the counsel to give them correct principles and let them govern themselves. Periodically, we review the state of the home in Family Home Evening and try to pin down problem areas, such as:

A. Whenever I want to practice, someone else is using the piano (so that's why I didn't get my practicing done.)
B. I got to reading this book after you left and just never did get to washing the dishes.
C. I'd have taken a bath but you used up all of the hot water washing clothes today.
D. I forgot that you told me to wash the tub when I was through.

Then we take a look at the "principles" involved:

A. Scheduling in the home makes it possible for everyone to progress
B. Work comes before play (first things first)
C. Cleanliness of home and self is necessary
D. Work charts that are written down make it easier to remember what our responsibilities are

115

Then we all make "rules" so that the "principles" will be incorporated daily to help living together run smoother. For instance,

A. Minds are clearer and absorb learning more readily in the mornings so we will accomplish practicing before school:
   a. Kathy: Piano (6:00 - 6:45) Violin (6:45 - 7:30)
   b. Carolyn: Violin (6:00 - 6:45) Piano (6:45 - 7:30)
   c. Family practice (7:30 - 8:00)
   (Everyone is dressed and beds made before practice)

B. Having chores done before school gives lots of free time after school. (You'd be surprised what can be done in ½ hour if you don't want to have to do them after school)

C. Mom will try to allow at least an hour before bath-time for the hot-water tank to fill up.

D. A work chart is made and they change around every week by initialing the jobs they agree to do "round-robin" style. All I have to do is look at a sink full of dishes, look at the chart to see who agreed to do them, and a short reminder is usually all that's needed.

They much prefer knowing what is expected of them than to get involved in something and then have me break into their "fun" by thinking of something that needs to be done.

We don't believe in spanking or hollering as training methods, but we resort to both occasionally. We feel it is unfair to our children to use those methods constantly though. Wouldn't it be sad if after they enter society, they wouldn't fulfill their responsibilities unless someone got tough with them. When we find ourselves in the position of having to get tough more-and-more frequently, then we know that it is time to call a family council and discuss the principle behind it. Some of these principles, besides the ones heretofore mentioned are:

1. Good health for more abundant living
2. Modesty
3. Respect for authority and rights of others
4. Respect for self
5. We take care of our own
6. Everything has its price

And thus, government is the tool for harmonious living and progress.

116

Meeting Problems of Modern Society

We have been advised that taking drugs is a symptom of unmet needs so we try to meet our children's needs of being wanted, increasing self-esteem, etc. Still, we realize it may not be enough, so we have taken the children to education seminars where drugs are explained. We became aware that we could be guilty of having a pill to cure every ill, so we have tried to curb our complaints about sicknesses and embarked on a better-health campaign in our home. We bought a wheat-grinder, and I make about everything now with wholewheat. We bought a trampoline, bikes and roller skates and have tried to establish better eating and sleeping habits. When someone complains of a headache, we prescribe more rest, and for muscle soreness, a hot soak in the tub. We have experienced far less illness in the family as we work to get rid of the medicine cabinet. We have had one child to the doctor, our baby, just once in two years!

Ron elected himself the responsible one to explain the facts of life and give sex-education to our older children. This he has done. When our eldest was asked by a reporter if she thought sex-education should be taught in the schools, Kathy told her directly that she would rather be taught by her father.

We feel our children need to see love properly expressed, and so we try to show our love for each other in small considerations and special comments about each other. We have made a policy not to joke about other men and women. We've talked about how we met, shown them pictures of our wedding, taken out our Book of Remembrance and shown them our histories. We hope they will want to live for good memories. When we choose to go to a movie, we make a point of looking at the possibilities and turning down immediately the R and X rated ones. When the children have asked why we have explained that time is too precious to waste it on something poorly done, with no value. We can only hope that if they do come across pornography, it will be foreign and unnatural to them. We have also tried to introduce good literature to them; particularly, biographies and autobiographies of great men and women. Helen Keller has become a family heroine lately.

We took the children on a "field trip" through Universal City and it really opened their eyes to see how movies and TV

117

shows are made. The result is that they rarely take them serious any more, but enjoy looking for evidence of behind-the-scene action. Much of television has lost its lustre and it is easy to encourage better ways to use their time.

If you really want to rid your family of any tendencies toward racism and "superiority complexes" and teach them love for all types of people, accept the Lamanite Program of the Church. There is great satisfaction in helping these young Indian students grow and develop, and it helps the family accept the ways of other cultures in a great many ways. We can learn and gain perspective from them. Plan to treat a daughter like an Indian Princess and watch a diamond in the rough begin to sparkle!

We read of the problems that are associated with rock music, and we watched our children's eyes begin to light up when they heard it. We thought, "What can we do?" Then we read in *The Instructor* that if children were educated toward classical music, they might go through a phase with psychedelic music but would soon recognize it for the cheap art that it is. We outlined a plan to build appreciation of good music in our family. Our first step was to enroll in the Community Concert Association. We began taking the children to concerts from the time they entered public school. We bought records and began building a library of Bach, Mendelssohn, Brahms, etc. Ron installed an intercom so that music was played every night for them to sleep by. After three years, we could see the change which had taken place. They no longer yawned or squirmed as they did at their first concert, but would sit entranced over chamber music, ballet, and symphonies. They began taking piano and violin lessons. At the concerts Kathy would crane her neck to watch everything the pianist did. Carolyn, our violinist, was all eyes and ears when a violinist came on the scene. The surprising thing to us was that each soon begged to take the other's lessons in addition to her own. When Kathy wanted to start on the flute, she worked hard and paid for it herself as we felt we just couldn't afford another instrument. Each of the older girls now "tutor" the younger children for a dime per 15 minutes tutoring. As a result, everyone in the family, down to our four-year-old son, plays the violin, and Ron plays the cello. We have been invited to play together often. Their piano teacher, Mary

Lou Cox, is now teaching them arranging and composing and they, in turn, teach me. Together we are having a marvelous and exciting time learning to arrange our own numbers and making up new ones. Our violin teacher, Mr. Gregor Agranoff, is a Russian Jew who defected during the Bolshevik Revolution when they slaughtered so many Jews. We receive a wealth of history, bits of all of his nine languages, and his marvelous expertise every time we go for our lessons. They happen to be all day Saturday. (What a shame they have to miss all of those cartoons!)

Oh, the girls still come home from school with the latest hits bouncing off their tongues and try to play them. They enjoy lighter music. But they look forward to the Community Concerts and are now begging to bring their friends. They never turn on rock music any more and seem to truly delight in the music they have learned to appreciate.

Sociological Principles

We have learned sociological principles from the interaction of our family members. We have especially grown to enjoy relationships with those less fortunate, with the lonely, with the aged and those in need of special help. Over the years we have taken into our home for various lengths of time:

A juvenile delinquent released by San Francisco authorities

A drug addict following hospital withdrawal

A Swedish immigrant who lost her fortune and had no place to go

A Negro, employed by us for four years, only to find he was an escaped convicted murderer

A Lamanite

Various aunts, uncles, cousins, and neighbors

To us, each of these individuals were friends of the family— some coming to help, some coming to be helped. We all formed lasting relationships of love and respect for each other. Both unhappiness and joy were experienced in these relationships. Time can only tell the effect these experiences have had on our children, but they do have some definite ideals and goals in life which these people have helped to shape. We hope these ideals will help our children skirt around the paths which lead to unhappiness and embrace those ideas, at any price, that lead to success and joy.

Languages and Customs of Other Lands

We feel the best way to learn is by direct contact with what we're studying. We wanted to learn about other lands, so between breaks in formal education and jobs we moved to Mexico City for a few months to go to school. There we toured the country, watched them excavate ruins, and visited little towns and hamlets. We learned the language and songs, learned to eat their food, and participated in some of their customs. It was a grand experience, and we have been able to use what we learned in hundreds of different ways. Ron is invited to speak at the Spanish Branch here in Washington and has been given the Spanish families to fellowship and home teach. He has been able to interpret for Mexican children and parents in the school district, and has expanded his ability to serve in many ways. Our children were speaking the language fluently when we returned, and two languages by the age of four is no small accomplishment.

We are now planning toward a similar experience in Germany. We play records at mealtimes in an effort to learn the language, and we are saving our pennies toward the trip. It is the land of my husband's ancestry and so we are excited about learning all we can about this country. How can we afford it? We drive a smaller, more economical car, put the difference away in savings, and try not to grumble for lack of leg room.

Also, we have had the privilege of housing three Swedish immigrants. While they were with us, they taught us their language and customs. We celebrated Christmas their way one day and our way the next day—a choice experience! Lilian Engstrom was a lovely LDS person whom we grew to love. Her nephew, Jorgen, (pronounced *Y*orgen) couldn't pronounce his *J*'s. They always came out as *Y*'s. It was so cute to hear that he "yumped" over the fence, he drank "yuice" for breakfast, and "by yimminy" life was good.

Two Japanese exchange students were in our home last year. It was their purpose to live in a home and learn how Americans live. They were both Buddhists but they attended Church with us and enjoyed the emphasis on family activity. They told us, "You have good church. I marriage soon. I like class to discuss life. Only old men go church. It better when family go, it more happy."

120

They taught us to eat seaweed on our rice, to make birds out of paper, to do karate in the living room without breaking the furniture, to say numerous phrases in Japanese, and to sing their national anthem. They gave us each a Japanese name and showed us how to draw Mount Figi. They also performed by singing: "Wanleetle, two-leetle, three-leetle In-dee-ahns..." These were choice experiences for us.

Religion

We are fortunate in our home classroom to be able to open and close each day with prayer and to be free to bear our testimonies often. We must *never* allow our religion to sit on a shelf to be admired only once a week. We must weave it continually throughout all that we do or it is of no real value. Our children must be able to see the gospel truly improving their lives, and must be able to experience real joy through it from time to time. It is vital that they participate in fasting and prayer, that they may learn for themselves an avenue through which they can communicate with the Father of us all. It is important that they understand how the Holy Ghost operates, that he will not violate our free agency but must be invited before he can truly help us. They must understand that their conduct while they are alone is the real test of good character and that regular attendance at Sunday School is only a "means to an end": that end being that we will learn how to live so that we can rejoin our Father in Heaven and be part of His Kingdom. They need to learn that the tragic punishment we may be asked to endure is to look upon that which we might have had and been and watch it pass by, leaving us with less than was possible. We insure our children's understanding of these principles by:

Holding Family Home Evenings regularly and meaningfully

Going to Church regularly and sitting together as a family

Praying morning and night together (We kneel together to have our family prayer, then each of us says a private prayer to himself for a few quiet moments)

Following the programs of the Church (year's supply, genealogy, tithing, budget, welfare, etc.)

Speaking well of others—especially those in authority

Accepting responsibility and doing our very best with it

121

All of these, as important as they are, will not have impact if the children see improper behavior at home. They need to see the family happy, industrious, and alive with creative approaches to growing and learning. We feel that the only training that really counts is the kind that says "follow me," and if they should choose to do otherwise, at least we have walked in a manner in which we believe.

With a large family, Church and community responsibilities, and those 101 other things that need to be done, we found complaints coming in occasionally that we had no time to be just alone with each child. We seemed to be creating our own generation gap. So we decided to organize our children into our lives as regularly as we scheduled any other appointments. I met with each and worked out a regular hour once a week where my time was strictly theirs—I was at their disposal. This has literally stopped all complaints and signs of jealousy. It was surprising to discover what meant something to them. One wanted to learn to sew so we made a pair of stretch pants, another wanted to bake, another put a scrapbook together. We ride bikes, or go downtown for a milkshake. It has been relaxing and great fun to me as well as satisfying to the children.

In summary, we believe that education is a process that takes place continuously and that formal education is only one medium through which to grow. We also believe that it is our responsibility as parents to introduce our children to as many avenues of growth as possible to the end that they may have true freedom of choice. We consider formal schooling only supplemental to our task. This doesn't mean we ignore it as an unnecessary part of society. Indeed, we do all we can to upgrade the teaching profession. However, because my husband is a school psychologist and is called upon to determine causes behind learning failures and disabilities, we observe that almost invariably these causes of poor learning originate in the home. So it is with impetus that we constantly review our own home as a launching pad for inquiring minds. We ask these questions often of ourselves:

1. Is academic education helping us in our parental role or taking our place?

2. Do we tend to dwell too much on the "know" and not

122

enough on the "do"?

3. Are we close enough to our children to be a guiding influence in their lives?

4. Do we stumble through life on our own, or do we pray continually for divine help in this all-important responsibility?

5. When answers come and the price seems high, do we courageously give the tasks a try, committing ourselves to our best efforts?

6. Do we recognize the power of an organized family unit and do our best to make it the "best organization we belong to"?

7. Do we recognize our need to continually improve our abilities by taking advantage of the training programs offered to us?

8. Are we truly assuming the responsibility of educating our children by conforming our actions to fit the words we preach?

9. Do we plan and prepare just as diligently for our family as we would if we were asked to teach a class at school or at Church?

10. If true education seeks to make men and women not only good mathematicians, proficient linguists, profound scientists, or brilliant literary lights, but also honest men who have virtue, temperance, and brotherly love—men and women who prize truth, justice, wisdom, benevolence, and self-control as the choicest acquisitions of a successful life, *how close to becoming truly educated are we?* We teach best what we are!

INTRODUCING—DORA D. FLACK

In our opinion, Dora is the perfect blend of talent, wisdom, experience, dignity, and willingness to tackle a challenging task and to see it through to its proper conclusion and fulfillment. She is mature, realistic, and unassuming—all qualities which have helped her to find joy in her role as wife and mother.

Our friendship with her grew as we edited her recent book, What About Christmas?, *and prepared it for publication with Horizon Publishers. It was soon obvious that here was a woman with self-discipline as well as talent. Each day she would set realistic goals, and each day she would rise to meet them. Dora is an accomplished author, with many writing awards to her credit. Her work is published in national and church magazines. She is the co-author of three books, including* Wheat for Man...Why and How, *which has a distribution of over 400,000.*

Over the years, she has presented literally thousands of book reviews before church, civic, club and school audiences in several of the western states. Her program hallmark is music. This, combined with a dramatic flair, never ceases to delight her audiences. Her talents keep her in constant demand.

Dora is married to A. LeGrand Flack and they are the parents of six children. Her programs have served as a means of aiding the oldest three to fulfill missions for the Church. She has the missionary spirit too, having previously served as a missionary in the North Central States Mission herself. Four of their children are now in college with the last two not far behind.

She is the typical capable and efficient Relief Society president, a responsibility she has twice filled. She is also interested in genealogy and has served on stake genealogical committees for many years.

Dora finds pleasure in performing homemaking skills well and has taught these skills to her children. In this chapter she passes on the secrets which have worked well for her. JDC & DSC

124

THE MIRACLE WORKER
by
Dora D. Flack

During the depression, I was a teenager and eager to earn an extra nickel. A nickel bought something then. Quite early one morning, I was summoned to the telephone. A neighbor pleaded with me to come and help clean her house. Great, I thought, that should be worth a lot of nickels, and I hurried over. On entering the front door, I was aghast at the scene of utter chaos.

The neighbor explained, "I've been away for a week with the baby and my husband has been here alone." At a glance I could see that he'd hardly been alone. Glasses, bottles, wastebaskets were all overflowing. The living room was a confusing obstacle course. I supposed (and rightly) the rest of the house was just as bad. Never in my life had I seen anything like that! But I had agreed to help her and I couldn't back down. She busied herself with the baby's needs all day, simply answering my questions of where to put things. Secretly I was sure the baby was her escape. I started at the front door and by four o'clock, order had been restored and the house was shining, even to the kitchen sink. As I walked home, the satisfaction inside overshadowed the thrill of the paper money (not silver) I grasped in my reddened hands. I had performed a miracle—and I knew it—by bringing beauty out of such confusion.

The dictionary defines a miracle: "An event that appears to be neither a part nor result of any known natural law or agency and is therefore often attributed to a supernatural or divine source. 2. Any wonderful or amazing thing, fact, or event; marvel. 3. One who or that which is of surpassing merit or excellence."

If we could comprehend God's laws which govern this world, they would cease to be miracles and might be as commonplace as my miracle listed above.

The laws which govern a homemaker seem very simple on the surface. Our tasks are repeated so often we almost lose our sight—or foresight. "Hindsight is better than foresight." So, looking back over more than a quarter of a century of homemaking, perhaps my

125

hindsight may give foresight to young mothers—mothers who may each be caught in the squeeze of too many demands of the "now" and the frightening realization that how she works, trains and teaches her "now" brood creates good or bad homes for generations of her future progeny. Happy, productive and well-adjusted individuals in the future years are the result of the miracles performed each day of the homemaker's life.

Homemaking—A Career

There is no re-run in the race of motherhood. Unfortunately you can't go back to the starting line after you've made a few bad trial runs. You must keep moving down the track, correcting and improving techniques as you race. Heavenly Father is your coach, sending flashes of inspiration and assistance, as you seek. Often the needed guidance comes from supporters on the sidelines: spouses, parents, siblings, teachers and associates. The race is not finished until life is completed. But the joy is in the running, not in the laurels at the end. If we can look back and see that we have created good homes, and have enjoyed doing it, then we can view a miracle. We're teaching our children every day of our lives, like it or not—even if it's what *not* to do.

This is your life's work. Whether you are a career woman living alone, or a full-time homemaker, you will always have quarters to keep. So learn your trade. And learning it earlier than later is the easy way. Barely keeping ahead of the Board of Health wears you down, teaches the same bad patterns to your children and retards your husband's productivity and advancement.

Every career involves a certain amount of routine and homemaking is no exception. Yet the homemaker's art offers the possibility of the greatest variety of any career in the world. Instead of turning on the TV for a dull, irritating accompaniment while you work, think and plan. The more things you can convert to habit, the more free time you have. Learn to do the monotonous in a hurry. Then you can utilize to the fullest the challenging, creative moments you have earned by your diligence, no matter how brief those moments are. Every woman needs re-creating time or study time. She can have it through wise planning and scheduling, cutting corners and eliminating unnecessary repetition and enlisting the children's help.

126

From a baby's earliest days, he is absorbing that which formulates stability or instability. Always remember that your husband and children are your first consideration. *Now* is the short moment of your opportunity. Tender, loving, intelligent care is as important as nutrition in forming the whole individual. As the baby emerges into childhood, he becomes capable of accepting responsibility and learning that work is part of living.

Attitudes are absorbed, not taught. If a mother works with a smile and a song instead of a sigh and a frown, a child discovers that work can be enjoyable instead of a drudge. Never allow yourself the luxury of admitting, even to yourself, that you hate to iron, for example. Your children will hate it, too. Getting the job done, and behind you, saves much nervous energy and physical fatigue. The more complaints and dreads, the harder the task becomes.

Mildred Harris Bradley, the mother of fourteen children, was asked the secret of her smooth-running household. She said, "Organization! I do things on a reasonable schedule, which I learned from my mother. If I don't feel up to washing on wash-day, I may feel worse the next day. I can't afford to let my work pile up. Keep up with your work and it won't get you down."

Using Caution

Before discussing specifics, perhaps a few general ideas should be discussed. First, buy and use a copy of *The Art of Homemaking*, by Darryl Hoole. The purchase price will pay you big dividends in shining results, peace of mind and those precious private moments.

Always be careful. Scrubbing and other related tasks should be taught as the child is big enough to handle the equipment. He must know the dangers of cleaning solutions and preparations. Take time to explain. He won't read the details of labels unless they are called to his attention. Keep all potentially dangerous chemicals out of the reach of the little ones and avert tragedy. Train older children to observe and practice this caution also.

Dustcloths, saturated with furniture polish, should never be stuffed in a drawer or garbage can—they're combustible fire hazard!

Electric motors can be a serious danger. Electric beaters can mangle fingers. A child sitting on the counter as you work is a no-no. I know a beautiful little girl with long hair who was almost scalped because her hair was caught in an electric beater.

127

Use of a vacuum requires instruction. Bedspread fringe must be kept up on the bed or it can be easily caught and burn out the vacuum motor.

Of course, there are many other cautions too numerous to include. Be aware.

Involving and Training Children

Remember—you're chief executive of a home and family, not a museum piece nor a showplace. The woman who browses through too many beautiful home magazines can develop a complex. She may think her home must, at all times, match the pictures of perfection on every page. First thing you know, she has a guilt complex if she falls short. Danger! Your home must be a haven for you, your husband and children. If they are driven to keeping a totally immaculate domicile, it ceases to be a home. Comfort and spirit should be your goal. They'll love you and remember you for it, and so will everyone who comes within your walls. A home that is too much like a picture creates uneasiness and a feeling of awe where one daren't sit for fear of disturbing the pile on a velvet chair. Your home is not your citadel, but also belongs to every member of your family. They can be taught cooperation in keeping it presentable but not be required to keep it sterile. "Cleanliness is next to godliness" and "Order is the first law of heaven"—but you haven't yet reached the celestial kingdom.

Let your offspring have a choice of work and don't confine them to the same routine assignments. For example, if you don't like to wash windows (but of course you've never admitted this) and your teen son loathes scrubbing the floor (and he's told you repeatedly), here's a possible solution. Ask him which he'd rather do—windows or floor. You'll be surprised how these little tricks work.

Lists or choreboxes are a mother's best friend. Darryl Hoole says: "Making a list is like a pep pill and crossing off the items is like a tranquilizer." Making a list of the tasks to be done and allowing the children to choose and divide them usually makes quick work of the day's tasks, with no bickering. They love to cross off and can experience the thrill of accomplishment, which is the reward of honest toil. Then they're free to choose what they want to do with their leisure time. Personally, I do not think children should be paid for the regular work they do around the house and yard. They're paying their board and each individual must realize he is part of a family. If everyone is to be happy and have a home where he can be proud to invite his friends, he must do his share.

Boys should learn girls' work and girls should learn boys' work wherever and whenever possible. Then both appreciate more fully the efforts of the other. Girls can mow lawns and do yard work and encourage plants to grow. A well-kept yard then becomes a satisfaction to the whole family. Who knows when each must substitute for the others? Who knows when misfortune or sickness will strike? Families should be self-reliant instead of waiting for the Relief Society or priesthood quorum to come in and take over. This is also the training ground for a good marriage and is the basis on which many marriages survive.

One of my young friends has excelled in 4-H work. She has won national scholarships for college through her cooking and canning. She's as capable as a woman of many years' experience. But her mother reaped the dividends of her early instruction when she became ill. The daughter has taken over the complete household for several years. Because she had learned young, she was able to manage everything, even while going to school full time. Few women escape without a serious sick spell—then come the rewards of her training, or the consequences of her neglect. When the emergency arrives, as it inevitably does, it's too late for the learning pains.

Of course there are numerous reasons for broken homes. However, too many marriages have been terminated chiefly because of the inability of every mother to train her daughter so she will be capable in her own home. In cases involving such incompetency, when a daughter returns in distress, bringing her children, the parents pay the heavy price of neglect—and that's when it hurts. There are three affected generations! And later ones to come. What a sobering thought.

Family Work Projects

Some of the most rewarding hours our family has spent together have been spent building and refinishing old furniture together. My husband has always worked with the boys, instructing them in manual skills. As a result, they can figure out problems on a job which cause most young men to wring their hands and give up. We have finished our basement ourselves. Family members, especially the boys who are the three oldest of our six children, have assisted their father as the building has progressed from one room to another. The family room was last and everyone got into the act. Then we furnished it with antiques—not all genuine, of course. We've salvaged furniture generally regarded as junk and have refinished it. Every member of our family is justifiably proud of that family room. It's their favorite room because they had such a hand in its creation. We took the pieces outside and stripped and sanded and sanded some more; even the youngest helped. As we scraped and slaved and refinished, we related to the children the background of each piece. I'm sure none of our antiques will be junked, because we've been informed we'll have to "will" individual pieces to each one, so there will be no bickering over who gets what of the salvaged items which are now works of art. There's a pump organ, a treadle sewing machine, an oak table and chairs, an 1880 clock, and many other pieces—all precious and beautiful. Even the children's friends respect these lovely items out of the past.

New Tasks for Growing Children

This is the miracle of creating a lovely home—far from perfection or extravagant beauty, but obviously where children learn to live within their means and where they will feel comfortable to bring their friends.

So let's itemize tasks and see how children can learn the small miracles which create the big miracle of a smooth-running, happy home. As the years go by, children increase rapidly in their ability to perform household tasks. Their new abilities should be matched with increased challenges.

Clutter: Learning to pick up his own toys after play teaches a young child orderliness. Make gaily-colored bags from fabric scraps, or see-through net bags, for toy storage. Size the bags according to the intended contents and pull a drawstring through a hem at the open end. A piece of pegboard masonite can be attached to the back of the door with metal hooks, on which the filled bags can be suspended. Then he's a part of the clean-up detail. Picking up before bed can be accelerated with the promise of story-time and singing-time. Make a game of it. Who can finish first? One picks up as another is bathed. It's a miracle to work out this timing—but with persistence, it can be done. At most difficult childhood situations, my mother always quoted:

If a string is in a knot, patience will untie it;
Patience will do many things, Did you ever try it?

A wastebasket in each bedroom is a must.

Put the closet clothesbar at the child's level and raise it as he grows; then he can learn to hang his own clothes. Shoeboxes in drawers for dividers improve most situations.

Bedmaking: If you take one side of the bed in the beginning, the small child learns to straighten the covers and pull them smooth. The spread pulled over the lumpy covers and stuffed toys that strayed in the foot of the bed during the night is good enough for him, unless he is taught the pleasure of seeing a smooth bed. As he snuggles down at night, call to his attention the pleasure of a straight bed in contrast to stumbling over the uncomfortable bumps. Of course, you wouldn't expect him to change the sheets and make the bed from the bottom up at first, but he'll soon learn.

Praise oils the machinery of doing, but it should be earned. He'll soon learn to do an acceptable job if you expect it of him and show your genuine pleasure in his honest accomplishment.

Dishwashing: A stool to stand on makes it possible for a young child to wash the dishes. He can learn to do a thorough job with practice.

Soft clouds of suds and plenty of hot water make dishwashing fun. You'll have to do them over sometimes (when he doesn't know it) because he (yes, boys should learn to do dishes, too) hasn't learned the sanitary need, unless you've taught him. His attention-span is sometimes short and occasionally he's plain lazy. If he gets too sloppy, give him the greasy knife or the fork with egg coated on it and an unclean plate. Explain the need for cleanliness with food and dishes. He doesn't want to invite the "rocky-mountain quickstep," does he? Don't despair if you lack a dishwasher. One person washing and another drying bridges the communication gap. "It's a lazy mother who washes her own dishes alone," one wise grandmother said.

Dusting: A dusting mitt made from soft blanket pieces or a crocheted yarn mitt make dusting fun for all ages. Demonstrate

131

the proper method. Remember that you didn't absorb all the details the first time. It may be as routine as drinking water to you, but keep in mind that he is learning. Don't expect perfection at first.

Sewing: Buttons are good for beginners—boys, too. They must depend on themselves when they're away on missions or at college. Learning to embroider paves the way for expert hand sewing later on when a girl takes up dressmaking. Knitting and crocheting furnish needed therapy from the pressure of "nerves." Surgeons crochet and knit to keep their fingers nimble and to relax. It's difficult to foresee a quiet time when possible limitations of the mind and body might keep us housebound and otherwise unproductive. Following a broken hip, my grandmother whiled away the hours, which otherwise would have dragged heavily on her hands, by crocheting and doing handwork. Idle hands make an unhappy mind. However, if you've failed to learn such skills very young, you may be wanting—wanting something to do, believe it or not—at some future sparse period.

When the girls want to make their own clothes, start with simple articles. Help—but don't do it for them, even if it waits undone.

Every time I complete an article of clothing, this is a miracle to me. The economy is no less a miracle. To be able to take a pattern and fabric and turn out a beautiful dress is truly a source of joy. Out of this process evolves one of life's great lessons. If I am haphazard about follòwing the pattern, I have a haphazard article. On the other hand, if I'm careful to follow instructions, the resulting creation is a work of art, embellished by my own initiative. This has a broader application to life.

Many years ago, my mother heard President J. Reuben Clark counsel the women to store, not only food, but fabric, against a time of need. She obeyed. During the war when fabrics, laces and notions were scarce, my sisters and I never went without a new dress when needed. Mother's trunk, stored with cloth, always had a lovely surprise. That warning has carried down to me with resulting savings. There may someday come a time of greater need than we've ever known. We may be glad we've saved the old treadle sewing machine, and happy we've mastered the miracle of sewing.

Washing: Modern conveniences have simplified washing. But

often white clothes don't stay white now, even with automatic washers. Sorting clothes and operating the machine properly must be learned.

Even small children can learn to fold clothes. Mating socks is good reading-readiness practice. And children must be responsible for putting away their own clothes.

Ironing: With so many wash-and-wear clothes available, ironing is almost a lost art. Fabrics of the future will require less. But ironing is still with us. Most of the dread of ironing stems from putting it off until the stack grows formidably high; then a mother is bowed down. As Mrs. Bradley said, "Keep up with your work and it won't get you down."

Teach children to do their pressing at ironing time. Then their clothes are always ready to wear. There's no frantic last-minute heating the iron for one skirt or pair of pants. Nothing tries a man's patience more than pleading for a shirt to be ironed as he's rushing to work or to a meeting. A homemaker's job is to see that her husband's clothes are presentable and available.

In interviewing his priesthood boys, one bishop found that the most frequent excuse for non-attendance at priesthood meeting was that the boy didn't have a clean, ironed shirt.

Shopping: Young children in the supermarket are a hazard. A mother is frustrated with their wheedling. When she reaches the checkstand, she finds items slipped in unawares. She does need her wits to shop intelligently. When children are old enough to figure, trips to the market can be valuable. Show your child how to compare weights and prices. Show him the different sizes of eggs, for example, and figure the price accordingly. Then comes the realization that he needs arithmetic. As you saunter down the aisles, think out loud to him so he knows why you buy as you do. Let him know you must live within your budget, then do it. The world is very cruel to the child who grows up thinking he can have everything he wants.

Basic Decorating: Guidance in colors should be a part of an individual's growing up. This begins when the very young child mixes and matches his clothes. He should have some choice in what he wears. Colors do affect a person's disposition, and this carries over to his home.

A former neighbor had her living room in somber beige and

133

maroon. Unconsciously I couldn't visit there very long without being depressed. I wondered what effect it had on the occupants. That couple were wise budgeters, and one day they accumulated the means to redecorate and refurnish the whole living room at once. This time an interior decorator was consulted. Now it's worse. The living room is a picture of flambuoyance and untouchable elegance. The children never set foot in that living room, but go to the unfinished basement to play. Possessing some basic knowledge of design and color harmony, that woman could have saved money and would have had a living room which reflected her own taste and personality. Consult a child in the redecoration of his room. You'll all enjoy the results more.

Cooking: "The way to a man's heart is through his stomach," is an oft-quoted adage. It's a smart woman who knows the value of nutrition. Advance menu planning is excellent training for all young cooks.

Food is fun if a child is indoctrinated from the beginning. Permit her to help when she first indicates an interest. Of course, you can do it so much quicker than she. But how did you learn? By repetition. Give her a job within her capabilities. One thing leads to another and soon you'll have her actually helping instead of hindering. With so many easy packaged foods, beginning cooking is easy. There is the satisfaction of having prepared something edible for the family—and it's really good. Later graduate to the "scratch" recipes. We do an injustice when we permit a child to cook and then clean up the mess for her. Clean-up should be part of cooking.

I knew two sisters whose mother waited on them totally, cleaning, pressing, ironing—the whole works. When the girls were married, they were helpless. Marriage was a terrible adjustment— not only for them but for their poor husbands. Fortunately, both married well-trained fellows who taught their wives the art of homemaking. The boys looked haggard before the girls could carry their end of the partnership. Not many men would have had that much patience. The mother had always said, "Anyone with any sense can read a cookbook." She didn't realize that craftmanship is the important part of successful cooking. There is far more to homemaking than preparing food.

Then there's my friend who starved her young husband for several weeks because nothing she prepared was edible. At last lamb stew tasted good to him, so she served lamb stew every night for two weeks. The result was open rebellion, and finally divorce. Neither has remarried—how sad!

So, for goodness sake, teach your girls and boys to cook. You never can predict which short end they might be on some day.

Encourage your daughter to keep a list of recipes she has conquered. When you're in too much of a rush to help her with dinner, she can consult her list, find the recipe, and you've received a dividend for your previous investment in time.

Cookie-making offers great variety in experience. Rolled cookies, especially, allow several children to get into the act. They love to use a cookie cutter. Let them use imagination, too.

At Christmas time I always garner my dividends along this line, because cookie-making is a big part of our Christmas. We make literally hundreds and hundreds of cookies, with many favorite varieties. For several years my brood has become so proficient that, if I'm rushed for time, they take over completely. Assembly-line decorating of the rolled cookies speeds the process, and there are often neighbor children included around the big kitchen table. There are Santa heads, trees, stars, gingerbread men—you name it. Plates of cookies, which the girls distribute to our neighbors and friends, are our own special Christmas greetings. This is traditional and they love it.

Since I was nine years old I have made bread. I love to make bread, and, although my girls can do it, they don't yet share my enthusiasm. But they like to eat it. With such an early beginning, it was quite natural that a good many years ago I became interested in cooking with stoneground whole wheat flour and using wheat which we had stored in great quantities in our ward. At the time (1950) I was a young Relief Society president. Following the Bishop's instructions, his wife, Vernice Rosenvall, my counselor, Mabel Miller, and I began a teaching experiment in the ward which became a long, fascinating adventure. We bought electric stone-grinding mills. The interest mushroomed. As a result of an illustrated article in the Church Section following a breadmaking demonstration on Homemaking Day, we received a bushel basket of mail, requesting recipes and help. Our whole wheat cookbook, *Wheat for Man...Why and How* was the result. It has sold some 400,000 copies to date. The royalties have helped to build three chapels. Our families were the guinea pigs for the testing.

As completion neared, all the delicious items for cover photographs waited on my kitchen table. One luscious sponge cake was almost an inch higher than the other. My year-old son sneaked up on the table and picked a piece right out of the top margin of the higher cake. Frustration! For the photo, I picked a piece the same size out of the lower cake and anchored it with a toothpick. But one edge raised a hair, and it shows in that photo! I never look at the cover without thinking of that little character—who is now a big character. His interest in cakes has continued. In fact, he's a professional part-time cake decorator.

As a missionary, he wrote from New York: "Please send me a lot of casserole recipes, the quick, nutritious, economical kind. You'd be surprised how few elders can cook." From New Zealand, where the eldest son served, came a letter from one of his Maori friends: "Your son is already a good cook. Now I teach him Maori cooking." When he returned home, he could prepare from "scratch" a better pizza than any purchased one. The middle boy served in Canada. His visiting companions praised his cooking. In fact, he had a mission-wide reputation for his pancakes, earning the nickname of Flapjack. See what I mean about boys learning to cook?

A loaf of fresh bread to the sick or grieving becomes more than physical bread. Children should share the pleasure of taking it. But do become an expert. Nothing is as tempting as good homemade bread, but nothing is as unpalatable as poor homemade bread. Remember: "If at first you don't succeed, try, try, again."

Preparation Progress Chart

You'll see a miracle in action in the future if you have adequately prepared your children for the time they leave home. Perhaps a preparation progress chart of essential skills is in order as your children look forward to Church service during their teens, college, mission, and marriage. Let me suggest these tasks:

CHURCH SERVICE
Artistic and creative ability
Develop musical talents:
    Lead the singing
        Play piano, organ or other accompanying instrument
    Develop speaking ability

136

Teach home evening lessons—on-the-job teacher training

Spark imagination (Social events are festive because of decorations and goodies. All through life, they have been progressing toward executing successful events, such as Beehive and Mia Maid honor nights, Laurel conferences, Explorer dinners, Relief Society and priesthood socials.)

COLLEGE

Getting along peaceably with others
Housekeeping and cleaning
Cooking
A recipe file containing quick, nutritious dishes
Budgeting
Washing
Ironing
Mending and sewing
Carrying a fair share (One girl found her time at college was consumed chiefly with learning how to complete her domestic chores in the apartment, which left little time for studying. College is too expensive to be learning what one should already know.)

MISSION

Washing
Ironing
Pressing a suit
Cooking
Recipes of quick, nutritious, filling dishes
Packing
Budgeting
Cleaning (A Relief Society president was asked by missionaries to clean the apartment they had just moved into, which had been left a little the worse for wear by the pair moving out. The elders had no idea of how to proceed—or were they finding the easy way out?)

MARRIAGE

All of the foregoing, plus: Knowledge of yard work
Desire to live within means "If you would be happy, decrease your wants."

Are you discouraged, now, as you view the obstacle course ahead? The real miracle is that we do survive.

137

INTRODUCING—JEAN D. CROWTHER

This introduction is different; no collaboration of editors here— Jean doesn't see this one till it's in print!

How hard it is for a husband to write objectively about the woman he loves so deeply, for thoughts of special little things keep obscuring the important ideas.

I met Jean fifteen years ago at the BYU. She was working at the desk of the reserve library and was every bit the sedate image of "Marian the Librarian." But that special attraction was there, and soon birds sang, bells rang, and love burst forth! Just as one can receive a revealed testimony of the truthfulness of the gospel, he can also receive the witness concerning who is to be his mate. That witness came to us, and it certainly had its effect on our courtship!

Jean is a Mesa, Arizona girl who was raised just two doors from the temple there and whose life reflects the eternal influence felt in that environment. She's a musician, a talented teacher of children and youth, a graduate in elementary education, one who goes the extra mile in every responsibility which falls to her. Her desire to live the gospel fully has been a stabilizing influence with many a class of Mutual girls, as well as with our six children.

Creativity is one of her many assets. She creates with the sewing machine, in the kitchen, with floral arrangements, with lesson plans. Her book, Growing Up in the Church, *has been widely read. Her song* I Love America *was part of a KSL-TV special which won a national Freedoms Foundation award.*

I know of no woman as well versed in the scriptures as she is. She has great stability, faith, and loyalty to the truth and to that which is right. When I first began to write, I dedicated a book to her: "To my wife Jean, who loves and heeds the words of the prophets"—that dedication is even more appropriate today than it was then. Jean, "Thee I Love," for your example of true womanhood has shaped my life for eternity. DSC

BUILDING SPIRITUALITY IN THE HOME
by
Jean D. Crowther

The sun was just setting as we dropped into the Salt River Valley of Arizona. A sweet fragrance of orange blossoms filtered into the car as we drove further down the mountainside onto the desert floor. I relaxed as a feeling of peace and contentment settled over me. This was my birthplace, and I was coming home after an absence of many years. I thought of my parents who were waiting in Mesa for our arrival—it would be wonderful to be home with them again!

Duane seemed to sense my feelings and teased me gently about where I really belonged. My reply was, "I will live happily with you in Utah, or Idaho, or wherever we have our home. I love you and our children. But when I come into this valley, this place of childhood memories, my heart knows it has come home!"

In one far-off day, each of us will drop into some area of eternity and our spirits will feel at peace and know they are home. Earth life is a preparation for that return to our eternal home, the presence of God. Our reunion with our Heavenly parents there will be glorious.

One of our most poignant hymns pleads,

> More purity give me,
> More strength to o'ercome;
> More freedom from earthstains;
> More longing for home.

Our spirits truly do long for our heavenly home and its glories while we are here in mortality, and the possibilities of eternity influence us in many ways. The objective of earth life is to constantly channel these longings our spirits feel for "home" into righteous living and preparation for our eternal future.

We can feel the upward striving of our spirit as we seek for eternal goals. Mortal problems fade as the spiritual side of our beings become dominant. Life falls into perspective as we place more and more importance upon the things of God.

139

When we identify the role God plays in our lives, we develop a confidence in Him. We trust in Him and know of His love for us and His interest in our progress. We obey His commandments, knowing that if we do so He will shape our lives for good. As we trust in God's willingness to direct and help us, we develop a personal relationship with Him.

Because of our knowledge of God and our relationship to Him, we strive to become like Him. We realize the importance of overcoming weaknesses and become receptive to the promptings of the Holy Ghost. The degree of spirituality we thus enjoy depends upon our seeking "first the kingdom of God and His righteousness." (Mt. 6:33)

Sanctification—The Process of Eternal Growth

We live on a series of levels. We may exist on the same plane for a long period until a problem or need in our life causes us to seek for guidance and progress upward. Then, as we rid ourselves of the apathy and weaknesses that hold us on the current level, we receive the inspiration and challenges needed to change our lives. We move up to a higher plane and the process is repeated.

We become candidates to that eternal kingdom which we will finally inherit by the levels of existence we have overcome. By this process we determine whether we will pass the remainder of eternity as telestial, terrestrial, celestial or exalted beings. Some of us are static and make little progress during our lifetime. Others, with greater motivation, gain increased understanding of the process and move consistently forward from one level to another.

The refining process results from a yielding of oneself to God. A righteous group of Nephites in Helaman's time experienced it, for

> They did fast and pray oft, and did wax stronger and stronger in their humility, and firmer and firmer in the faith of Christ, unto the filling their souls with joy and consolation, yea, even to the purifying and the sanctification of their hearts, which sanctification cometh because of their *yielding their hearts unto God.* (Hel. 3:35)

As we refine our characters and live on higher and higher planes, we become more Godlike. Indeed, the Spirit strives with our spirit, teaching us what needs to be changed and corrected in

140

our life. If we accept these promptings and repent of the attitude or sin, we prepare ourselves for additional promptings that allow us to be aware of other ungodly tendencies. The Spirit will continue working with us as long as we accept His guidance. This process, described frequently in the scriptures, is called "sanctification." It is the key to mortal progress and to eternal glory and exaltation.

Tasting Early Rewards from Meeting the Challenge

"Jean, would you be willing to join me in an experiment? I want to choose a day and try to live it perfectly—as if I were sanctified and the Savior was staying in my home. I want someone else to share the experience so we can compare our feelings together..."

The invitation came from a close friend in a nearby ward. I felt the idea was actually a personal challenge, and knew it would require me to rise to new heights of self-discipline. And yet, we had been teaching in our respective Spiritual Living Lessons that the purpose of earth life was to become perfect. If I really expected to arrive at this goal, couldn't I try to live it for one day?

I enlisted the help and cooperation of my family and we tried the experiment three different times that month, and each time we gained new insights. On these days, the children were sent off to school by a calm, cheerful mother and the housekeeping chores were done quickly. There appeared a sizeable block of time that usually wasn't there—hours that I used for gospel study. I was able to organize our home more effectively and the days were filled with harmony and contentment. Even our pre-schoolers played happily together. The joyous spirit lasted, with some self-reminding on my part, past homecoming time and supper, throughout the evening.

Those were days when we made the effort of exercising complete self-control. We diligently sought to fulfill Moroni's admonition to "deny yourself of all ungodliness" (Moro. 10:32), and we tasted the early rewards of meeting that challenge.

Thinking, speaking, and acting in a Godlike manner, as if the Savior were there beside us, was difficult to sustain, however. We soon found that it took a complete commitment and absolute effort from every member of the family. The task of living a perfect day couldn't be imposed by one person on the rest; it required

141

a willingness and determination by each individual. If even one of us let down and spoke a cross word or made an impatient remark, we could feel the Spirit leave. It was difficult to maintain our conduct on that plane. We discovered, also, that we couldn't go out "into the world" for very long without diluting the feeling of living close to God.

We found it was possible for our family to live an almost perfect day but that it was difficult to sustain the effort for much longer. Why was it so hard? Should it be such a struggle? And then we realized—we were doing things by conscious effort which should have been matters of habit. We couldn't enjoy the constant influence and companionship of the Spirit until we had made the necessary changes within ourselves—changes that would cause us to do instinctively and habitually what we were then doing on those special days by exertion of great energy and will power. We needed to correct and refine our conduct by actually changing our characters. Then perfect days could be lived. We needed to develop our spirituality, and do it in such a way that it would reach our entire family.

We haven't fully mastered the challenge yet, but we have made real efforts in a number of areas. From time to time we repeat the experiment and try to live a perfect day. It has helped us to understand the things which we must incorporate into our lives and projects we must pursue to increase spirituality in our family.

Seeking Family Spirituality Requires Parental Cooperation

Elder Arwell L. Pierce, who was president of the Arizona Temple, counseled Duane and me prior to performing our marriage. He emphasized that we must begin to function as a team, working together to the fullest extent. We have tried to follow his counsel and have found pleasure in helping each other with our duties.

Seeking to increase our family's spirituality has been a joint responsibility in our home. We have found that as we work together our duties have fallen easily into two closely-related divisions. It is my husband's duty to preside in the home. He honors his priesthood and keeps himself worthy to perform the ordinances needed in our family. He has accepted and fulfills the responsibility for conducting our formal religious activities. But we have come to

142

recognize that mother sets the emotional climate in our family, and that this determines the success or failure of many things we undertake. My attitude toward a duty or responsibility will generally be mirrored by the children. I can, through my reaction to spiritual things, create either reverence or indifference, acceptance or rebellion against them. Many times our responsibilities overlap, but generally:

My husband calls the family to prayer, invites a member to offer the prayer and encourages private prayers. My duty is to schedule and organize the family so prayer can be held regularly and at an appropriate time, have the small children ready to participate, and help the little ones learn to offer their own prayers.

Duane schedules our Family Home Evenings, conducts them, oversees and usually gives the lessons, and makes assignments to all of us for various types of participation. Again I must encourage the children to participate and help them prepare their parts, organize the evening so time is available (this includes having an early supper so the little children don't tire during the lesson), keep the evening free from tension and a quarreling spirit, and supervise refreshments. I sometimes give the lessons, particularly when visual aids are required, drawing from the resource files I have developed over the years.

My husband assumes the duty of encouraging church attendance, getting us there on time, and helping us all to be aware of our teaching, speaking, and priesthood assignments. I must create a pleasant environment on Sunday so we can participate with a minimum of "fuss and bother," guide the children into proper Sabbath Day activities, and willingly support church activity. It is my duty to see that clothing is pressed and ready, our home is clean for the Sabbath, and that meals are prepared with little effort.

Duane supervises our financial obligations to the Church, arranges to pay tithes, offerings, and other contributions at the proper time, and helps each child to do the same. I encourage the children to assume responsibility for their own obligations willingly, to keep track of their paper route money and allowance incomes so that they can compute their tithing

143

properly, etc.

This type of relationship is maintained in many elements of our family life. We have found that some areas of responsibility in seeking spirituality, however, are less easily defined. They become joint tasks for the two of us. Recently, Duane and I realized that our impatience was causing many problems in our family and that it was preventing our gaining of many of the goals for which we were seeking. We resolved to pull back and control our first verbal reaction in each situation which would arise. It took a lot of self-discipline because our bad habit was deeply ingrained. Yet as we held our tongues we could feel the peaceful atmosphere we desired return to our home in spite of the hectic lives we often lead. Harmony not only makes the home a pleasant place in which to live, it also makes it possible for the Spirit to function unrestrained in the home. We had to make this change *together* for it to be effective.

We have together tried to help each child discover who he was, his purpose for life, and his relationship to the eternal plan of our Heavenly Father. The importance of this effort has become evident to us on many occasions, but it became most vital in the summer of 1966 when we discovered that our daughter, Laura, only four years old, had contracted leukemia. When the possibility that we might lose her became real to us, we spent every minute we could take with our family explaining the steps of progression in the plan of salvation, the nature of life after death, and the blessings of the gospel. We feel that it made her passing easier for her and also for us. She died suddenly as we were traveling homeward to Utah after speaking to an M-Men—Gleaner encampment near Richland, Washington. Our oldest sons, Don and Scott (then six and seven), were in the car with us when she died. This could have been a very traumatic situation for them, but they accepted her passing calmly and with maturity far beyond their years because of their preparation and knowledge of the nature of death. As our other children have grown, they have been told about Laura and have a strong desire to be worthy to live with her in the future. We feel that by sharing our knowledge of the nature of life after death rather than the physical loss we have helped all of us to better accept her passing.

Faith-promoting experiences happen that can be meaningful

144

in our efforts to increase spirituality. But if they are not treated correctly the family soon may forget them. Reinforcing by discussion and retelling can make the same incident an important building block in a child's testimony. For instance, when our oldest son was four, he was often troubled by severe earaches. Medication was obtained but the infections persisted. One night the earache was particularly severe and Don was in real distress for several hours. He asked his father to administer to him as we had taught him to do. As my husband gave him a blessing he promised Don that the pain would completely disappear at that time but cautioned that it might recur with less intensity in the coming years. Even before the blessing was over the ear ceased to ache. Don was still occasionally troubled with a bad ear for a few years but each time the pain was less. He took comfort from the blessing he had received. We sought to remind him of it from time to time to build his faith. This incident is now part of his testimony of the healing power of the Priesthood.

Children accept the attitude of their parents very quickly. If husband and wife work together and treat the building of spirituality as an important objective for the family, the children will respond with the same feelings. They will learn to emphasize and regard as important what is valued by their parents. The building of spirituality should play a major role in family life.

Growth and Comfort from Priesthood Ordinances

The ordinances of the Church serve as guides for our conduct and also provide opportunities for individual growth. We feel they play an important part in the developing of family spirituality.

They can be classified in two categories: ordinances of progression and ordinances of comfort and blessing. Baptism, confirmation, priesthood ordinations, the endowment, temple marriage and sealings are all ordinances of progression. They constitute rungs on the ladder to exaltation and are essential steps that must be taken. Ordinances of blessing and comfort include the blessings of babies, patriarchal blessings, being set apart for positions of responsibility, administrations to the sick, fathers' blessings, and the dedication of homes. While the ordinances of progression are those which are required for growth toward exaltation, we've observed that the other ordinances have greater potential to influence individuals and to strengthen testimonies because they often have immediate and visible results which are faith-promoting. They help us to see that priesthood power is real and tangible. As we observe their fruits we can gain faith in the ordinances of progression where results are less immediate and more difficult to perceive.

Holders of the Melchizedek Priesthood have the right to give their children a father's blessing. The guidance in the blessings my father gave me when I left home for college, the night before I married, and two years ago when I had a serious health problem has been very special to me. Also, I am privileged to have a very special father-in-law who gave me a father's blessing on one occasion when I needed particular help. Much comfort and direction can be received in a blessing of this kind from one who is close to you and loves you.

We found great peace of mind by dedicating our home. We felt prompted to do so shortly after we moved to Bountiful, Utah. We regard the dedication as a seeking of God's protection from unrighteous influences, both seen and unseen, and also as our pledge that our home will be used for righteous purposes.

Administrations to the sick have taught our family reliance upon the power of the Lord. Often we have knelt together in family prayer before the administration to unite the faith of the family and concentrate it on a single goal. We feel that medical problems should be treated by a doctor, but we know that administering to the sick will relieve suffering and bring complete healing on many occasions.

Our youngest son, Billy, when he was six months old, was in his baby seat in a grocery cart as I was shopping when his brother David (then 2½) tried to climb into it. The cart tipped over and Billy was thrown out onto the concrete floor, landing on his head. The doctor examined the huge bruise on his head but found no other injury. Billy screamed all the time he was being examined and continued screaming for several hours. I rocked him, snuggled him, and did everything I could to quiet him, but my efforts were to no avail. Then my husband anointed him and, as he blessed him, commanded him to stop crying and to go to sleep. Within ten minutes the baby was quiet, asleep, and had no further trouble. This is the power of priesthood ordinances!

During his first year of life David suffered from something

146

which caused him to scream with pain many nights but we didn't know the reason for his distress. Medical tests were made and the doctor suspected an allergy, though he couldn't pinpoint the actual cause. He was unable to treat the source of the pain and distress until he could determine the problem by observing David as he was in pain. Sometimes when the baby was crying we sought the relief that could be gained by administration. I remember our pediatrician, a fine LDS man who was a member of our ward, scolded my husband on one occasion, saying that if we didn't allow him to examine David before he was administered to, the doctors would never be able to determine his problem—the administrations kept removing the symptoms!

We have tried to nurture our children's desire for a patriarchal blessing. Our children are aware of their parents' blessings and the guidance which these blessings have furnished in our lives. We have read ours to them on several occasions and have pointed out ways they have been fulfilled and have shaped our lives. Their Grandfather Crowther has been a patriarch for a number of years and our children have talked with him about his calling and about the blessings which he gives. They are preparing themselves to receive their own patriarchal blessings in the next few years.

Such experiences related to the ordinances of comfort have led our family to have faith in all the priesthood ordinances. We begin working with our children about six months before an ordinance date to prepare our children for baptism, confirmation, and priesthood ordinations.

Ordinance days are made important by inviting grandparents and gathering other family members around. These days are times for special meals, photographs and other memory-building efforts. We hope that these things will add to their understanding of the importance of the ordinances and their recall of the important events of that day.

We try to prepare them for future ordinances such as Melchizedek Priesthood ordination, receiving their endowments, and temple marriages, by relating our own experiences to the children. They have access to our "Temple Marriage Book" and other scrapbooks and are aware of the stories surrounding these events. The desire to be married in the temple is strong in their lives. We pray they can fulfill it and they do too. From early in their childhood

147

they have been taught to pray for major life goals: to be able to go on a mission, to graduate from college, and to be married in the temple.

Drawing Near Unto God

Prayer is man's communication with God. As we open our hearts to him we truly do receive comfort and guidance for our daily tasks. I remember as a child occasionally coming into my mother's room at different times during the day and finding her kneeling in prayer. I knew that she was troubled by some problem and was seeking help and guidance. As I grew older, I became aware that she did receive the comfort and assistance she sought from these prayerful consultations. Through her unspoken example I learned that prayers can be offered at any time when they are needed as well as in the morning and evenings. My mother's prayers taught me to better understand the inspired counsel given by Amulek, a missionary in the Book of Mormon:

> Humble yourselves, and continue in prayer unto him.
> Cry unto him when ye are in your fields, yea, over all your flocks.
> Cry unto him in your houses, yea, over all your household, both morning, mid-day, and evening....
> But this is not all; ye must pour out your souls in your closets, and your secret places, and in your wilderness.
> Yea, and when you do not cry unto the Lord, let your hearts be full, drawn out in prayer unto him continually for your welfare and also for the welfare of those who are around you. (Al. 34:19-21, 26-27)

My little ones have also come upon my private prayers and have occasionally knelt beside me until I finished. This is a sweet acceptance of my problems and attempts at solutions.

When I was in high school I shared my room with my sister, Elaine, who was then only three years old. It was my responsibility to help her with her prayers when she went to bed. One evening she refused my assistance, saying "I know how to pray myself—you just kneels down and bees quiet." I have come to realize how correct she was in her observation. Many of our prayers seem to become short, rather demanding, petitions for specific blessings. It

148

has been said that meaningful prayer should contain as much time spent listening for guidance as we spend asking for it. I wonder if God gets tired of a demanding child as we do as parents?

Prayer is a privilege, not a duty. When we spend our time only in repeating trite petitions that have become habitual, we may lose great blessings which could be ours if we truly offer our petition with a contrite heart. A personal prayer offered in haste because the bedroom is cold will not be more than duty fulfilled, or a family prayer offered during the commercial of an exciting Wednesday Night Movie on TV has little chance of being a meaningful communication with God.

As our family gathered in prayer together we sometimes have had hurried teenagers admonishing slow pre-schoolers about the time it was taking to pray. It seemed like the only thing we were accomplishing was gathering all the family together. We spent one family night this spring re-explaining the purposes of prayer and then walking around the neighborhood looking at the beauties of nature and expressing our gratitude for them. We have attempted to incorporate this grateful spirit into our prayers. Duane often summarizes the family's needs and blessings as he calls upon a family member to pray. We have also found that a regular time and place for family prayer helps us all to be better prepared, more reverent, and more in tune. The children learn to respect this time and we have less confusion.

Often the desire to express gratitude for our blessings will come independently from other needs. Children naturally feel wonder at the marvels of the world about them. Let us teach them to express this wonder in their prayers.

We need to have prayers answered to build our faith in prayer. Sometimes the answer can be quite dramatic and the incident will become a touchstone for faith. As poor, struggling, married, college students at the BYU we found ourselves without food money and many days before a pay check. We were both working, both student teaching, and both going to school, but we had organized a small dance band to help finance our way through college. We knelt together and explained our predicament in prayer to our Heavenly Father. Even before we had finished our prayer our telephone rang. It was a ward MIA president desperate to find a band for that very night. The next week Duane's uncle

149

came for an unexpected visit. When he saw how destitute we were, he quietly went to the store and returned with a car full of groceries, including many items we had been getting along without all of our marriage. I know he enjoyed doing that for us but I don't believe he even yet realizes how he was an answer to our prayers. We truly sensed God's watchful care over us as a result of that week and have shared the memory of it with our children several times.

We know that we have been blessed as a result of family prayer before trips. We have driven thousands of miles after offering the petition that we be protected from harm, from danger, and from serious mechanical difficulties. With the old cars we drove in the early years of our married life we have had our share of serious car troubles, but they never seem to occur when we are traveling or far from help. Several problems that could have meant major repairs or serious accidents have been recognized and remedied in service stations as we journeyed rather than leaving us stranded in the middle of nowhere. We are sure that our prayers for personal safety and the mechanical well-being of our car have been answered.

People allow disrespect to creep into prayers by using poor grammar and improper prayer language. Words of respect have been given that dignify prayers. We must help our children become familiar with them so they can use them freely and without awkwardness or a feeling of self-consciousness. This is a small thing, but just as we dress our best and act our best on the Sabbath, we should use the best possible speech in our communication with God.

We have also learned that one doesn't just ask for blessings and express gratitude. We need to kneel before God with the attitude "I am here and ready, what wouldst thou have me do?" As we show a willingness to be led and open our minds to inspiration, our thoughts will often open up and specific ideas or answers to problems will flood in.

Our children are invited to participate in prayers for help with serious problems. I remember as Laura was sick, our children, and also many of her four-year-old friends and cousins, participated in fasting and prayer for her.

When I was sixteen, my grandmother became very ill. She had suffered from a serious heart condition for several years and then cancer spread throughout her body. The doctors couldn't alleviate the pain caused by the cancer without seriously endangering her heart. I remember how our whole family fasted together in their various homes all one weekend and then offered their prayers at the same hour. Our petition was that she be allowed to go peacefully and not have to suffer any longer. She died immediately. The impact of this answer to prayer was very great on the testimonies of her grandchildren.

The purpose of fasting is to humble ourselves so that we become more receptive to the promptings of the Spirit. We can increase our level of communication with God if we actively strive for this goal rather than merely deprive ourself of food.

Our three older children have learned to fast with a minimum of discomfort because of the attitude we helped them adopt concerning this gospel principle. The first few times they fasted, as six- and seven-year-olds, were difficult for them. We have encouraged them to take a drink of juice or of milk to sustain them rather than give up their fast completely. Some children have a more difficult time than others, but a matter-of-fact "you can do it" parental attitude seems most successful in helping them. Lisa now is experiencing the maturity and pride of accomplishment that emerges as she realizes more and more that she can control her body.

On many fast days we talk together and choose a common need in our family for which to pray. Fasting just because it is Fast Day ignores the blessings which can be obtained. The united effort of concentration and prayer also pulls the family together and eliminates tension and distractions. Of course, fasting should be used as a tool with prayer more often than Fast Day if the need arises.

Building Testimonies

A religious testimony is knowledge that something exists, is true or is correct. A testimony comes by observation, by experience, by prayerful study, and by revelation. It comes, not all at once, but a bit at a time. We are prompted that this doctrine, then that principle, then another, is correct and true. A testimony is knowledge, not just belief. It is based on personal experience, insights and knowledge gained personally or revelation personally received. It must be as certain as testimony offered in a court of

151

law. Mere belief or suspicion is not valid evidence there. A religious testimony based on belief and not on knowledge is only a statement of desire, intent, or allegiance, masquerading as knowledge. There is no real substitute for an actual testimony—it requires knowledge, usually received or confirmed by revelation.

Many people can identify an incident or date that marked their gaining of a portion of their testimony. I recall two events that have given me a testimony that the gospel is truly Christ's plan and that the prophet of the Church is His spokesman to lead us in that plan.

The first was in 1953 at a Church meeting in Arizona. President David O. McKay was visiting. As he came into the room I felt the Spirit flood my mind and heart with the knowledge that he was truly a prophet. Although I hadn't been searching particularly for a testimony of his calling, I felt the Spirit bear witness to my soul that this man was the prophet of God.

That summer my grandmother died. I had been very close to her and was greatly bereaved by her death. Her funeral was held in the Assembly Hall on Temple Square. My grandparents had been personal friends of President McKay, and he was the speaker at her funeral. I still remember him standing at the pulpit dressed in a white suit as he bore a powerful testimony of the plan of salvation. I felt the truth of the gospel plan with all my being as the Spirit burned within me. Both of these experiences have made lasting impressions upon me and formed the beginning basis for my testimony.

We have the obligation to our children to help them understand the nature of a testimony and its necessity in their life. As they increase in their own spirituality, they need to recognize the promptings and witnesses of the Spirit when that guidance comes to them. It is our responsibility to help them especially when they reach the teenage years and are actively seeking and questioning. Often a teenager feels he is different or wrong to be searching for what he feels he should already know as a result of his previous religious training. He must understand that it is right and necessary to search, to test, to evaluate, and to wrestle for a testimony of each gospel truth. If he can be helped to realize that his task is to personally accept that which he has been taught and gain revelation and confirmation concerning it, he can feel secure in his questioning.

Although most young children have not reached this point of conversion, they often desire to bear their testimony. I feel that we should help them understand the reasons for bearing a testimony and then allow them to do so as soon as they like. They don't need to parrot adult wording but should bear a witness of what they understand and know. They need to begin early to gain knowledge of the truthfulness of elementary gospel principles and then express that knowledge. To do so requires practice. A good place for this to begin is in home testimony meetings, perhaps as a conclusion to an appropriate family night. If all the children know they can and will be expected to stand along with the parents, even the most reticent child will try something. Soon the time will come when they feel confident to bear their testimony in a ward meeting.

Loving encouragement, without bribes, threats or dares, will do a lot for a child who is slower than others to desire to express the testimony which is his. But if we can encourage children to participate before older grade school age, they will be more likely to overcome shyness and social pressures later.

If children do not hear parents bear testimony in public or express convictions in private, it will be harder for them to desire to do so themselves. We have an obligation to them, as well as to ourselves, to bear our testimony often.

The bearing of testimonies doesn't guarantee a child's complete conversion, however. Our constant goal must be to teach and convert our children through lessons, discussions, examples, and stories just as a missionary does with his contacts. Doing so will strengthen our own testimonies and create a basis of communication as our children mature. Remember "the art of teaching is the art of assisting discovery."

Building on the Strengths of Our Ancestors

In this day of "identity crises" and searching for "who am I?", it is comforting to know of our ancestors and their lives. Most LDS families have knowledge of their grandparents and earlier progenitors, family traditions, life histories, and stories of conversion to the gospel. Sharing these stories with our children, augmenting them with incidents from our own and their earlier lives, will build a foundation of identity for them. We have found great

153

pleasure in keeping scrapbooks and other memorabilia in a permanent form. This helps children to know who they are because they can better recall who they used to be. We feel our efforts to help our children be aware of their place in the family help them to build confidence in themselves and gain courage to overcome problems.

Faith-promoting accounts from family histories can play a significant part in strengthening testimonies and aiding knowledge of spiritual powers. Our children have loved true family stories such as:

Great-grandfather Thomas Crowther, an impoverished early Mormon pioneer, was told he could borrow his neighbor's oxen for spring plowing if he would get them in off the winter range. He searched all day in the hills above Cedar City, Utah, but was unable to locate them. Footsore and hungry, he knelt down and pled for guidance. An audible voice told him "They are up in Coal Canyon." He went there immediately and soon found both oxen lying down, seemingly waiting for him.

Great-grandfather Jesse Smith and his wife had lost two babies in Wales. Their remaining son lay seriously ill with diptheria. He left their Lehi, Utah cabin and went to the woodpile to pray for the life of his baby. As he did so, he saw a man dressed in white whose feet did not touch the ground enter the cabin and come back out carrying little Jesse. He knew from this that the baby was safe with God, even though dead to him.

Grandfather Louis Decker, a twelve-year-old sheepherder in northern Arizona, and his sister, Inez, were accosted by a group of Apaches in full war paint. The Indians demanded first the sheep, then the gun, but finally settled for the children's lunch when Louis courageously refused to yield to their demands. Grandfather was blessed with the courage to stand up to them as the result of a prayer he offered hurriedly as the Indians approached.

Grandfather German Ellsworth was President of the Northern States Mission when the Church negotiated the purchase of the Hill Cumorah and other nearby land of historical importance. He was walking on that hill early one morning when a voice spoke to him saying, "Push the distribution of the record taken from this hill; it will help bring the world to Christ." At this time the Church had drawn back somewhat from using the Book of Mormon as an

154

initial proselyting tool. The impetus he gave to the reuse of that sacred book as a missionary tool spread across the Church and altered the course of proselyting methods for years.

These stories and many others which are similar are dear to our family. We often build a talk or lesson around them. My parents have undertaken the task of writing down and distributing to their children histories of many of my ancestors which has been a blessing to us. We have read these and other printed histories to our children as part of our story hour. It makes Church history vital when you know a family member played a part in different incidents, and it makes names on a pedigree chart come alive. As we were preparing to attend a recent family reunion Don asked, "Is Kristine the little girl that came across on the boat and then walked all the way to Utah?" He was willing and even anxious to meet the people that descended from that brave woman. We are seeing an increased interest in genealogy work as our children mature and we attribute much of it to a familiarity with the lives of these people.

Our sons have been able to help in genealogical research for our family also. On several occasions they have gone to the Genealogical Library with me and have worked quite accurately there. It is enjoyable to work with them and to share in their enthusiasm. We have encouraged the attitude that they also help in this work when they aid in family routine and child care to free me to go to the library to continue our research. Duane is a set-apart worker in the Salt Lake Temple and performs vicarious baptisms each week. Several times our oldest sons have been privileged to go and participate in this work with their father baptizing them, which has strengthened their interest in the entire genealogical and temple work program. The family all helps when my husband publishes the *Crowther Chronicles*, the newsletter for the William Orson Crowther Family Organization. All these activities help us to build on the strengths of our ancestors.

A Time for Holiness

God, in his wisdom, has given us a special day each week to be devoted to increasing our spirituality. With the commandment "Remember the Sabbath day, to keep it holy," He defined our task: to make ourselves holy, or Godlike. That is what we are to

155

accomplish on this special day. Church attendance and resting from our labors are commanded as aids in achieving that objective.

The Sabbath is the day set apart to draw near to God and to learn of Him and His ways so we may emulate them. Families should be together, attend their meetings together, and make a definite effort to perfect their life on that day.

The Sabbath is a change of pace which creates the blessing and opportunity to have a peaceful, holy day in the family. By changing from our busy daily routine we find ourselves with additional time to get into the spirit of worship and contemplation. The proper spirit comes when housework is kept to a simple minimum and family problems are greatly reduced.

Experience has taught our family that if we are out late Saturday night, we make less progress toward our goals than when we begin the day well rested. We've learned that going to bed Saturday night with a straight house, clean clothes and plans for Sunday menus helps us also. The children's song that says "Saturday is a special day, it's a day to get ready for Sunday" is certainly stating a wise principle. Our observation is that young children react to the Saturday preparation and soon realize that Sunday is a different kind of day. When the family uses extra care in keeping the home in good order all day Sunday it adds to the "specialness" of the day also.

In some households mothers prepare elaborate meals for Sunday dinner. I've found that when I do this, it keeps me from experiencing the proper spirit of the day, it takes hours that should be used elsewhere, and I sometimes even resent the apparent leisure of the rest of the family. We've decided that Sunday meals should be simple, prepared ahead of time if possible, and cleaned up easily at our house. When we limit the kitchen duties, I am able to attend Sunday School as well as Sacrament Meeting. This sets an example and I can take advantage of the gospel lessons made available by the Church. In the Crowther home, Scott and Don help fix foods that can be left baking in the oven as we attend Church meetings before they leave for priesthood meeting. Potatoes wrapped in foil can bake for 2-3 hours without drying, or we have a simple rice dish that can bake for three hours. Roasts, chicken or round steak are often browned and left to bake while we attend Sunday School. Lisa can prepare Jello salad on Saturday, tossed green salad is easy

156

to fix, or we often have a dish of fruit. These, plus a vegetable, round out our menu and the items require little preparation on Sunday. Duane has encouraged the tradition of everyone pitching in to help with final preparations so we're usually able to eat dinner within a half hour after our return from meeting. Since I usually make an attempt not to serve the same menu during the week, there has been little complaint with having similar meals each Sunday.

Sunday supper is casual, often bacon and eggs, toasted-cheese sandwiches, or an easy scone recipe that can be fried in an electric fry pan. I have tried to teach my children that Sunday isn't the day for a lot of cooking.

Many parents, I believe, find it hard to set and hold to rules concerning proper Sabbath activity for children. Several years ago we made a few decisions that have helped in our family:

1. *Dress nicely.* After returning from Church meetings, all our younger children change from Sunday apparel into fairly nice "school type" clothes, with girls in dresses, rather than into their play clothes. This automatically eliminates certain inappropriate activities.

2. *Television stays off.* We reasoned that if it is not in keeping with the Sabbath to go to a movie, it is just as wrong to watch that same movie or other entertainment on TV at home. We feel this decision has helped the spirit in our home very much, even though it eliminated many "good" shows from our viewing. Occasionally we have relaxed the rule for a movie with religious aspects such as **The Robe.** Of course, general conference and the Tabernacle Choir broadcasts are allowed, but the television is on only for that time period and then is turned off. Our children have grown up with this practice and it has been well accepted by them. We don't have Sunday television arguments.

3. *Inside activity only.* This is the one decision concerning Sunday conduct we have found most useful. It eliminates all the frustrations of "Why can't I play basketball, or ride a bike downtown?" Play inside by the younger children is also geared towards more quiet activities. What is the difference between a Saturday or a Sunday afternoon in a child's life if the same play and activities take place? How does a young child learn to identify Sunday as a special day unless his conduct varies for the Sabbath? Friends

157

can be invited over if the activity is quiet and appropriate. Projects like scripture study and preparing for priesthood goals are encouraged for our older boys. They also work on scouting or read good books.

4. *Everyone goes to church.* We have made it our policy that everyone in the family is expected to attend all their church meetings and to be in their proper place during those meetings. We reccognize the wisdom of the oft-given counsel that we sit together as a family.

"The chapel doors seem to say to you shh—be still." Reverence is important, but we feel more than just being quiet in our chapels is expected of us. We attend church to worship, and worship requires communication with God. We've tried to teach our children to participate fully in the meeting, singing the hymns, following through the sacrament and sermons or lessons with a prayerful attitude, and keeping their thoughts centered on the service. Our daughter's Primary teacher gave each of her class members personalized pocket hymn books last year. How pleasing it has been to see the delight Lisa takes now in singing the hymns in Sacrament meeting. Religious services are times for personal prayer. We've encouraged our children to pray for those in charge or speaking during the meeting as well as for personal needs.

Our very young children have needed something to keep them quiet (unfortunately our babies have never slept well in church). We have found that a small selection of books, soft toys, or a quiet book help more than a large purseful of distractions. We choose our "church toys" with the questions, "will it scatter easily?" "will it make a noise if it is dropped?" "will it distract others trying to listen?" "is it appropriate for the Lord's House?" We've found that young children don't need entertaining in church much past the age of two, especially if older children are not allowed to play with them. Future problems are created by providing children with play things and books in church when they are capable of doing without them. Books may keep an older child occupied, but they only hinder his interest in the service and thwart his real reasons for being there. Our three-year-olds are usually able to sit still without any toys, talking, or tending, with arms folded during the sacrament service. With proper preparation before the meetings they recognize this as a period during which they must be quiet. Sometimes they offer an audible sigh as the Bishop stands at the conclusion of the Sacrament, but that training pays real dividends later.

We have tried to use our family night lessons to teach that the sacrament is not a "treat to keep me from being hungry," that congregational prayer is their prayer too and should be followed mentally and ended with a spoken "Amen," and that the sacrament is a renewing of the baptismal covenants.

Sunday is the Lord's day and should be honored as such. It is a day for us to find ways to improve our lives and to make ourselves more holy. Much growth can be enjoyed if parents will develop a positive attitude and treat proper Sabbath observance as a joy rather than a duty.

Learning the Ways of God

I sometimes wonder if I am progressing or if I am stagnant. It's a good thing, I believe, to compare our present with our past and ask, "Am I a better person now than I was five years ago?" "Am I moving forward toward clearly-identified goals?" "What am I trying to accomplish this *month*?" "What will be the eternal results if I live the rest of my life on this level?"

The key to growth, I have found, is to draw new knowledge and inspiration from the scriptures. We need to study, and ponder, and seek out the concepts which can guide our lives for good. But it is a rare woman that can discipline herself to study and read the scriptures consistently on a daily schedule, without some outside motivation. The women of our neighborhood have greatly enjoyed a study group in which we each read privately about ten pages of scripture and then meet each week for an hour together. As leader I have made extra preparation by reading several outside sources from Bible scholars and Church leaders and have led the discussions. We have had a faithful group attend and, in the three-and-one-half years we have completely read and discussed the *Bible*, the *Book of Mormon*, and the *Pearl of Great Price*. At this time we are starting the *Doctrine and Covenants*. We make no effort to go into deep discussions of philosophy. Our attempt is to learn the things of God.

Another excellent project we have undertaken several times in the past is an actual scripture memorization program. When our

159

three oldest children were still very young, we learned with them the Articles of Faith, the Ten Commandments, the names of the books in each of the four Standard Works, and about forty other basic scriptural passages. It was interesting to see how readily they learned. As Lisa, David, Billy, and Sharon have come along we have found it harder to find time to teach them these things and we find that each year as they grow older their ability to memorize really diminishes.

We have found accomplishment in neighborhood scripture groups also. Twice, when we first moved to Bountiful in 1967, my husband gathered groups of about twenty children of grade school level, motivated them, and memorized one hundred passages with them. We repeated the process with teenagers and adults and learned several hundred passages more. Most of the success in scripture memorization programs comes when you are challenged and know you must repeat the passages to someone by a certain time. But what a blessing it is to be able to feel confident of your knowledge of the scriptures on many vital topics!

One of the best methods we have found to regularly teach our children is "story time." Because Duane usually finishes supper first it gives us a few minutes at dinner time: everyone continues eating as he reads to us for ten to fifteen minutes. Since this is an integral part of our supper hour everyone stays at the table and listens quietly. We have been doing this for almost eight years and have now read about sixty books. Most of the books have been stories of the scriptures such as *A Child's Story of the Book of Mormon* by Deta Petersen Neeley, *The Book of Mormon Story* by Mary Parrish and Ron Crosby, *Story of our Church, Bible Stories,* and *Book of Mormon Stories* by Emma Marr Peterson, and the Seventh-Day Adventist *The Bible Story.* Several of these have been repeated twice and three times. But we find that our children, ages two to thirteen, are also able to understand and enjoy the actual *New Testament, Doctrine and Covenants,* and *Pearl of Great Price* with occasional parental explanations being interjected. We have also included a few poetry books and some histories of my ancestors. We highly recommend this method of reading to any family. Our children have a knowledge of the scriptures that far exceeds their age levels.

The Church leaders have given us another tool that will aid

us in raising the spiritual level of our home. The Family Home Evening program of devoting an evening a week to family activities is a vital program. Much good can come even if we only follow the program as outlined, but far greater good can be accomplished if we adapt the program to fit the personalities and needs of our family.

Many of the saints across the country have the opportunity to view the sessions of general conference on television. To many, I believe, the challenge to gain something specific from conference goes unanswered. We turn the TV on and then go about our regular duties with the speakers providing only a background for our other activities. I have found that doing something stationary in front of the TV, such as ironing or mending, is better for me. But the most successful plan, short of attending in person, is to leave my home chores and sit down and observe as if I were in the tabernacle. The years that I have taken notes on each talk have been even more productive. Sessions that can be enjoyed in this way are discussed later in the evening with the family more knowledgeably than "I can't remember who he was but the first speaker told an interesting story today" level.

There are thousands in the Church who cannot see the conferences televised. For them, as well as the rest of us, there is the blessing of *Church News* coverage of the talks and the complete conference reports in the *Ensign* magazine. These should be read as avidly as the continuing story in *Good Housekeeping*. It requires discipline to learn from the teachings of our General Authorities and to change our life as they direct us for good. Beginning with the recent change in the Presidency of the Church, my husband has resolved to keep a complete file and prepare a detailed outline and analysis of every discourse made by the Prophet which is reported in the Church periodicals.

Our responsibilities as mothers is to keep the spiritual level of our family life moving on an increasing upward direction. We must keep aware of the gospel attitudes held by our family members. As we strive to open communication to the powers above through prayer, we learn to listen to promptings of the Spirit that will help us as a family. "Listening is wanting to hear."

The priesthood is the leadership of the home. We should strive to help our husbands and sons develop their priesthood power.

161

This will build up a shield of protection for our family to help us overcome temptation and adversity.

We must endure to the end, but we cannot merely remain static—we must progress towards meaningful goals that we have set for ourselves and our family. We must weed out all that is degrading and sinful and substitute Godlike qualities. Every person has this responsibility for himself.

We are here on earth learning to know, to do, and to be, so that we may eventually reach exaltation and godhood. We have the necessary opportunities. As King Benjamin said to his people,

> This much I can tell you, that if ye do not watch yourselves, and your thoughts, and your words, and your deeds, and observe the commandments of God, and continue in the faith of what ye have heard concerning the coming of our Lord, even unto the end of your lives, ye must perish.

(Mosiah 4:30)

The key to achieving this goal is to foster true spirituality in our lives and in the lives of our family. It must become the dominant theme, which affects our choice of all the other things we do. With that accomplished, we can be ready to reap the revealed promise that "If you keep my commandments and endure to the end, you shall have eternal life, which gift is the greatest of all the gifts of God." (D & C 14:7)

INTRODUCING—ALICE W. BUEHNER

Looking for the well-rounded woman? Try Alice Buehner. In the biographical sketches she furnished to us she writes, "I love to travel! I've been to Japan, Hawaii, South America, the Dutch West Indies, the Bahamas, and Europe. I love water skiing and snow skiing. I'm a certified scuba diver and lifeguard. I like to sing and play the piano. Writing and painting and reading are my favorite hobbies."

Alice was named "Mrs. America" in 1965 and found herself catapulted into the role of radio and television personality, model, and public speaker. These opportunities were superimposed over the tasks of homemaker and mother of five young sons and a daughter—that would provide a real challenge for any woman. She met the challenge with the aid of her husband, Don L. Buehner, a co-owner of Electro-Controls company in Salt Lake City.

A home economics degree had previously been the result of Alice's study at Utah State University in Logan, Utah. She then worked as an airline hostess flying to Hawaii, Wake Island, and Japan for a year and as an interior decorator. She and Don were married in the Salt Lake Temple in 1954.

Church assignments have had their claim on Alice's busy schedule. She's been in presidencies of the MIA, the Primary, and the Relief Society, has been a Junior Sunday School coordinator, and has taught in all of the auxiliaries.

Like many·of the authors in this book, Alice has taught classes for the Brigham Young University extension division. Her course on self-improvement for women has continued for a number of years. Lecturing is a pleasant experience for her.

Every person has a need to develop a plan for personal growth. In this chapter Alice discusses the universal need for individual goal-setting and development in mental, physical, spiritual, and social areas. We commend her thoughts to all who recognize their need for self-improvement. JDC & DSC

PLANNING FOR HAPPINESS
by
Alice W. Buehner

There's a story about Johnny Lingo who bought his Polynesian wife for the unheard-of-price of eight cows, when the going price was only two or three. His young bride, who had for many years thought she was worth nothing in her father's home, suddenly realized she was worth more than any other woman in the village. Of course she soon developed into an "eight cow" wife simply because her attitude toward herself changed.

Thinking Positively

Before a woman can realize her full potential she must first develop a *positive attitude.* It has been stated that "as a man thinketh in his heart, so is he." What a profound truth that is! We alone can determine what our attitudes will be: either positive and happy, or negative and miserable.

We all know people who are constantly complaining and looking at the dark side of life. And we all know people who are continually happy and exuberant, who seem to find joy all around them, in spite of the problems of everyday life. Which person would you rather be like? If you study the two types, it soon becomes obvious that the pessimist attracts gloom while the optimist attracts happiness.

My brother, Bob Welti, is a marvelous example of an optimist. Several years ago my husband and I, our 10-year-old son, my brother Walt, and my then 72-year-old father went on a canoe trip down the normally placid Green River with Bob. A strong wind came up which soon turned into gale force making white caps on the river. My father's boat capsized twice, chilling him so thoroughly that he was determined to walk back!

Sand blew into our provisions, making it impossible to eat that night. We finally could go no further, and luckily docked our boats near an old farm. In the darkness, we found an old shed where we slept fitfully in damp sleeping bags. In the morning we discovered to our distaste that we had been sleeping in what was once a chicken coop! In spite of the inconvenience and discomfort we were experiencing, Bob exclaimed, "Isn't this great! Just think what you'll have to tell the folks back home!"

His happy, enthusiastic attitude made the whole trip fun!

So first of all in our plan for happiness, we must develop a positive attitude. Get rid of "I can't." Instead, use "I can and I will!" Remember, success comes in cans; failure comes in can'ts.

From this moment on, blot out every negative thought that you've ever harbored. If one pops into your mind, immediately erase it and replace it with a positive thought. Feed the good habits and starve the bad habits. We are victims of habit and your way of thinking becomes as habitual as the way you walk. It takes conscious effort to change a habit, but that is just what you must do. Each day when you awaken, kneel down and thank your Father in Heaven for your life and pray that this day may be one in which you practice positive thinking continually. You can do it with His help!

Soon you will find that life is looking rosier and that you are feeling peace of mind. We are on earth for such a short time, compared to eternity. We want to enjoy every moment! "The fruit of the spirit is love, joy, peace." (Gal. 5:22)

A Model for Balanced Growth

God's plan for us is that we might prove ourselves worthy to enter back into His presence. In other words, we are here on earth to perfect ourselves. Wouldn't it be folly to try to bake a cake for the first time without a recipe? Just the same, it is folly to try to live a perfect life without a plan and a set of rules. God has given us the rules for happiness but we must make our own plan.

Every principle for happiness can be found in the holy scriptures. For instance, there is a useful outline for a balanced approach to living in Luke's description of the boyhood of the Savior:

And Jesus increased in wisdom and stature, and in favour with God and man. (Luke 2:52)

Jesus grew four ways: in wisdom (mentally), in stature (physically), and in favor with God (spiritually), and man (socially). What better outline for a well-balanced life could we have? Now let's relate each of these areas of growth to ourselves:

Growing Mentally

Are you increasing in knowledge and wisdom, or have you ceased to grow and progress intellectually?

Many men lament the fact that their wives become uninformed and uninteresting after several years of marriage. They become weary of hearing only about children and household duties. Some wives actually render a minute-by-minute report of their daily routine when their husbands return home from work. If you are guilty of doing that, you can be sure your husband would rather hear about some interesting news item or about a book you're reading, or even silence.

Many mothers complain that they, in fact, are bored. Talking with young children day after day is not particularly stimulating conversation, but as Belle S. Spafford once said, "A woman should realize that until her children are all in school, she is semi-retired." You must dedicate many years to helping new little minds blossom, but certainly not let your own mind lie dormant. Although your duty lies at home with your small children, there are many avenues of mental growth open to you. We can always find time to do what we really want to do, so there is no valid excuse for not keeping mentally alert.

If being a slow reader is holding you back, get a book on how to read faster. Remember - *you can do it!*

Find out what time the news broadcasts come on and listen to them at least once a day. This keeps you informed about current events and provides a topic of conversation with husband and friends. A good way to remember a story is to tell it out loud to someone (even yourself, if necessary), while it is still fresh on your mind. If you wait, you may forget details.

Whenever you hear a word for which you don't know the meaning, write it down, then look it up; use it five times in a day and it will be yours!

Learn to budget your time just as carefully as you do money. I know a woman who has learned to make use of her "waiting moments." She keeps a paperback book in her purse to read while waiting for children at lessons, or anywhere else. She keeps a weekly news magazine in her bathroom. You'd be surprised how many "waiting moments" are spent there!

166

The mind, like the body, improves with exercise. And certainly the more you feed it, the more it is able to feed back. The human mind is so amazing! Just imagine, everything you have ever seen, or heard, or read, or experienced, is recorded there! Isn't it logical that when judgment day comes along our mind will serve as the complete and accurate record of our life on earth? That is why it is so important to fill our minds with only wholesome information. We are free to choose what we read, see and hear. Let's begin now in our plan for happiness to set time aside for mental growth.

Developing Physically

Have you looked in the mirror lately? Do you like what you see? If not, it's time to do something about it!

Most men agree that all women are beautiful, only some behave as though they are, while others do not.

You announce to the world how you feel about yourself in many little ways. Let's explore the visible characteristics that lead to beauty.

Health and Cleanliness: I have always felt that a healthy body is the most important physical attribute a person could want. We must make the most of whatever God has given us at birth. I'm a believer that food in it's most natural form is what God intended us to eat. I avoid foods with preservatives in them whenever possible, even though they are easier to prepare. Cooking can be a great source of enjoyment, and nutrition is a fascinating science. It is a wife's and mother's responsibility to learn all she can about good health. I would never want to cloud my lungs with tobacco smoke nor numb my senses with alcohol or drugs. A woman should take excellent care of herself—so many lives depend upon her.

Just as a positive mental attitude is reflected in your expression, so is a healthy body reflected in your sparkling eyes, shiny hair, radiant skin and queenly bearing. If you want to look impressive, stand with erect posture, walk a little faster and smile a lot more.

When you think of femininity you automatically think of cleanliness. It's imperative for a beautiful woman to be immaculately clean and sweet smelling.

167

Figure: Americans are very diet conscious. A favorite topic of conversation among women is how overweight they think themselves to be. It's a good idea to avoid drawing attention to your shortcomings. We are our own worst enemies at the times we tell everyone our faults.

Rather than talk about your weight, do something about it! Turn talk into action! Begin by setting a realistic weight at which you would feel good. Then tell yourself you *can* and *will* achieve it in a certain amount of time. It is a matter of disciplining the mind, in most cases.

If you feel tired-out and lethargic lately, chances are you need exercise. It's a fact that the more exercise your body gets the better you feel. When you exercise, your lungs receive more oxygen and your heart pumps the blood faster through your body to revitalize every part of it. Compare a mountain stream that is constantly moving to a pond of immobile water. The stream is fresh and sparkling while the water in the pond is stagnant.

If you want to feel more energetic and look better, plan to exercise at least three days a week regularly, whether it's by playing tennis, skiing or just plain old down-on-the-floor exercises.

Skin: A thing of beauty is a joy to behold! With a healthy body you are bound to have good skin. Four requirements for a lovely complexion are: eat properly, drink plenty of water, keep your skin clean and get plenty of rest. In one chapter it is impossible for me to explain how to do these things in detail, but my purpose in writing this is to *motivate* you to want to find out what to do.

Hair: Clean, shiny hair is a crowning glory for a woman. If your hair is a problem, the best thing to do is to get professional help. Most women can keep their hair glamorous now days with the extensive knowledge and many hair-care products available to us. If all else fails we have the aid of numerous hair pieces.

Makeup: Too much makeup can make a woman look harsh or even frightful. But a little makeup, used correctly, almost always improves the looks of a woman. The more natural the makeup looks, the prettier will be the effect. The major role makeup should play is to add color and highlights to the face. It should only enhance the facial features, never cover them up.

Clothing: I have long ago stopped thinking it important to be "fashionable." Instead, I like to choose clothes that look especially well on me. I don't need very many clothes, just as long as what I have looks stunning. A wise woman chooses colors that make her come alive and plans her wardrobe around them. She learns to mix-and-match and to accessorize her outfits to make the most of what she has. The important thing to remember is to be immaculately groomed at all times. Even as a homemaker, which is usually a woman's full time profession, she should be attractively dressed. We all know that "when we look nice, we act nice." Other people react more favorably to us also.

I have made it a habit, when I get up in the morning, to wash my face, comb my hair, get dressed and put on a little makeup before I do anything else or it never seems to get done. It never fails that on the days when I don't do it, someone comes to call.

One last word of advice: You're never completely dressed unless you're wearing a smile.

Increasing in Spirituality

I've been saying how important it is to look well, but there is something much more important—to act well. Pick up any book on how to be happy or successful and it will state that to like yourself is an important requisite to success.

Since our prime responsibility in life is to perfect ourselves so that we'll someday be worthy to enter the Kingdom of Heaven, it stands to reason that the closer we come to perfection the more we will like ourselves. This, then, is the challenge we all face—to perfect ourselves.

It is our main duty to study the scriptures and to learn the laws pertaining to our salvation. Through doing so, a new world of enlightenment opens up before us and wonderful blessings flow forth in abundance. Through living God's commandments we become less self-centered, more interested in others, and the end result is happiness. One of my favorite sayings is: *Care* for yourself but *think* of others.

In my life I have had spiritual experiences which enable me to testify of God's influence. I have a strong knowledge within me that God lives and answers prayers. He does not always respond

169

the way I would want Him to, but nevertheless He does answer them. I love God with all my heart, and the more I read His words the happier I become. Through searching the scriptures women can find eternal happiness!

Maturing Socially

A young missionary told a visiting General Authority that he was very unhappy in the field. No one seemed to like him or pay any attention to him. His companion, on the other hand, seemed to attract people's friendship and love wherever he went.

"My companion," he complained, "is so phony! Yet people like him in spite of it."

The General Authority thought for a while and then wisely said, "During tonight's meeting, why don't you show me how your companion acts? Pretend, just for tonight, that you are your companion."

During the meeting, the young missionary was seen exuberantly shaking everyone's hands, saying "hello" to everyone with an exaggerated smile and generally acting as his companion did.

You guessed it. Suddenly everyone took notice of this now-friendly young man and began to be interested in him. He noticed the results and shyly admitted that he got the message.

If you haven't already discovered the secret of being happy, let me tell you. It is attitude.

A simple phrase to help you get along socially is, "Act as if!" It may not be gramatically correct, but nevertheless, it works! When you are with other people, whether it's a social group or your own family, act as if you are friendly. Act as if you are thoughtful. Act as if you are the kind of person you want to be and you will become that type of person. It is not at all phony to try to improve yourself. Practice will make it easier and soon it will be as natural as breathing.

There are certain desirable qualities that help a person to be socially acceptable. They all hinge on the same principle: focusing your mind away from yourself and onto others!

A good conversationalist is someone who is interested, as well as interesting. To be interested, we must learn to listen. One of the best listeners I have ever known is Kathryn Ricks, the sister of President David O. McKay. She was our next-door neighbor in

Logan, Utah, when I was a little girl. She would always ask us children about what we were interested in and then listen with rapt attention. We thought she was the world's best conversationalist!

To be interesting we must be knowledgeable. This doesn't mean to eat shredded encyclopedia for breakfast, but it means to have a genuine knowledge and love of certain subjects which you can share with others.

A pleasant speaking voice helps to make us more attractive to others. Several characteristics are important in acquiring one: a good quality, a desirable pitch, and a volume no stronger than the occasion demands. It is much more impressive to listen to someone speak who enunciates well. If you are lazy at this, try biting a pencil between your upper and lower teeth and speaking clearly, using your lips with marked exaggeration.

It takes practice and effort to develop a pleasing personality. One of the best ways to acquire one is to notice characteristics about other people that you admire and, taking one at a time, concentrate on securing that trait. It may be that you want to become more friendly. Notice what friendly people do and then set out to do just that. Work at it until it becomes a habit, then start working on another characteristic. That's what makes life so much fun!

Now that we have discussed the four areas of growth, let's conclude by making a goal chart. An organized plan, in writing, is a key to progress and success. If you really wish to improve yourself, set meaningful goals, resolve with full commitment to fulfill them, and then *begin!*

My Goals For:	MENTAL	PHYSICAL	SPIRITUAL	SOCIAL
1 year				
2 years				
5 years				
10 years				
lifetime				

Setting goals is simply a way of committing to yourself that at a given time you will accomplish certain things that you want to do. In making up a chart, you can see where you are going and how you are progressing. It takes a great deal of thought and time to plan your future. Pray for guidance as you do it. Weed out the unimportant things you may be doing now. Keep a positive attitude while you set out to accomplish your goals. Life will be full of happiness!

INTRODUCING—CHARLOTTE S. MAXFIELD

Charlotte is widely known for the personal development and modern woman courses which she has taught. These courses have been sponsored by the Home Economics Department at Weber State College, the Brigham Young University Adult Education and Extension programs, the Utah State University Home Economics and Extension units, and by various school districts through their adult education outlets.

Salt Lake City was Charlotte's home in childhood days. She graduated from East High School, then went on to the University of Utah. She reigned as royalty for many events: as the Heart Fund's "Queen of Hearts," as "Miss Sugarhouse Centennial," the "Day's of 47 Queen," the "Dream Girl" of Delta Phi, the queen of the U of U Military Prom and then as U of U Homecoming Queen. In 1958 she participated in national competition and was named "Miss United States of America." As Miss USA she also took part in the Miss Universe Pageant that year. In the midst of all these activities she completed her bachelor's degree with emphases in speech, theater, and vocal music.

She married M. Richard Maxfield, and they are now the parents of seven children. Richard has been a seminary teacher, head of the Data Computing Centers for the state boards of education in both Utah and Alaska, and is currently completing his PhD in educational psychology. During the early years of their marriage Charlotte taught speech and theater on the high school level and voice and diction as a graduate assistent at BYU. Like many of the other authors, Charlotte has given extensive church service including callings in Presidencies of Relief Societies and MIAs and on several stake boards.

Charlotte's chapter deals with many of the relationships between husband and wife. We know her views will be widely discussed because of their thought-provoking nature. JDC & DSC

A HUSBAND—TO HAVE AND TO HOLD
by
Charlotte Sheffield Maxfield

...from this day forward—for better, for worse—
for richer, for poorer—in sickness, in health—to
love and to cherish...

First, I want to say that I feel it an honor to be asked to write a chapter in such a special book. There have been days when I have sat down to work, not knowing what to write. After prayer, I found the ideas coming so quickly that I could hardly write them fast enough. I sincerely hope that the ideas presented here will be valid, and that they will not be distorted by any weakness in my own nature.

Are You Really Happy?

In the past ten years, I've been asked to teach extension classes in wards, stakes, and on university campuses, adult education courses, and education weeks. These experiences have led me to share rather intimately in the lives of quite a large number of women. I have been stricken with the fact that though most of their neighbors would say that all is going peacefully at their house, many of these women feel a real frustration. I suspect if I were to ask them very sincerely, "Are you really happy?" that they would look away for a moment with a long stare and slowly say, "Not really." I suspect that these feelings are not just limited to the areas in which I have lived, but are also very prevalent in the lives of many of the so-called "modern women" today, especially in America.

Contrary to the feelings of Betty Friedan in the *Feminine Mystique*, which tells the woman to go out into the world and fulfill herself, or the cries for day-care centers and liberation from the "slavery of the traditional female tasks" vociferously shouted by the feminist movement, I feel that the real solution to the strange and uncomfortable feelings which much of our female population is feeling today is to be solved within each individual.

174

"But this inner search is a very deep and foreboding experience," you say. That is just what I used to think. Because I felt so, I read volumes of books and articles, took exacting notes of hundreds of lectures, and pondered deep into the hours of the morning many times, trying to plan for better living and to face the things which bothered me, but all was to no permanent avail.

The change which has finally brought peace within me has actually been a gradual process, and a very painful one as well. It has brought greater happiness and peace into our home than we have had in 13 years. It is evidenced in every facet of our home life from housekeeping, the children's attitudes, and most important of all, the relationship with my husband. It is very, very difficult to change, especially if such truth is threatening to you, but as far as I can see, the only answer is to take a grave and honest look into yourself, to make a diligent search for the proper course of action to improve toward your goals, and to make a prayerful commitment to yourself and God. After that it's self control, work, and great amounts of faith. In the hope that these principles might help some other women, I would like to share some of them with you.

What Kind of Wife Are You?

The pressures of modern society have wrought many changes in the role today's woman plays. Changes in the husband-wife relationship have influenced many marriages. Because the role relationship hasn't been functioning correctly, many men have stopped giving freely and lovingly in their marriage. Their wives have become demanding, vindictive, and grabbing and the men have had to defend themselves. Sometimes a man will resort to divorce to get peace.

In Holland they have another word for a *nagging wife.* They call it "fussing." Dr. Ann Jansen organized a group called "Fussing Anonymous" for wives who can't stop complaining. She warned, "The wife who constantly fusses *at* her husband may succeed only in driving him into the arms of the first attractive woman who will fuss *over* him."

Although most of us women like to turn away from this possibility in horror, it is a very real fact. Even if we don't want to face it, these situations are occurring all around us and we must

175

look to our homes to improve what is necessary. It is going to take all the strength, ingenuity, study, faith and prayer we can muster to honestly search our souls, change our attitudes, and adjust our behavior every time we slip back into our old patterns of responding and thinking. If we don't appreciate our man then maybe someone else will. Here is a letter sent to Ann Landers:

Dear Ann Landers:

This is not a confession but a word of warning to The Wife. I am the Other Woman. I am younger than you, more sensitive, more cultivated, more interesting and more responsive to your husband's needs. I'm not a sex queen or a raving beauty, but I know quality when I see it and Lady, he's got it.

If you don't want him, just keep on nagging, complaining, being a frump and a bore. Make him feel like a heel and he'll continue to escape from that igloo that is more of an icebox than a home. I'll see to it that he finds plenty of comfort in my warm and loving arms.

We are in love and it's pure magic. No guilt, no shame, and no future. No future, that is, if you see yourself in this letter and go to work to get him back. Half of me hopes you won't—because I want this man more than I've ever wanted anything in the world. But the other half of me knows that he must have loved you once and his children need him. No man leaves a wife and family without paying a tremendous price.

I'm writing this letter because I need to go on record. I must tell myself, "You warned her. You gave her a blueprint. You tried to wise her up but she wouldn't listen." I hope, with all my heart, that you will ignore this letter. He will then be mine.

Patience[1]

This kind of woman can't demand anything from your husband because she has no rights guaranteed by the law, as you do. She has only his sincere and appreciative loyalty for her devotion to him. She doesn't criticize, question his judgment, complain to him, make fun of him in front of others, order him around, or take

---

[1] Ann Landers, "Letter from the 'Other Woman,'" (Salt Lake City, Utah: *Salt Lake Tribune*, January 16, 1972).

over and do things because he isn't capable. To her he is as perfect as a Greek God—intelligent, wise, and capable of making correct decisions. Often he provides for her every need and more.

She yearns to be with him. She thinks of things which would please him, and make him happy. He relaxes in her company, and delights in her in every way. She makes him feel "ten feet tall." She caters to his wishes, and when he expresses a desire, her first wish is to fulfill it. When he is displeased, she doesn't make excuses, justify her behavior, blame him or someone else, hate him for finding fault, or cry in self-pity. She sets about to rectify it, because it pleases her to please him. And he worships her for it. Of course, I have greatly generalized this, but I hoped that it might make us think about how far away from completely satisfying our husbands some of us might have drifted.

Often in our American society today, you will hear of a man leaving everything for such a relationship. It must mean that some of us are failing in our loving devotion to our husbands or it wouldn't be happening so often.

The woman he leaves, to all intents and purposes, is a perfect housekeeper, keeps the kids spotless, well trained, and well fed, but he still gave up on all of it—such a price—for what? Someone who made him feel like a real man. The *mother type* I just described may sound perfect, but maybe she was just too perfect. At home he may have felt like he was just a little boy and his wife had taken over everything. She handled the bills, dickered over prices at the market place, arranged for everything, and the decisions seemed to always be "her idea." She may have put on a lot of weight and looks more like a mother than a sweet wife. Her clothes may have become severe or even rather mannish in style. Her hair may be kept extremely short because it's so practical. Can you imagine the thrill her husband must have running his hand up her bristly neck. Everything about her is so practical—never frivolous, impulsive, or feminine.

Her voice has gradually become less musical and more whiny, harping, or demanding—like a general. And she is always right. If you dare cross her, she'll talk incessantly to prove it. And worst of all, she is very, very self-righteous. She has become a judge of the law (which is only God's right) and not a doer of the law (charitable).

177

Howard Whitman wrote "The shrewish wife is as much a menace today as she was in the Bible, when it was written, 'It is better to dwell in the corner of the housetop than with a brawling woman in a wide house.' " Can you imagine how living with such a woman would wear on a man, and cause him to yearn to be the master of his life.

The *competitive wife* is another type which can have an unsettling effect in the life of a man. Samuel Kling, a divorce lawyer, said, "Some women have over-reacted to their new-found freedom. They are shrill, aggressive and emasculating, becoming rivals and competitors of their husbands instead of their helpmates, believing that anything their men do, they can do better. Such wives have lost their charm, allure and most precious asset—their femininity." This wife may be very intelligent or highly educated. Rather than be content to sit back and have the limelight fall on her husband, she is scurrying about with her fingers in "every pie." Social patterns, television, magazines, and neighbors all tell her she is a sharp, modern, sophisticated gal if she can manage to handle everything efficiently. If a woman takes upon herself all the burdens of dealing with the harsh letters from a loan company, the aggravated phone calls of a bill collector, the unscrupulous charges of a dishonest repairman, the physical exertion of fixing the broken water pump on the washer, and "talking down" the prices of things she buys, she loses that gentle softness which a woman should ideally possess.

Man is made to cope with these things. He is by his very nature built to thrive on competition, responsibility and decision making. Problem solving to him is a challenge, and a real man glories in it. A woman should resign to letting her man deal with all this kind of business and leave her free to deal with her own responsibilities. Because of her nature, she can better cope with the small, meticulous, often repetitive and exacting tasks which care of the home, meals, and children require. If a woman expends all her energy in the wrong channels then she hasn't the time or strength or peace of mind to effectively fulfill her major responsibilities.

The *partnership marriage* is often spoken of as an ideal. Is it? In this kind of marriage everything has to be fair. The husband probably has enough masculinity that he doesn't "give in" all the time. He may have found that she is so clever and often coercive that he has to keep an even balance on things. Because they have often been on opposite sides of an argument and fighting has proven undesirable, they have decided to compromise. "I'll do this if you'll do that." To avoid fights they might even set up rules. Here is what one expert has to say about such an arrangement:

> Another obvious approach is the 50-50 rule. Everything... is a balance-of-power, a co-equal division, a partnership. But that doesn't work either. People aren't statistics and marriage just doesn't work on percentages. The old idea is misleading. In most marriages somebody has to make it 60-40 now and then or 90-10. The people who are constantly watching to see whether the one is delivering his full 50%, and being very careful to supply his own but no more, are likely to miss the real wonder of romance. You find most romance in marriages where people are trying to see who can give the most.[2]

This woman described might find herself more comfortable in pantsuits than in feminine dresses. She also finds that she can have her hair styled in a short neckline and keep it fairly decent-looking for about a week with a lot of hair spray, if she uses the right kind of cap, pillow case, and doesn't move around when she sleeps. Can you imagine how exciting and unrestricted her husband must feel sleeping with her? How dashing, capricious and wildly romantic it must make him feel!

This gal may be full of apprehensions about her appearance and about growing into middle age. Someone was "supposed" to have "made a rule" that a woman cannot have long hair after the age of 30 so she doesn't dare have a long, natural, soft-falling style around her home, for what would the "swingers" say? She is so frightened of the void of the years after 40 that she may fight this by assuming all sorts of current behavior, and faddish or stereotyped clothes, to prove that she still has value on today's sophistication market. Enjoying her own individuality and her true femininity are a mystery to her. She may never have taken the time and occasion to sit down and get acquainted with herself, to establish

---

[2]Howard Whitman, "Who's Boss?", (Salt Lake City, Utah: *Deseret News*, November 20, 1962).

just what her true values and goals in life are.

Then there is the *disorganized woman.* She sounds familiar. She's just living in a "whirl"—from one meeting to another appointment. Fixing a casserole for this and answering the phone for that. Everything seems to close in on her. Someone suggests that she try to relax by taking a class in something, join a group, write poetry, or take up a new hobby. All this does is add to the already staggering schedule and only temporarily alleviate the pressures which her life forces upon her.

She may often get frustrated and angry about it all, and wonder when the peace and joy are supposed to come. But she doesn't even know who to get "mad at." She may have developed some physical ailments, and she finds it hard to sleep or get up in the morning.

Her work seems an unending drag, and the children seem to get on her nerves all the time. And she feels guilty for not spending more time talking closely to them and showing them affection. This guilt often tempts her to let them get away with things which might not be good for their development, but it sometimes seems nice just to have them out of her hair for a few minutes of temporary peace.

She knows she should have some sort of schedule, but that seems to make her feel like a prisoner for some reason. When her husband needs that shirt which she hasn't ironed, she feels resentful toward his complaints. He just doesn't understand. When she needs more money for certain things, asking her husband for it turns out to be a bad experience. She has been known to pout.

She finds it harder to have the meals ready on time, or to remember to mend that pocket or sew on that button. He never takes her out to the things she likes. They seem to spend less and less time together now. What is going to happen when the kids are raised? It scares her to think about it. Their love life isn't the same any more. It almost seems habitual, but—after all—she is doing her duty. It isn't exactly unpleasant. She would hate to think they could survive without it.

Those of us who run around following such a hurried life have trouble saying "no" because we haven't shaken ourselves and weighed what is truly important to us and then organized and established guidelines to reach the kind of goals that we truly desire as a couple and as a family. It would be sad to find ourselves alone some eternal day and mourning because we realize how many little, actually unimportant, things we placed before our major loyalty—the person whose role it will be to awaken us into exaltation.

The Wife's Effect upon Her Husband

I heard the head of a family relations department relate a story about a middle-aged couple who had reached a deadlock in their counseling. He asked the woman what she felt her duties were as a wife. She said, "Keep the house clean, serve good meals, teach the children, ..." etc. He replied, "I didn't ask you about your duties as a housekeeper, cook, or mother—but as a *wife!*" It then began to dawn on her that her entire attitude toward her marriage had been wrong.

The professor revealed to us that many people get married to become Father and Mother not Husband or Wife. The children should never become more important than *he is* to her. One child psychologist told a class, "Your child will grow up okay if he is never more important to either parent than they are to each other." Your husband was there long before the children ever existed and will still be there long after they have departed—if you are wise.

I once heard a sociology professor discuss the situation of role identification in this way: "When Prince Charming carries the princess away on his white charger into the sunset, someone has to be in front guiding the horse. It is the prince. She is the one in the back who is holding on to him adoringly and tightly." I try to imagine what kind of look he has on his face. Is it a Casper Milktoast look? Never! He is full of vigor and confident manliness. That's pretty exciting!

Can it be that by trying to grab hold of the reins, criticizing the way he holds them, or fighting with him for control of the horse, we are losing something wonderful? What has happened to the face, the bold manner, the brave confidence of our prince because of this? Will he ever become the king for which he was foreordained? If not, whose fault could it be? Are we robbing him of the right of "trial and error," and to make his own mistakes, and to learn to manage the kingdom around him so that he will be prepared for his possible destiny?

When we yield responsibility to its rightful owner—our husbands—it relieves us of a tremendously heavy burden. If he chooses, he may delegate some of it back to us and we should obediently do as he wishes. There is a security, a peace and a loving respect which will follow when this occurs. We will have a portion of the dominion which he has placed in our care. We will be responsible for its success and will rule over it. Billy Graham said, "I believe the Bible teaches that women have a noble role, and they will be happiest, most creative—and freest—when they assume and accept that role... As queens in the home they wield the powerful scepters of faith, trust, loyalty, and justice, and impart them to their husbands and children. ... Women cannot abdicate the greatest power of all—the power of shaping the world through the influence of a godly home."

I believe with all my heart and soul that the gospel is true, and that it is the means which our wise and good God has given us to follow along his path to return to him as a couple. It is these diligent couples who will be God's jewels, His greatest prize, His most steadfast children, His most valuable refined materials for extending His glory in worlds to come.

Let's do our part, and develop within us the true feminine nature which is our most beautiful gift. Many women in their wisdom have long known this; others are doing well, but see room for improvement; others may find the things we have been discussing a stark revelation of what has been wrong all this time. I am still striving along this road to improvement myself, but would like to share some of the suggestions which may help women to awaken within themselves the soft, responsive, "following" nature of femininity which is within her.

Becoming More Feminine For Our Husbands

Have you ever noticed a cute little girl who has been out in the mud playing, and then seen her later, all dressed prettily and at her best for Church? Isn't she irresistable? She is so precious that you want to pick her up and cuddle her. I once heard someone say to such a little darling, "You look so yummy, I could gobble you up!"

We can learn a lot from this example. It is easier to be loved if you make yourself lovable! You can't ignore all the ingredients which make a woman delightsome and just dare your man not to adore you—because he's supposed to. Try making it easier for him. In fact try making yourself absolutely irresistable. It really helps!

There are many very basic differences between the way men and women move, speak, feel, think, and dress. If a woman is smart, she will exaggerate the differences between them, because this great variety "calls out" to her man. It is a natural, unconscious attraction—one which he can't even explain. It simply mystifies him and he finds these differences extremely fascinating.

The basic simple rule then, would be to behave, dress, and feel completely and sweetly womanly—as completely opposite from masculinity as you can.

Devote your energies to improving your appearance. Always try to look clean, neat, and feminine in all ways. Remember a nylon with runs or lingerie which is discolored or clothes which need mending all give you a "used" appearance.

A queen dresses and moves with dignity. She dresses privately instead of in front of her children, especially when they approach puberty. Remember that your children will carry a visual picture in their minds in later years of the way they used to see you dressed most of the time. Will this image be one of frayed levis and a faded blouse with a button missing, of a long brightly-colored lounging gown, or of a fresh, clean, pretty, comfortable dress?

Try using these tips for a more feminine appearance:

1. Select shoes which slenderize your ankles and have more delicate lines, rather than heavy heels and lines which give you a matronly appearance.

2. Wear colors which are soft, clear-toned, and along the warmer feminine shades. Brash colors, loud or confusing patterns, muffled or subdued darker shades are more masculine.

3. Choose patterns which are smooth, flowery, flowing, and smaller in size. These are more feminine than plain, geometrical, mod, rough, or tailored patterns.

4. Buy materials which are soft, filmy, light, flowing, and smooth. These seem more feminine than rough, nubby, thick, or other more masculine fabrics.

5. Add trims which are ruffled, flowing, and soft. These are more suitable than tailored, abrupt, boyish, or military types.

6. Select designs and patterns which are different from masculine lines and styles.

183

7. Slenderize and tone up your figure. This is imperative. It is not only important to your health, appearance and disposition, but good muscle control is very important in all aspects of your relationship with your husband.

8. Keep your hair styles long, soft, and with natural lines. Your husband should be able to touch and muss it at any time of the night or day. If the style is suitable you can fix it quickly and easily without much trouble. The color should definitely be natural-looking and feminine.

9. Strive to keep your voice soft. If you have become more accepting and peaceable in nature, you will find that you will have less to say. Men find whining, piercing, nasal, screeching, raspy, shrill, or rough aggressive qualities very annoying in a woman's voice.

10. Train your movements to flow freely and in a relaxed manner. Jerky grabbing or overdone aggressive movements irritate men. A tomboy is never feminine.

11. Keep all of your skin as smooth and soft as possible. Imagine how caressing rough, uneven, unkempt skin would feel, but recognize how blissful your baby-fine skin could be.

12. Don't ignore the magic of essence. Fragrant hair, powdered skin, sacheted lingerie, fresh clothing, and a suggestion of elegant perfume have more of an effect than most women realize. Have you ever passed by such a sweet smelling woman, and found her fragrance there after she has left the room? Surely this is one of the trademarks of a real "lady."

13. Smile, and let your enthusiastic optimism radiate to all those who come in contact with you. Think of all the positive power you can generate.

14. Behave as if you were beautiful. I don't think it hurts to aim for a queenly manner. I think of such a woman as mature, dignified, unselfish, dependable, generous, appreciative, understanding, cultured, poised, and loving. Surely these are qualities to be desired and emulated.

15. Constantly observe the women around you. Notice excellent examples of true femininity in dress, manner, and attitude. Emulate such qualities.

There may be a limit to the amount of gold or diamonds in the world, but there is no limit to the number of women who can enhance their natural beauty if they will but learn and put forth the effort to do it.

The women I have known, who have done this, still remain vividly in my memory. Even their voices and aroma were enchanting. The world needs beauty. It is a priceless gift. It uplifts all those who partake of its presence.

The woman who cultivates herself isn't necessarily proud. It's the woman who neglects herself who is suffering from a deflated ego and a damaged self-concept. She should encourage more love and respect and dignity toward herself. Nobody respects a doormat or a self-styled martyr. If a woman can develop a confidence and assurance of herself, then she can forget herself and devote herself to others.

Many of us have "let ourselves go." We are in pretty bad shape. Once we can dedicate our inner self to becoming more feminine in nature then we must tackle the outer appearance. Many changes, such as facial expression, voice, movements, will start to occur naturally as our inner nature changes, but other physical problems will require more effort. There are many books available on charm, self-improvement, and beauty. They are worth the time used to read them.

As you begin to establish a new feminine wardrobe and look at the whole world through peaceful, loving eyes, everyone around you will behave differently toward you, because you are different! It is a special and wonderful experience. Your whole manner will be beautiful because your thoughts and attitude are that way. As the dowdy old maid was told by the vibrant, but kind salesman in the play The Rainmaker, "You're not plain. You've got to think in your heart, 'I'm beautiful,' and then someday your mirror will be the eyes of the man who loves you."

Improving Marriage Relationships

A normal, healthy man loves every quality of a whole woman. If a wife doesn't work to develop every aspect of her mind, body, and spirit—her whole personality—she is robbing her husband. He will never be able to taste of the special joy he could experience if she possessed capabilities and used talents freely within the holy bonds of their marriage. She can represent all women to him, all that he could ever want or need. This can be her great gift to him.

185

When the Lord said, "Therefore shall a man leave his father and mother and cleave unto his wife and they shall be one flesh" (Gen. 2:24), I don't think he meant that the height of her devotion should be a casual "Hi, how are things at the office?" when he comes home.

You meet at the door with a kiss. . . you've been doing that religiously since you married. You would never think of eliminating that kiss, but what's happened to it. Take special notice of that kiss the next few evenings. Will it be something like this? "Hello Harold, I thought you were going to phone (peck) this afternoon. Why didn't you?" Why bother to kiss at all? To be blunt, either put some oomph into it or don't kiss. There is nothing so ridiculous as a husband or wife kissing as though they were a couple of old aunts meeting at a Sunday School picnic. They got married in the first place, assumedly as male and female under the delightful spell of mutual attraction which such polarity affords. Why break the spell? . . . When the wife's role becomes diluted and the husband's role is no longer clearcut and vigorous, these two begin to live together as friends instead of loved ones. The powerful polarity which holds marriage together is weakened, so that the opposites which attract become, instead, like the poles which repel. [3]

A woman has the power within her to be so adorable and fun when she allows herself to be. This playful spirit can lift her husband out of the depth of despair and relieve him from the extreme pressure which his great responsibilities place upon him. One of our Social Relations lessons in 1972 in Relief Society cited a talk where our late President Joseph Fielding Smith quoted the Prophet Joseph Smith:

Let this society teach women how to behave towards their husbands, to treat them with mildness and affection. When a man is borne down with trouble, when he is perplexed with care and difficulty, if he can meet a smile instead of an argument or a murmur—if he can meet with mildness, it will calm

---

[3] Howard Whitman, "It's Not All Platonic," (Salt Lake City, Utah: *Deseret News*, November 24, 1962).

down his soul and soothe his feelings, when the mind is going to despair, it needs a solace of affection and kindness.

When you go home never give a cross or unkind word to your husbands, but let kindness, charity, and love crown your works henceforward. . . . Who are better qualified to administer than our faithful and zealous sisters, whose hearts are full of faith, tenderness, sympathy and compassion.

It is a blessing for the whole family for the parents to occasionally get away together privately to let loose from their burdens and enjoy each other completely for awhile. When they return, there is a united bond which strengthens and unifies the whole family. The children know that they are truly in love with each other. It is good for children to see their parents playfully joke and tease each other occasionally or to witness a sweet embrace once in awhile. They enjoy it immensely and sometimes even come up and hug both of their legs to get in on how wonderful it feels to share this warm love together.

I remember hearing a wise woman state that she felt that there were enough hard times in the struggle to raise a family that a man and wife need as many blissful private memories as they can build to hold them through the hard times. She felt that a couple should not neglect to have a Sweetheart or Date Night together at least once a week and that their children should respect it as a valuable time for their parents as individuals and as a couple. She felt that there should be memories of picnics together in fields of wild flowers, on mountain tops or in forest glens, or sailing to a wooded island in a lake.

All too often we adults work so hard at our "fun" that we really don't enjoy ourselves at all. . . . The cause of our fatigue, tension, and anxiety is—we've forgotten how to play and recapture the thrill of being alive. A child doesn't ask if what he's doing is worthwhile. He plays as an end in itself. . . . For him the moment is everything, he has spontaneous and infectious joy, with a quality of freedom, of "letting himself go." We grow ashamed of being spontaneous. . . . Go for a walk, listen to a bird or watch a squirrel, sit on a bench in the sun. Giving in to one's impulses for a few minutes does not automatically lend to lazy irresponsibility.

187

Quite the reverse: it can lead to greater efficiency and productivity, for it refuels the reservoir of self and nurtures an inner core of being that needs to be lovingly refreshed.[4]

The same woman blushed as she related how she thought that every business man should have a surprise visit from his wife where, behind a locked door, she could snuggle up on his lap for a few minutes after work. Can you imagine the warm reminiscent smile which would come across his face as he sits there and remembers it from time to time?

One night as we were preparing for bed, I dropped something. My husband, who loves to tease me said, "You butterfingers, you're always dropping and breaking things, and I never break anything!" At that moment he boldly sat down on our old bed, and it fell flat on the floor! We looked at each other and burst out laughing!

Another wife in one of our classes said that she delights in slipping a couple of new adorable items of nightwear in her suitcase when they are going to travel on a trip together and this surprises and pleases her husband. She feels that money spent on these is far more important than money spent to impress "the girls."

Some women who complain that their husbands don't talk to them anymore are telling on themselves. I don't feel that a man who divulges a problem wants to hear his wife give him a list of solutions. It makes him feel that she's really setting herself up as his superior by getting things all worked out. He wants appreciative sympathy and understanding. In the past she may have divulged many things of a private or personal nature which he has confided to her, and he lacks trust in her ability to keep things to herself. He might also feel that she is cheapening something special between them if she shares it with others. And, of course, he may just be "sick and tired of problems" and doesn't want to drag them home from the office to his peaceful refuge of home.

Many times when a woman dedicates herself more to her man and increases her devotion to him, these special thoughts will flow from him again as he becomes more sure of her trustworthiness

---

[4]Edna J. LeShan, "The Secret of Having Fun," *Reader's Digest*, (October, 1969), pp. 116-120.

and sincere lack of demands upon him. Her sweet allegiance to him has merited his trust. Any woman who has spent hours of sincere loving closeness cannot doubt a man's gratitude when his hand reaches out toward hers and the words "thank you, sweetheart," pour from lips which don't utter such words commonly. The deep penetrating look of love which he gives seems to repay her for everything she has ever done for him. Her own tears down her cheeks are enough to tell her that.

As married couples become more intimate in their confidences, their trust, their exchange of philosophies and confessions, their appreciation of strengths and exposure of weaknesses, they become more intimate too in the physical aspects of their oneness. . . . In successful marriage . . . the relationship develops over the years to heights of satisfaction undreamed of in the first blush of the honeymoon.[5]

What impressed me was that many of the women who made these comments in our classes were not new brides, but were women whose children were grown and leaving home for successful lives of their own. They found that their married lives were full of excitement and promise. It grieved them to see couples all around them who were separating, whose futures were dwindling into loneliness. This should be a time for a deeper love to grow:

There is an opportunity for new romance that can bud in the mid-years of marriage. It is no longer romantic infatuation, but romantic love—and there's quite a difference. . . . Infatuated girls mention he's "good-looking, a cool dresser, smooth, exciting," but married women, deeply in love with their mates say, "He's considerate, tender, masculine, and loyal." . . . We live in an age which panders to romantic infatuation, but has little to say of romantic love. . . . But the love we knew at the altar is only an opportunity for achievement of love. "You don't fall in love—you climb up to love." The man in the shiny, blue serge suit is real. Can you love him. . . when the first bloom of love has passed, when you no longer thrill to the mysteries and discoveries over which you once sighed. . . . We should look ahead to the dawn of a new era in

---

[5]Howard Whitman, *op.cit.*

the growth of love which is brighter, more radiant, more resplendent and more glorious than all that has gone before. . . . Mature love is the opportunity for romance which makes youthful infatuation look like the childplay it really is.[6]

Whether a woman likes to accept it or not, it is most usually up to her to provide much of the imagination and spontaneity in their time of loving, and this should come from an attitude of warm appreciation and wholehearted acceptance of her man.

Do you think that all women really feel this desire toward their husbands as often as they should? Several studies which I have read recently indicate that from 60 to 80 per cent of American women don't ever respond completely as they should in their love lives. Does this sound like "Thy desire shall be to thy husband?"

Many women would like to put the blame upon their husbands' prowess or artistic ability, but who do you think may have killed it? Guilt is an awful thing to face and such matters can be vicious circles in their cause and effect upon a relationship. If things have progressed to such a sorry state then improvement must begin somewhere:

> Man, biologically and emotionally strong, needed the seasoning of tenderness that woman alone could provide, and she in turn required man's strength and leadership qualities to complete her, to give her fulfillment.[7]

If a woman is completely honest with herself and God, she has to admit that she knows that God has placed the man as leader of the home and that it is his tremendous task to guide the family. The Lord didn't say to follow him—if you feel like it, if you've had a good day, if he hasn't crossed you lately, if he is home on time. He said to follow him! When a woman rebels against God's plan, she is placing her family in great danger. She attacks the very foundation which holds the family together. She sets an unforgivable example to their children that may come back as rebellion later to torment her eternally. How I pray that

---

[6]Howard Whitman, *op. cit.*

[7]Rev. Billy Graham, "Jesus and the Liberated Woman," *Ladies Home Journal*, (December, 1970), p. 42.

this curse might never be the lot of us.

Love is the climate in which all living things flourish, and sometimes a single touch can evoke the atmosphere. . . . But in the last few decades, especially in Anglo-saxon countries, we have persuaded ourselves that there is something weak, dubious or wrong about showing affection physically. We pride ourselves on our restraints, our well-thought-out verbal and written communications. But actually we are isolating ourselves. . . . Closeness. Tenderness. Touch. These are the ingredients that can be put back, if their importance is understood. . . . A father ruffles his son's hair lightly and in that casual gesture expresses infinite pride and joy. A husband, helping his wife on with her coat, rests his hands for a moment on her shoulders—and thus says "I love you" as clearly as if he had written the words in letters of fire.[8]

Another ingredient which can aid a couple on the "bumpy road of life" is having a good sense of humor. My husband used to tell me that when we were first married, he would make a joke about something and I would take him seriously, and then he didn't know what to do. Sometimes it made him feel terribly mean.

I think that this humor should be two-sided, though. Ridicule and biting sarcasm can do a great amount of damage when aimed at someone vulnerable. We should use this humor to see the funny side of things. Many a touchy situation has been saved by the proper use of humor. I have heard this attitude called the "play spirit." What a relief from tension it is. I remember hearing about a wife who arrived home late because she had been "gabbing with the girls." Her husband was determined to be mad at her. As she tiptoed up to him standing there with his arms folded in his gruff manner, she snuggled up to his side and reached up and gave his ear a little bite, and said, "You're not going to go and get all mean at me, are you?" She was in just too good of a mood to have a fight, and he had already said what he would have to say a million times anyway.

He couldn't hold his indignation. He reached over and spatted her and picked her up and carried her off, saying, "You little

---

[8] Smiley Blanton, M.D., "The Magic of Being in Touch," *Guideposts*, August 1, 1965.

character, you just can't stop chewing the fat with your girl friends can you?" She threw her arms around his neck and said, "I know, isn't it awful?" What happened after that, I'll leave to your imagination. This life is a beautiful thing; let's spend more of it being happier instead of being a glum, pessimistic, old grouch!

One thing which I appreciated learning is that many times a husband will "bark" when he is feeling bad or his needs seem neglected. Our men will not always come out and tell us if they have had a bad time at the office, they will just find that everything is bothering them at home.

A keen woman will sense what is behind it all and meet the need or the real problem instead of the symptoms which are showing up on the surface. Mrs. Billy Graham said:

> My part as far as Bill is concerned is the part any wife plays in her husband's life—just to try to be the wife that he needs. ... My husband has a need when he comes home to recharge his batteries, he needs quietness, and then on the road he needs to have a sense that things at home are cared for, so he doesn't need to worry about them. ... God has created woman to be a 'helpmeet' unto man, a help suited to man's needs. ... A wife is to fit into the life of the husband.

A New Look at Our Husbands

As a woman becomes more feminine and submissive to her husband, she will find two things happening to her vision:

First, she will begin to have the "scales fall from her eyes." She will begin to see her husband differently than she has before. She will see endearing qualities, manly traits, depth in his character which must have always been there, but which she has not been consciously aware of with such appreciation.

She will also see how vulnerable he is, how much her support is important to his success and well-being, not only physically, but mentally and spiritually. Because of the internal strife and conflict in their marriage, she may have been stifling his effectiveness in every respect. With these internal struggles eliminated there can be no end to the growth which can take place, especially if she is right there at his side taking orders as fast as his clever intellect can send them her way, and unhesitatingly fulfilling or delegating them as efficiently and quickly as she possibly can.

192

Why do you think a good secretary can make a man more successful in his field? She is worth her weight in gold to an employer. She uses all her training, professional experience and allegiance to obey and support him and help him unquestioningly, as a loyal servant would. How much more so can a good wife be a blessing to her man?

I read an exercise for increasing your love for your mate lately. It was suggested that we donate about 60 seconds a day to look at our mate with detachment as though we were observing from another planet.

See him as a person. Who is he? Another struggling human being striving to make harmony with life? With all the inner pressures, conflicts and complexes, the frustration, the doubts and fears that all flesh shares. . . . He is a somewhat lonely soul, perhaps a bit more frightened than he is willing to admit . . . looking for a little warmth. . . .Can you bring it to this man across the breakfast table? . . . Love in the true sense, is not getting something. It is an out-going process. The joy of living is the joy of giving. The pleasure of love isn't the loving. What it literally means is, "I desire your well-being."

Detach yourself, and try a flashback. See him, as a little child. Think of the child at 6, full of wonder. At 11, growing serious, yet dizzy with dreams. At 16, full of faith in life, aspiring to great things, believing in the inevitability of happiness. That man across the room is this same child . . . you are the prime reservoir of life's promises, you have the power to give life to dreams, to shape them, to create happiness or to stifle it . . . This is a new perspective on this child-grown-into mate who shares life with you. . . . Appreciation sees things in a different hue. George is a wonderful fellow—he's my fellow. He gives his best and he has bundles of talent that the stupid old world hasn't even found out about.[9]

The second thing which will happen to her vision is that she will no longer see his faults. When this happens her tendency to criticize and nag will be gone. Just this single thing can change a relationship tremendously. Her self-righteousness has fallen into

---

[9] Howard Whitman, "Take 60 Seconds," (Salt Lake City, Utah: *Deseret News*, November 20, 1962).

sweet submissiveness and humility. A strange and marvelous thing takes place. He just may start to turn into her hero.

I recently had the privilege of hearing a special couple from the BYU faculty speak at our Mutual Marrieds' fireside. The wife, a mother of a very large family, was telling of the period of frustration which had confronted her in the last few years. She had every reason to be completely happy, but something was wrong. After much study and prayer, she arrived at the answer that she was to "increase her love for and complete dedication to her husband." The answer which she received from the Lord was to put him first.

As she set about to accomplish this, she found her whole outlook toward him changing. She began to realize that her attitude toward him was extremely important to his welfare and eventual growth—even after this life. She said that she began to pray for him. "If I don't pray for him, who is going to?" she confessed. After she mentioned the beautiful changes which had been occurring in their marriage and family life, her husband spoke. You could see what a difference it had made in his life. The amount of love he felt for her was so deep that we could all feel it, as he recounted some of the experiences which they had shared together recently. Everyone left that meeting with greater resolve to develop a deeper love for his partner. Such an attitude is expressed here:

> Most husbands want most of all to know that his wife has confidence in him. He wants to know that to her, he is always the "great man." . . . So often the outside world makes the husband feel very small. . . . The boss may fail to appreciate George, and George can take that, but if Mary fails to appreciate him, love may be dealt a mortal blow. Mary, if she wants that love to flourish, must truly see George as her hero. If the boss doesn't promote George, it's the boss who is stupid. If a younger man is edging George out, why anyone can see it's just politics. Don't worry, someday they'll wake up and really appreciate George. He's smarter than all of them! Build up that man. . . . [The wives who are most admirable] are those who have been able to transform their marriages from weak ones to strong ones by building up the virility of their husbands by making them feel that they are successful

194

males.[10]

I recently heard an interesting example of this principle. It likened a man to a cake. It's edges were rough, coarse in texture, uneven on the edges, etc.—all truly manly characteristics. This cake has a few imperfections which were small chunks which have fallen from the sides—representing faults.

Then it compared the wife as the frosting, which must contain the correct ingredients. This frosting had to be whipped and beaten down until it was free from imperfections or rebellious lumps which might tear the cake apart. What might these lumps represent?

These are the big boulders that can crush the love of a husband, but there are also the nasty little stones that can trip that love too often that eventually it won't get up for more. ... Most marriage bonds are not broken on the rocks in the great storm; they are worn away by the endless battering of pebbles—sarcastic words, wanton irritations, petty acts of vengeance, intentional slights and embarrassments, nagging and accusations.[11]

If this frosting is stiff and clings to the bowl, its usefulness is ended, because it has crystallized and hardened and never fulfills its purpose to go forward to newer and greater purposes, and it is cast aside. But if it becomes refined, smooth, and pliable, it will then be used by the Artist's hand to pour out of the bowl where it has been prepared and over the cake to help its parts adhere together where there is an imperfection, instead of going around it and saying "Look at this fault everyone," she smoothes herself over it, and fills it in. She covers it with evenness so that no one is even aware that it exists.

The cake is finally completely covered by her smooth and flowing nature, because there was plenty of frosting. It represents love and the fluidity a wife provides for her husband when she loves him.

The finished cake is the important thing, but it is the unity with the frosting which has produced a complete result and useful

---

[10] Howard Whitman, "How to Hold the Love of a Husband," (Salt Lake City, Utah: *Deseret News*, November 23, 1962).
[11] *Ibid.*

offering. She decorates him, shows him off, is light, pretty, and special. He is still a cake without her, but she is necessary to his complete fulfillment. Now, everyone says, "Isn't that a beautiful cake," not "Look at that lovely frosting." As Henry Wadsworth Longfellow wrote on such unified partnership:

> As unto the bow the cord is,
> So unto the man is woman;
> Though she bends him, she obeys him.
> Though she draws him yet she follows;
> Useless each without the other.

A strange and wonderful thing happens to the cake as it begins to grow. The larger and bigger in importance the cake grows (the greater and more important the man grows), the less need there is for the frosting to hold the parts together or cover imperfections. Now the frosting's purpose is to decorate, to embellish, and to compliment him. Her harder work is over and she is supported by his inner strength. Her burdens are lightened and more joyful as they share their appreciation for each other. I like these suggestions for learning to have greater interest in each other after the children are raised:

> Marriage is a living, growing state—don't settle for a status quo. Nature hates to stand still.
> 1. Take up an interest together. Enthusiastically learning to do something new can add vibrancy and cause your marriage to move forward.
> 2. Ask questions about books, or movies, events, issues, and show an interest in what he thinks.
> 3. Discuss new ideas. Alert minds which run swiftly and smoothly are interesting.
> 4. Soul talk. Get out under the stars together. There is a little poet in every adult. Sing together. No human being can be told "I love you" too often. Tiny acts of love are often so monumental, such as picking a flower, sending a card, bringing a little gift.[12]

I remember hearing one marriage counselor speak to a group

---

[12] Howard Whitman, "Love Unlimited," (Salt Lake City, Utah: *Deseret News*, November 23, 1962).

of women. He stated that we often hear that there are many kinds of love. He felt that there is only one kind of love, but that we feel it in different degrees and show it in different ways to different people. The thing which I enjoy about loving is that it is limitless. There is no end to it. You can always find more. It was the whole purpose of Christ's ministry, and we all have heard that "God is love."

Love is not a finite thing. It is not that the individual contains just so much, as a pitcher may contain just so much water, so that if more is offered to one love object there will be less remaining for the other. Love is infinite. As Dr. Frank Crane wrote in his essay on love, "Give it away, throw it away, splash it over, empty your pockets, shake the basket, turn the glass upside down, and tomorrow you shall have more than ever.[13]

I should think that such love in a person's life would be worth any price we can muster. Many of us take a class, read something, and say, "That's nice," but never do anything about it. If you find this happening to you occasionally, I will spend the remaining portion on a possible concrete manner of approaching the goal of greater love and service to your husband. To some it might seem radical, others just what they have always believed. I suppose that the only way we can really know is to sincerely pray about it and honestly endeavor to make it come true in our lives. The Lord knows your particular situation and what is best for you. He is the one who can help you discern which things are best suited to your particular problems. Take it before Him in prayer and He will help you to discern the proper steps to take and give you the strength and wisdom to accomplish those steps. Here is the experience of a woman who accomplished success in this respect:

A wife in her thirties recently said to me, "For the first ten years of our marriage I felt I was in a state of war with my husband. Each of us seemed to be out to subdue the other. It was pretty miserable. But as I passed 30, I seemed suddenly to grow wise. I somehow recognized love as a surrender of the

---

[13] Howard Whitman, "The Children," (Salt Lake City, Utah: *Deseret News*, November 23, 1962).

197

self and not the conquest of another. I began to yield instead of oppose. Only since then do I know what happy marriage is. Now that I no longer thwart my husband, he seems to dedicate his life to pleasing me.

There you have it; the gain is giving. Ambrose Pierce said, "Marriage is a community consisting of a master, a mistress, and two slaves, making in all two."[14]

The Answer

Paul said it:

Wives, submit yourselves unto your own husbands, as unto the Lord.

For the husband is the head of the wife, even as Christ is the head of the church. . . .

Therefore as the church is subject unto Christ, so let the wives be to their own husbands in *every thing*. (Eph. 5:22-24)

The solution I suggest to you for overcoming your problems in marriage and bringing peace to your family is exactly what Paul commanded: *Submit* to your husband in everything!

It's crazy, you say? It can be done, and I've seen it accomplished many times. The changes and blessings it brings are so great that I can hardly express the difference. I have seen several hundred women accomplish it in their lives and as they relate the results of their change in behavior and the reaction within their whole family, their happiness brings tears of joy to your eyes.

Can you dare to do it? Have you the courage and faith? What have we really got to lose that is of eternal importance? Search into your deepest soul and commit yourself: Give away all your haughty rights, prejudices, opinions, even the right to a divorce, even the children (actually they are his anyway, aren't they?).

Ask his advice on things, without even thinking what you would like first, and accept it. (You may slip back from time to time, but let him know that it isn't permanent and that you are still dedicated.)

When something bothers him, change it immediately. Straight-

---

[14] Howard Whitman, "Who's Boss?", (Salt Lake City, Utah: *Deseret News*, November 20, 1962).

en that cupboard, and get rid of that piece of furniture as soon as he mentions it. If he expresses a wish, make it the first thing on your list. You may feel his request is pretty silly, and he may test you a time or two at first, but soon he'll stop testing you, because he'll know that you really mean it—forever—from now on!

Don't allow yourself to have hurt feelings. It is a sign that you are not truly dedicated yet, and are indulging yourself in childish self pity and it is a form of rebellion against him. If you have displeased him, just honestly tell him that you are sorry and that you'll correct it. When you really mean it, he'll know by your actions and respect and worship you for it.

Your single and most compelling desire is to obey and please him 100%. As you do this you'll never have to worry about yourself again: your needs, wants, or welfare.

The women who have succeeded in this attitude have found that their husband has become even more confident and manly, more fully accepting of his authority and the responsibility for the welfare of everyone's needs. Soon, before she even realizes that she has a need, he has provided for it.

One woman said, "He knows more fully that I am his, and he is responsible for my happiness. This feeling seems to arouse within him such masculinity and power in his role that he is able to accomplish unbelievable things. Although I expect nothing, he has begun to lavish more love, attention, gifts, money, privileges, extravagances (and to earn the extra money to pay for them) upon me, because he now owns me." In a woman's soft submission, her husband must look after her, because she is totally geared to thinking of his wishes and not of her own any longer.

I must give a warning. Never start on this pledge because you want to change him or to manipulate things to get something out of it for yourself. A woman should never embark on this journey as a fling, a trial run, or a lark. It is absolutely serious. If she does it half-heartedly, without searching and pledging herself inwardly, she is likely to "reap the whirlwind," and the wrath of her husband will be lashed against her like thunder. He'll know that it's phony, and that she is manipulating and playing games with him. The hurt and the deceit that he will sense will make him hate you for treating him like an object or a plaything to be toyed or experimented with.

199

A woman should never begin this commitment unless she has pledged to completely accept her man for what he is, to forgive him for any past grievances, and to love him entirely. She should promise that she will refuse to see fault in him or criticize him even in her mind from then on. She will obey him unquestioning. Then, with the help of God, she can prayerfully begin her quest of thorough dedication to his support, upliftment, and the deep love of her heart to the head of her family which God has placed over her.

After she has searched herself and made a sincere commitment with an honest and contrite heart, then she will begin to relax and discover what becoming completely feminine and responsive as a woman can mean. Her wishes and desires will be his from now on.

The marvelous blessings that are in store for her as she begins to change her ways of feeling, behaving, and reacting, are so glorious and limitless that it is impossible to describe them.

When he is sure of your true dedication to change, he will begin to open up to you his thoughts and dreams and plans and deepest feelings more than he has before. All these things take time, but you have the rest of your lives to grow in your love for each other. He may even ask your advice, but you won't have much, except what he wants. He'll start to remember the gentle manners—long forgotten, to bring certain personal gifts at unexpected times which indicate that he has been thinking of you. He may telephone for no other reason than he misses you and wants to visit. His loving may become less mechanical, longer, more poetic, and with spontaneous and tremendous enjoyment. He'll sincerely compliment you on your more feminine way of dressing and moving. He may allow you more and more freedom and delegate more responsibility to you because he trusts you to follow through just as he would wish if he were there.

And the joy of it all is that since you expect nothing, and don't calculate, your whole relationship begins to have a new spontaneity and freshness which is very exciting.

I know that there are some women who might read these things and the idea of complete submission sends chills of agonizing fear into their hearts, but I have heard fear referred to as lack of faith. In order to succeed in this challenge you must believe that your husband is good. It is frightening to place yourself

200

at the mercy of someone else, but you will find that it will become the most glorious dedication of your existence. The two of you shall reach such realms of exalted joy in your lives together that you will finally begin to know what "home—a heaven on earth" really means.

Anything which is truly worthwhile requires effort, risk, and work. If you are willing to pay the price you will find such sweet and tender feelings swelling from within you that you didn't even know were possible. You will no longer think of yourself as a separate person, but as part of him. When you are apart there is an incompleteness, a yearning for his return. If your love life has lost much of its luster, you may have read about this yearning and wondered what they were talking about. Soon you'll know. Perhaps you are one of the wise ones who has this already.

Let me talk to the woman who might tend to feel that she wouldn't dare to obey everything her husband tells her, because he isn't perfect and therefore doesn't have the right. This kind of woman is usually manipulative. Though she's deathly afraid to admit it to herself, others can see it. She may be the kind of woman who has been unconsciously looking down on her husband in self-righteousness, and treating him like a child who is not permitted to grow into complete manhood. Such a woman will often laugh at such an approach to her future happiness and try to find some logical reason why she couldn't possibly do it. This justifies her failure to commit herself. It is easier to condemn something as foolish, impractical, faulty, and ridiculous than it is to say, "I haven't the humility or faith to do it," or "I'm scared." Remember "Thy desire shall be to thy husband, and he shall rule over thee." (Gen. 3:16) Some women would like to erase that from the scriptures, but I don't think that our Father in Heaven could have made it more clear.

The only reason a woman will look for an excuse to rationalize or justify her behavior is because she is defending her inside self who is frightened of the truth and afraid of having to humbly dare to change.

You must have faith. It is difficult to believe that any man who is entrusted with the welfare and safety of a loving woman who has completely sacrificed all her selfish desires and wishes and pledged her undying obedience unto him would ask such a sub-

201

missive and delicate possession to commit sin. If he did, I feel that the sin would be upon his head, if she were obeying God's law. And I cannot believe that any of our husbands are that corrupted.

You must have faith in him and in yourself, and in God—that He will bless your sincere efforts. I believe that He will answer you beyond your most vivid imaginings. Ask, knock—for His greatest desire is to have heavenly marriages. Remember that you and the Lord are an "invincible team."

After all, isn't that what the Lord is asking of you? He has commanded us to place nothing before Him in importance. That means that there is nothing (your clean house, your baby, your career, club presidency, your eyes, life savings, your hobby, your best friend, your favorite antiques, your jewelry, your most valued earthly possession, or craving) that you would not gladly lay aside with no begrudging feelings, to show your willingness to sacrifice yourself for the gift of the remission of your sins by repentance and forgiveness through His grace and His great loving sacrifice on the cross. I once remember my husband giving a talk when he was a seminary teacher during which he said, "I believe that the Savior loves you so much that, even if you were the only person alive in the world, He would have died on the cross just for *you*!"

Well, are you willing to set aside your—pride? Are you willing to obey God's law? Can you willingly obey the head of your home as a similitude of your love for your Savior as Eve did? You know what your husband can become, but only if you will cease to resist and fight him. Your pride may be the only thing which is stifling his spiritual growth into what he can become.

Is there any price too great to pay for this promise? If we are to become worthy of this tremendous reward, we must practice and grow now. We must take those few frightening babysteps with faith and courage and humbly pray to the Lord to guide us. I have faith that He will.

Great blessings are in store for you if you can now give life to the words and beliefs you have merely been giving a nodding lip service to all these years.

To those of you who have already discovered these truths and are reaping the rich rewards may I say that I admire you for your wisdom and your strength. To those who are still struggling toward it—God be with you, is my prayer. . . .

INTRODUCING—JOAN FISHER

Friendliness is the keynote of Joan's chapter and of her life as well. We didn't know her, except by reputation, before The Joy of Being a Woman *was started, yet we feel drawn to her now because of our friendly conversations together while the book was in progress.*

Her sweet spirit led to her being chosen "Mrs. Utah" in 1968 and then being selected "Mrs. America" for 1969-70. This competition was a real challenge—ten days in length, and based on a variety of homemaking skills. As the final curtain fell on the pageant her husband, Byron, was talking with one of the judges, a gracious business woman from Chicago. He commented that making the choice must have been very difficult. She replied, "The choice wasn't so difficult for, you see, in Joan's personality I find a little bit of God."

Joan graduated from BYU in 1961 with a degree in elementary education. After some brief experience in teaching she and her husband began the raising of their family. They have four children at this time, with another child due shortly after the book's release date. She truly enjoys her life as a wife, mother and homemaker and feels that her happiest times are spent with her family, whether enjoying home evenings together or vacationing across the country in their motorhome. She also enjoys music, cooking, and socializing.

At the present time she is teaching the cultural refinement lessons in Relief Society. Much of her church activity, however, has been devoted to the Mutual, where she has filled almost every position from sports director to president.

As Mrs. America, Joan traveled over 150,000 miles, visiting most of the states and also the Virgin Islands, Europe, and South America. Since that time she has been active in civic work and has done some work in local politics.

Joan is genuine and unpretentious, and this spirit is reflected in "The Art of Friendship." We think you will enjoy it. JDC & DSC

203

THE ART OF FRIENDSHIP
by
Joan Fisher

"Oh, the comfort, the inexpressible comfort of feeling safe with a person; Having neither to weigh thoughts nor measure words, but to pour them all out, just as they are, chaff and grain together, knowing that a faithful friend will take and sift them, keep what is worth keeping, and then with the breath of kindness blow the rest away."

—Dina Maria Mulock

Just as happiness was born a twin, so also is friendship. To be a friend you must be a friend, both within and without. To consider the friends in our relationships requires that we consider us as individuals, and how we can improve ourselves in becoming better friends.

Meeting and Gaining Friends

The most important challenge in meeting and associating with other human beings is to *be yourself.*

Prior to my competing in the national Mrs. America contest many friends gave me advice and help, but I felt the best advice I received was from Alice Buehner, who was Mrs. America three years before me. She told me, "Joan, the most important thing in the contest is you, so be yourself. When you walk into your judges' interview, just make believe that they are all your Relief Society sisters, and you won't have any trouble at all!" How vividly I remembered that advice when I faced those six judges for the first time. And, how much that advice helped me to relax and to be myself.

Remembering names is a key to building friendships. When meeting people for the first time, listen to their name and associate the name and the person you are meeting with something familiar to you. Sometimes associations can be quite humorous. For example, an acquaintance of mine has the name of Klomp. The first few times I heard his name, I had trouble remembering it. Then I associated it with the rhyming word "stomp," and I have never forgotten his name since. I once met a man who, after meeting a whole room full of people, for the first time, could repeat their names and something interesting about each person. This is a talent that I truly admire and one that I would like to enjoy myself. This talent of remembering names and people is one we can all learn, if only we would take the time and interest to do so.

A good beginning is to be genuinely interested in the person we are meeting. At a dinner in Wisconsin, we were introduced to a gracious hostess for the first time. She knew my background and interests even before we met and she expressed them in many ways during the evening—like, "Did you enjoy teaching school" and, "living so near the mountains, I'll bet you ski; tell us about your skiing experiences." Finally, out of curiosity, I asked how she knew so much about me. She said that earlier that day she had called the newspaper library and they had given her a biographical sketch. It was this simple, effective interest that so impressed me of her genuine desire to become a friend.

Regardless of how hard we try to remember casual acquaintances we have met, those embarrassing situations when a name simply slips our mind may still occur. Often I have had to apologize and ask a person to please refresh my memory. I'd much prefer doing this than to spend part of the evening trying to recall a name. My husband, Byron, and I have a method of helping each other remember names. We always try to repeat aloud the names of those whom we are greeting. Then if one of us has forgotten the name, it is mentioned without a formal introduction; many times this has avoided an awkward situation. For example, he would say, "Joan, you remember meeting Jim and Pat Smith." And, although I might have forgotten their name, I don't have to be embarrassed or ask them.

Being a good listener is an important quality in meeting and associating with people. This is an area where we all can use some improvement. Be genuinely interested in what another person is saying. We learn so much more from listening than we do by talking. We also make more and better friends. When you converse, put in enough details to make it interesting, but not so many as to bore your listeners and lose their attention. Make conversation stimulating and interesting; encourage conversation in which all present can participate. Occasionally, it is interesting to leave something unsaid that can be added by someone else. As married couples, we should develop group conversations that include both spouses. Avoid the type of conversation where the husbands go to one corner and talk over the last pro football game, while the wives are in another corner discussing the birth of their last child. Many qualities are important in meeting and conversing with people. You must want to meet others, and be willing to let others become acquainted with you. What is most important is to...be yourself.

Maintaining Personal Standards

As we work toward being ourselves, it is also very important to be an example of the norms in which we believe and for which we stand. Regardless of what your personal standards, ideals, goals, and religion may be, it is important to be a good example of what you actually are and of your way of life. Others notice so easily who and what we are, very often without our being aware. One day as we returned to our hotel during the contest I was sitting by Mrs. Rusty Seiger, Mrs. Hawaii. I complimented her on the fine presentation she had made that day in the competition—for truly she had. Her reply was "Thank you Joan, but you have something that I don't have." When I asked her what that was, expecting it to be related to another part of the contest, she said, "You have an inner peace, and my other Mormon friends in Hawaii are the same way." I thought how ironic it was that while we were involved in a secular, homemaking-type contest, she saw something very different in me. Be yourself, and be an example of who and what you are, especially as you meet and make friends.

As LDS people we live a somewhat different social life than others, especially when it relates to our Word of Wisdom. It has been happily surprising to me to learn there are many other people who, for a variety of reasons, also do not partake of alcoholic beverages or tobacco. Most important, I believe, is that when offered, we turn down items which conflict with our beliefs in a graceful manner. The easiest way is a polite "no thank you." When you are seated at a banquet table, simply turn your coffee or wine glass upside down. But do so as inconspicuously as possible.

I will never forget what happened at a luncheon in Texas. I neglected to turn my coffee cup over and the person next to me,

206

seeing I was about to get a nice hot cup of coffee, but knowing my beliefs and practices, turned my cup over for me and the waiter passed me by. How kindly I felt towards this person. Truly this friend not only respected me for my standards, but even helped me to keep them.

Social activities in today's society often begin with a cocktail hour. Many non-drinkers shun such events or go as late as possible just to put in an appearance. These can be good times to meet lots of people, make new friends, and enjoy conversation. For the non-drinker, many beverages used as mixers are always available, such as Ginger Ale, 7-Up, tomato and orange juice. The only problem I've had is learning to drink my soft drink slowly. If I don't someone is always refilling my glass (and me).

It is considerate to let your hostess know ahead of time that you are a non-drinker. Then, if she is a good hostess, she will be prepared to make you feel comfortable. While we were in London, England for five days, one of our activities was to have tea with the Lady Mayoress at the Mansion House in the heart of London. This gracious lady, the wife of the Lord Mayor of London, has a house staff of thirty-five, which should give you an idea of the size and stature of the Mansion House. I had informed the people who had arranged for our "tea" that my husband and I were members of the Mormon Church, and did not take stimulating drinks, including tea. When the servant entered with the silver tea service, included on the tray was a large glass pitcher of orangeade. However, what impressed me most that afternoon was that the Lady Mayoress joined us in a glass of "orange crush," "Because," she said, "to tell the truth, I really don't care that much for tea." She was a gracious, lovely lady and a fine hostess. I did not expect her to change her pattern of living and join me in a glass of orangeade, any more than I would change standards and join her with a cup of tea. What was important was that we had mutual respect for each other. The golden rule of "do unto others..."surely applies to situations like this. Meeting others who may have a different background and beliefs than you can be a rewarding and meaningful experience. Be anxious to learn of others and their way of living. In this way, we broaden our own life and our circle of friends. As LDS people, we should always uphold our own standards, but at the same time re-

207

spect others for their individual ways, just as we want and hope for the same mutual respect.

The Attributes of True Friendship

In considering what we want in a friend, I think it is important to apply the characteristics of a good friend to ourselves. Then we may be that kind of a friend to others.

Trustworthiness is one attribute that is all-important in friendship. One whom you can trust is one you want for a friend. It is fun and sometimes necessary to share confidences, and it is so important that those with whom we share them have the self-discipline not to hurry to their telephone and tell what we've said to someone else. There are times when we seek the counsel and advice of a close friend. We must be able to know that our confidence will be kept. Those who are experiencing marital problems may seek counsel from a friend and trust their very happiness in keeping that confidence. The friend may not offer any counsel at all but helps by being sympathetic with problems and failures.

Another criterion in seeking a friend is to seek a person who wants the best for you according to your way of living. A friend is one who accepts you for what and who you are, not one who tries to change you into something or someone else. Good friends respect your personal desires and are considerate of you and what you enjoy. I'm reminded of the night we got off a plane in Connecticut and were met by a man from Chicago who worked for the company we were representing. It was rather late and I knew he must have been very tired. I also knew he'd enjoy having a few drinks before going to the hotel. But he thought of my desires first, sighed, looked at me and said, "Well, would you like to go get an ice cream soda?" I told him that I doubted we'd find an ice cream parlor open so late at night in Hartford, but that I appreciated his thoughtfulness. This was a simple example of one who wanted the best for me according to my own way of living, not according to his way of life.

One of the people whom I truly call my friend has a great criterion for choosing friends. She searches for a friend that can make a constructive addition to her life—one she can learn from and gain from—a person that will help to make her a better individual. Early in our marriage, I worked outside of the home until

208

our first child came. Then, even though my husband was a struggling law student, I stopped teaching school and became a full-time mother and housewife. At first I was so involved in the tasks of motherhood that for a while I really did very little to stimulate my mind. How grateful I was for a friend who got me, and a few other young mothers like me, interested in art and the life of the Great Masters. We spent many hours visiting the National Gallery of Art and reading and learning of the works contained in that cultural center. This was a friend who helped make me a better individual. She made a fine contribution to my knowledge of some of the cultural things of life.

Loyalty is another vital quality of friendship. How grateful I am to say that I have a loyal friend. A mutual acquaintance once said of this person, "No one can ever say anything negative about you, Joan, when she is around. She'll always stand up for you." She is like this to all of her friends, and you can be sure they are plentiful. How much I appreciate a friend like that and hope someday to have a similar thing said of me. Friends are not like a glass figurine: "fragile...keep away from children...do not touch." Children also should be exposed to our friendships and shown by example the value and fun in having and being a friend. Make a friend with your own as well as with other children. It is rewarding to see the comradery that can grow between youth and adult. I think of the love I still have for a teacher in our grade school who never taught me in the classroom, but made a friend of me and others like me. How I loved and learned from her, and still enjoy visiting with her when I return to the neighborhood where I was raised.

We should encourage our children to make their own friends. I believe it is important to guide, suggest, and to help show them what to look for in a friend. Impress upon them the importance of their being a good friend too, and encourage them to be the type of a friend that they'd like for themselves. Remember, though, that they still need freedom to choose whom they want for friends.

Truly Caring For Others

Life's greatest joy comes from service to our fellowman. To keep a friend, find something to do for him, share with him, and give something of yourself to him. We all have opportunities to be

209

of service, and should take advantage of them. I remember when preparing for a trip to Palm Springs a friend of mine who had arranged for my visit called and asked if I could take an extra half-day and speak at a benefit luncheon for The Retarded Children of the Desert Foundation. There also was the Sunday when we took time from our South American travels to give 2½ minute talks in Sunday School to a small branch of the Church that we visited in Peru. These experiences and others like them are what bring real personal joy and satisfaction.

I was once asked by reporters in Minnesota what was the greatest single thing that happened to me during my reign as Mrs. America. My answer was simple: the personal growth I have experienced. So much of this growth came because of the joy received in doing good to someone else.

There were times when I would begrudge having to take time from my family or from a fun personal activity to speak to a group. In fact, I remember being in tears for 20 minutes on our way to a Young Marrieds Fireside one night where my husband and I were scheduled to speak because I wanted to stay at home with my own children. However, the group that night was so responsive and appreciative to us that I smiled during the ride home with a warm glow and feeling in my heart that only comes when you give of yourself and your time to others.

When you make an effort to help the other person, it is you that always benefits the most. If you have problems that sometimes seem to be too much for you to handle, the best advice I could give for overcoming your own troubles is to serve your fellowman.

Spur-of-the-moment service can often be a source of real joy. One day, I misread a cookie recipe and when I corrected my mistake, I ended up with far more cookies than our family could consume and still remain healthy. A few minutes later, I learned that a neighbor's child was hospitalized that day with an infection. How fun it was to find a good place for those extra cookies. I have wondered since just what was the real reason or cause for getting my recipe too large. That was one mistake I was grateful that I made.

It is always easy to do something we enjoy doing for someone else, but what about things we don't enjoy? I recall a Relief Society President who took over the ironing of a sick friend. Now that, was

210

true service. My husband finds little time for working in our yard, but he is always anxious to help a friend build a new fence. My favorite story of unselfish giving concerns my own mother, who always has enjoyed being a friend to those around her. There was a dear lady in our ward that Mother visited monthly as a visiting teacher. As this woman grew older, it was necessary that she be placed in a rest home. I'm sure she had visitors, but what she missed most was her closest companion, her German Shepherd dog. Few people even knew what had become of that dog, but Mother located him. Although Mother never allowed a dog to come in our home, or ride in our car, she would take that huge German Shepherd in her own car out to the rest home to visit its mistress. This is an example of service in its finest form.

The principle of joy through service to others works in reverse too. The best way to make a friend is to ask him to do a favor for you. It is more blessed to give than to receive, but receiving is sometimes harder than giving. We, as friends, must allow others the opportunity to be of service to us, and we should accept this service gratefully and cheerfully. I remember a meeting once where afterwards the speaker was quietly asked to take the centerpiece of flowers home to enjoy. The person making the offer was almost prepared for the speaker to say something like, "Oh no, I couldn't do that, you keep those lovely flowers for yourself." So often this type of refusal occurs. Instead the speaker smiled and said "Thank you, I would be honored to receive such a lovely tribute from you." Later the speaker received a note saying how warm this person had felt to have her flowers so graciously accepted. Be a gracious receiver as well as a giver. It is so rewarding to give to someone, or to do something for someone, who truly appreciates it. All of us enjoy serving others when we know that our acts are appreciated. Thus we must be certain to show our appreciation.

Although we should always remember to show our appreciation to others, we, personally, must not always expect to be thanked or rewarded for things we do. It is fun to practice being a secret friend and to do something for others without their knowing or with no thought of receiving thanks. One evening I suggested that my children and I bake a cake for a widowed neighbor who was celebrating her birthday. We placed the cake on the porch, rang the bell, and ran home. What a warm feeling we all had as we

211

shared our special secret. Learning to enjoy doing for others without expectation of thanks or praise is a fine attribute to teach and to practice, for then we have the true, unselfish spirit of giving.

Preparing For Friendships

Friends are not just made; you build a personality that will accept friends. You should attempt to develop enthusiasm for life and what it offers you. These feelings radiate to others. Practice being more out-going in your associations with others. For example, cross the room to meet a friend, or when conversing in a small group, open your circle to include him. Don't always wait to be invited—if you desire to do something with another person, do the planning and inviting yourself. Don't feel that you are pushing yourself on others. Many are seeking friendly associations, but are backward in planning an occasion to get together.

There is value in being somewhat dependent upon other people. There is wisdom in seeking others to help enjoy and enrich your life. I know a dear woman who does many kind acts for other people. She is always knitting handicraft items to give away to those she knows. She loves to make donuts, pies and cakes and share them with her neighbors. Yet this woman is so self-sufficient that she seldom allows others to enter her world and to become her friend. We need to rely on others if we are going to make friends of them.

Developing A Positive Attitude

In making friends with others, we must first make a friend of ourselves. We must first like ourselves before we can have the capacity of liking others. Who are you, and how do you feel towards yourself, are questions that I believe should have a positive answer before you have positive thoughts toward other people.

You are an important person! You are someone of great worth! You are daughter of our Father in Heaven! These are three positive statements of you—now it is up to you to expand on them. To whom are you important? What is your worth? What can you do well? Where lie your talents, and your strengths? I was once invited to speak to the wives of our Church Authorities. I felt myself most inadequate to that responsibility. Yet, I remembered that I, too, am a daughter of our Father in Heaven and that I had had some experiences that had been different from theirs. In that capacity, I should be able to give them something to broaden their lives. The few hours that I spent with those fine ladies are very pleasant to remember. I'm grateful that I could think positively enough about myself to enjoy their association.

We all have faults and areas in which we'd like to improve. Sometimes this knowledge gives us a tendency to think negatively and to tear ourselves down. A positive thought takes us much farther than a negative one because it is a constructive, rather than a destructive, idea. Gain a positive attitude toward yourself as an individual. When you have accomplished this you are much closer to being and gaining a friend.

Gaining Self Confidence

How important it is that we have confidence in ourselves. I believe if any job can be done in this world—you, as an individual, have the ability to accomplish it. What is important is that we try. Our procedures and results may not be the same as someone elses but still we can do it. Let me share with you an experience in my life that taught me self confidence. Regardless of my joy in being a homemaker, I have never taken a home economics class in school since the eighth grade. My knowledge and talents, whatever they might be in the homemaking field, are strictly the result of experience and were not received in the classroom. Knowing this, you can understand that while I had been sewing some of my school clothes in high school and college, I was amazed at my fiance's suggestion that I create my own wedding gown. "Why I could *never* do that," I said, "I don't sew well enough." "Why not?" said he. Although I could think of many reasons why not, none of them seemed valid. So, I made my wedding dress. Now it took me eight weeks, and had a fine seamstress looked at the flaws and rough edges, I'm sure she would not have judged it as much of an example of the art of sewing. However, to me, it was a great source of pride and accomplishment. And the day I wore it, that gown was the most beautiful dress in the world because it was mine and because I had made it.

It is amazing how self confidence can grow if only we give it a chance. The following year when we moved into our first unfurnished apartment, we had more time than money, and nothing to cover the bare windows. Surely if I could make my own wedding dress, I could make a simple pair of curtains! And later on I thought, if I could make curtains, why not try making drapes? And many years later when I was asked to demonstrate my creative talents I was at a loss—what talents?—until I realized that I could take pictures and samples of the different window coverings I had created for every room in my home. By accomplishing a task in sewing that I didn't think I could handle, I gained the confidence to try more and different things. It has been surprising to me what can develop from overcoming that little obstacle—"I can't do it." What is important is to try and try, and later at a slightly different or harder task, to try again. Remember, if it can be done, you can do it! Develop a confidence in yourself.

Someday, I hope, dear reader, I may call you my friend. Until then, let us strive to gain confidence by exercising a positive attitude towards ourselves. When we meet, I will find in you those qualities which make you a person that I would like to know. When we meet, be yourself and leave room in your life that I might add something to it as you will add to mine. Then friendship will be a twin: friends without are friends within.

INTRODUCING—REBECCA B. GLADE

We feel a close kinship with Rebecca, though we have yet to talk with her face to face. We've enjoyed her performances several times in Promised Valley *and watched her excellent portrayal of the wife of John Adams in 1776. But what draws us so close to her is the many similarities between her interests and ours. She has a composite music education degree, studied music at the University of Utah, taught music in the Salt Lake City public schools, has been a private music teacher, and has been involved in a number of musicals and productions. That's Duane's background too!*

Rebecca was winner of the first place vocal award at the Utah State Fair, an honor highly regarded by budding Utah musicians. She toured South America for the State Department as part of the cast of Annie Get Your Gun *and has been active in many musicals presented by the University of Utah. She has served as drama director for the U of U Opera Workshop and has sung professionally throughout Utah. Coaching and directing groups of young singers has occupied her talents on many occasions.*

Musicians always find their talents needed in the MIA. Rebecca has served there as both a president and as activity counselor. She's also filled callings as stake music director, ward chorister, choir director, and Relief Society teacher.

She is the wife of Royden J. Glade, who was recently called to preside over the Chilean Mission. They, with their two-year-old daughter, Jennifer Lynn, moved to Chile right before her chapter was due. Rebecca assumed the responsibilities for the mission-wide Primary, Relief Society, and MIA programs, yet still made time to share her thoughts for the book. Her typist, Betty McDonald, rushed the copy to us as final deadlines were approaching.

With our special interest in music, we share her understanding of the happiness music can add to people's lives and fully support Rebecca's admonition to "be a music maker."   JDC & DSC

215

BE A MUSIC MAKER
by
Rebecca B. Glade

The Joy of Music

"If thou art merry, praise the Lord with singing, with music, with dancing, and with a prayer of praise and thanksgiving." (D&C 136:28)

Music is a delightful means of expression. It has a dimension to it that other forms of communication do not have. It touches the emotions and enriches the soul.

The Lord has said, "My soul delighteth in the song of the heart; yea, the song of the righteous is a prayer unto me, and it shall be answered with a blessing on their heads." (D&C 25:12)

Most people are aware of the blessings of music. Some of the richest experiences in our lives come through participation in music. It introduces us to many choice friends and helps us express feelings and emotions that we cannot convey in any other way. Music makes us a part of many exciting activities and opens the door of opportunity for all that will use it.

There has always been a great emphasis on music in the Church because it enriches our lives. The pioneers while crossing the plains were oftentimes sustained and uplifted by joining together in song. I imagine the warmth and unity that came to them as they sang around their campfires is similar to the feeling we have today when we join with Church members to sing praises to our Heavenly Father. Music draws us closer to others and provides a time for contemplation.

Harmony in the home is a primary goal for all Church members. Music can be a source of help. A home filled with good music is likely to be a happy one. Music fills an important need in our lives.

President McKay spoke to the Tabernacle Choir in 1958, after they returned from a successful tour. He said at that time that "Music is the fourth greatest need of man. First he must have food to sustain life. Raiment or clothing for the protection of the body is next. Shelter is the third greatest need, and then comes the necessity of music for his soul."

We are fortunate to live in an age when so much good music is available for us. Radio, television, and record players make it possible for all of us to be acquainted with the finest music.

Television has much to offer that is educational and beneficial. It provides wonderful entertainment and allows us to see professional performances with the flick of a switch. However, there may be a tendency for us to be watchers, instead of doers. It might seem easier to watch or listen rather than to participate. If we are not careful we may miss the happiness that comes through creative expression. The joy one experiences through active participation is worth the effort required.

Methods for Finding a Good Teacher

If you, or other members of your family, are interested in obtaining professional instruction in music, it is of great importance to find a qualified teacher. Music degrees or the fees charged for lessons are not always an indication of the quality of the teacher. Many of the different techniques employed in teaching music are successful. Since it can be confusing and frustrating to change from teacher to teacher, it is worth the time which may have to be spent in finding the right teacher for you. In your eagerness to begin learning, you may accept instruction from someone who is not qualified or who teaches incorrect principles. This restricts the development of your talent. And in addition, time and money may be wasted.

The following are some of the best methods for finding a good teacher:

1. Observe the students produced by the teacher. Do you like the way they perform? Are they progressing well for their age and ability and the length of time they have studied?
2. Visit recitals. Listen to students in concert.
3. Ask the opinions of respected musicians.
4. Ask yourself if the teacher is one who will inspire you to do your best.

217

5. Make your decision and put forth your best effort to learn from the teacher you have selected.

Then, if you find you are not making the progress you wish, and if you are sure you have given yourself time and your best efforts, change teachers. Do not let emotional ties keep you in a situation that will not promote growth. Most teachers have the welfare of the student at heart and will be happy to recommend or accept a change if you are not progressing properly. However, it is important to realize that in the development of a talent, you will have many ups and downs. After you have studied for a while, you may arrive at a plateau in your learning. Consult with your teacher about your progress. He should be able to counsel you correctly.

Opportunities for Expressing Your Talent

You can always find good opportunities to express your talent. Begin in your own home. Your development and achievement will be stimulating to you and your family. Perform often for family members. They will be your best critics. If you can survive their judgment, performing for others will be easier. Take advantage of family home evenings and special events in your home. Music can be an integral part of family gatherings.

In my early life, most of my performing was at home where we were all invited to participate for special occasions. I still look back upon those experiences and feel that the sincere encouragement I received at those times prompted me to continue studying music.

You may want to participate in a musical program presented in the community. Since it is unusual to start at the top, be willing to accept smaller parts or chorus parts initially and thereby learn from those who have had experience.

Many successful performing groups are comprised of individuals who organized themselves to perform for a family or Church function. If you take advantage of these opportunities and perform to the best of your ability, someone may see you, like your work, and engage you for another program. It is fun to use your imagination and work out a program that is your own creation.

One of my most enjoyable experiences has been with a group of individuals who met while performing in a musical. At the con-

218

clusion of the musical we decided to arrange a program of our own, using some of our favorite songs. We selected a theme and wrote a special dialogue to tie the songs together. At the conclusion of our program, we were invited to perform for other functions. Frequent requests encouraged us to prepare new material. As time went on we selected songs and themes to fit the special needs or occasions for those for whom we performed.

The Church gives the individual so many opportunities to use his talents, but you need to let it be known that you have an interest in performing. Some people have no opportunity to perform because they have not made their wishes known.

You don't have to perform for thousands to have a rich musical experience. It is not necessary to be famous in order to be great. If you can lighten one person's heart, (it might be your own) or bring happiness into your home, you will be well repaid. Nursing homes, shut-ins, the lonely and discouraged usually welcome musical groups.

When You Audition

You will be involved in auditions if you are going to do much performing. Decide first of all if you really want to be in the production or group for which you are auditioning. If you are successful in the audition you will be required to spend the necessary time for practices and performances. You show your interest in an audition by putting forth your best efforts. If you are not selected the first time, but perform well, those who are auditioning may remember your performance and select you for some other occasion. You may want to consider the following when preparing for an audition:

1. Prepare your music properly.
2. Practice in front of a mirror.
3. Perform for your family and friends before you audition.
4. Make certain your appearance is neat and appropriate.
5. Be positive. Recognize that some nervousness can be valuable and stimulate you to perform well.
6. Concentrate on how you want to perform, not on how you do not want to perform.
7. Keep in mind the intent of the composer of the music, rather than what the judges are thinking.

219

8. If possible, practice in the place where you will audition. Check the facilities—piano, lights, mike, etc.
9. Smile when you first present yourself. It will make you feel better and will help the judges feel that you are happy to be participating.
10. Persistance and optimism often determine those who are successful. You may fail several times before you succeed.

Overcoming Discouragement

Discouragement is a deterrent to the successful development of a talent.

You will have failures and make many mistakes, regardless of the greatness of your talent. We learn and develop from our failures. As a child learns to walk and talk, he makes many mistakes. He falls down again and again. If he were afraid of what people would think, or if he waited to take the first step until he was sure he could walk, he would never walk. If he waited to say his first word until he could form a perfect sentence, he would never talk. If you wait until you can sing or play perfectly, you will never perform.

In my teaching experience, I have found that some students, after only one failure, such as not being accepted into a school choir, decide to give up any hope of developing their talents. Other students have accepted the failure as a challenge, and some have turned out to be lovely soloists, or joined with groups and found a way to express their talents.

The development of a talent should not be discarded simply because of one or more failures. We do not discard a piano and call it worthless because of a few bad notes. The piano should be tuned and so we choose a qualified person, an expert in this field, to tune it. So it is with the development of our talents. If you do not succeed at first, try to determine the reasons for the failure, correct your course, and carry on. We are all a little out of tune on occasion.

In order to be successful as a performer, you must have a sense of your own worth. You must feel that you have something to offer and share. Each individual is special and is endowed with gifts differing from other people. You must find these gifts and talents and be willing to develop them.

220

It happens sometimes that a woman who has many years of special musical training behind her feels frustrated because she is not using this talent. Perhaps she feels her children, home and Church duties require so much of her time that she cannot express herself through music.

There is always time to do those things you really want to do. If you want to practice for an hour a day, you will find the time. You may have to get up one hour earlier than usual, skip a luncheon or a phone call, or let something else go, but it is a matter of personal priorities. You must decide what is most important.

Each situation is different, but the developing of talents and continual growth of the woman cannot help but benefit the family. If a mother can organize her time properly and discipline herself, and accomplish all the things she plans, this will be a great example to her children and encourage them to set goals and achieve them.

You may feel that perhaps you are too old to begin the development of a new talent. Let me tell you of my grandmother, Mrs. Milton Bennion (Cora Lindsay Bennion). She is one of the choicest people I know. After her children and grandchildren were grown, and when she was into her nineties, she began the study of the organ. In her mid-nineties she broke her hip in a fall and during her recuperation period found a great deal of pleasure practicing the organ and the piano. She has played the guitar until recently, but now her fingers give her too much difficulty. On one occasion, when the lights in her neighborhood went out for a short period, her daughter called her to ask if she could help her in any way. Grandmother replied, "Thank you, but don't worry about me. I'll just sit down and play my guitar for a while."

The continuing development of talents and interests has helped to make this lovely woman a tremendous influence on all those about her. Her life has been full throughout her many years and she has never known a period of inactivity. Consequently, she has had a unique way of drawing people to her and influencing many lives.

An interesting story is told of a young man whose hands were injured in an automobile accident. When he was taken to the hospital he inquired anxiously of the doctor if he would be able to play the piano after his hands were operated on. The doctor gave

221

the matter a little thought, and then replied that he was certain the boy would be able to play beautifully. The boy then said, "That's strange...I've never played the piano before."

When we see someone perform beautifully, we may think to ourselves that the individual has surely been blessed with unusual talent. We wish we could have the same ability. We fail to realize the tremendous amount of effort that has gone into the development of that talent.

There is no substitute for hard work. It would be unreasonable to expect that a talent could be developed without effort. If you are discouraged perhaps you have not put forth enough effort to accomplish that which you desire.

Discovering Your Potential

A favorite story of mine concerns a baby eagle who was separated from his mother. He was found by a farmer and placed with some baby chickens. The eagle grew, much in the same manner as the chickens, picking at the ground and never flying. One day a man traveling by the farm, saw the beautiful bird in with the chickens, and being a lover of eagles, he was concerned for the welfare of the bird. He asked the farmer why the eagle was kept with the chickens and received the reply that the eagle believed himself to be a chicken and acted accordingly. The traveler asked for and received permission from the farmer to free the bird. The farmer felt this would be a waste of time since the eagle had never known any other life. Nevertheless, the traveler picked the eagle up and holding him high he said to him, "You are a great bird. You should be soaring in the sky. Your wings are powerful and your feathers are magnificent. Spread your wings and fly."

The bird looked confused and jumped back on the ground. The farmer told the traveler again that he was wasting his time, but the traveler was persistent and urged the farmer to let him spend the night and work with the eagle. The farmer agreed.

The traveler spent a great deal of time with the bird that evening. He explained to him that eagles were strong powerful birds, that they were known for their freedom and courage. He lifted the bird upon his arm and said, "Eagle, you are a great bird...spread your wings and fly." This time he felt the wings of the great bird flutter, but the bird jumped down after a short

222

period.

The traveler retired for the evening. He arose early the next morning before the sunrise. Just as the sun was rising over the mountains he lifted the great bird high in the air. He said, "Eagle, you are a rare creature. You are powerful. You have beautiful wings. Your home is in the mountains. Spread your wings and fly."

The bird's keen eyes caught the glimpse of the sun. He heard the words and caught the vision of his potential. He felt the strength of his wings and desired new life. He fluttered his great wings, turned his head to the mountains and soared off into the sky.

All of us have tremendous potential which has not been realized. We may need a traveler (a teacher, parent, friend) to help us discover what we can become.

The development of a talent requires the help of others. We must be willing to listen to those who can give us help and advice. Like the eagle, we should be willing to cast out fears and doubts about ourselves. We must have the courage to spread our wings and seek a better life. We need to challenge ourselves to develop the very best that is within us.

As a mother and father want their children to succeed, so does our Father in Heaven want us to succeed. He has a greater capacity for love than we can understand. He has blessed us all with many gifts...music being one of the greatest.

Every talent or gift has an appropriate price that must be paid. Desire and hard work are necessary ingredients to unwrap the gifts which we have been given. We must not allow ourselves to get discouraged easily. We should take advantage of opportunities to perform and follow the advice and counsel of those who can help us.

A true source of happiness comes from accomplishment. I hope that you will find satisfaction through the development and use of your talents.

Music delighteth the soul. "If thou art merry, why not praise the Lord with singing and with music, with dancing, and with a prayer of thanksgiving."

INTRODUCING—MABEL JONES GABBOTT

It's easy to get acquainted with a noted author when she lives in your stake and her daughter is your secretary. Mabel lives in Bountiful, Utah, and we're quite aware of her accomplishments. During the past year we've read several of the articles she's written in the church magazines, enjoyed a lovely fireside presentation she gave to our neighborhood study group, and joined many others in shedding a tear or two as she was honored with a bouquet of flowers in our stake Young Artist's Festival *for the lyrics she had written for one of the compositions in* Sing a New Song. *But more impressive was the honor of being able to join with Mabel and her family in the temple when President Harold B. Lee changed her daughter's signature from Sue Gabbott to Sue Dewey. (Who can appreciate a talented and capable young lady most, her mother or her "boss"?)*

Mabel has many accomplishments as an author and poet. She has been an editorial associate at the Ensign. *Three of the hymns in the LDS hymn book carry her name, and eight of them in the children's song book* Sing With Me. *She has won the Deseret News Christmas poem contest, been a finalist in the Relief Society Eliza R. Snow poetry contest, and has a collection of her poems,* A Woman's Way *in print. She was poetry editor for the* Children's Friend *for eight years and has been active in local writing groups.*

For many years Mabel has been a member of the General Board of the Young Women's Mutual Improvement Association. She is a former Primary Stake President, a member of Relief Society, MIA and Sunday School stake boards, a genealogy teacher and a Cub Scout leader. She is now an inservice teacher trainer.

She and her husband, J. Donald Gabbott, are the parents of five children. Don is owner of a photography studio in Bountiful.

Mabel went out of her way to make helpful suggestions as the book project got underway. We appreciate her help!

JDC & DSC

224

CREATIVITY AND THE WOMAN
by
Mabel Jones Gabbott

Do you remember the story of *Our Town*, as told by Thornton Wilder, and the climaxing scene when Emily, who is dead, receives permission to return for one day to the land of the living? She chooses her twelfth birthday, remembering it as a day when everything was perfect. Yet she becomes greatly upset because her family is so unconcerned about time passing, their relationships with each other, and about the world. Emily cries out: "Oh, earth, you're too wonderful for anybody to realize you. Do any human beings ever realize life while they live it—every, every minute?"

To see the world as Emily challenges us to do—to see ourselves and our loved ones with a deep abiding awareness, demands special creative powers. It requires continual exercising of our perspectives, of our imagination, and of our creativity.

How often I have said, "Yes, dear," to my husband's account of his day, with my mind already wondering what to get for dinner. Or I have listened to a child's recounting of a wonderful thing he saw with my eyes on the clock and the next task.

Being creative means to be totally and completely alive and absorbed in the living of each moment of life. It means giving the whole circle of feeling and concern and delight and joy to each instant that demands attention.

Creative living is an attitude, a way of thinking, a way of looking at life. A creative woman has a positive attitude toward life, an affirming of all the joys and tears, the frustrations and the blessings. Knowing that there are the hills and the valleys of life, that there are the "everlasting yeas" and the "eternal nos," she moves always forward. She finds joy in the hills, the high periods of living; she crosses the valleys, the lows of life, with endurance. She lives with determination to look forward, to reach out, to see and overcome in spite of all shadow, and she emerges with a maturity, a wholeness, and a gladness of being.

To the extent that you are alive and eager for life in every part of your being you are a creative person. Creativeness lies within the creator. The creative woman has abundant vitality which is under her control. She has empathy for others and can look into another person's life. She can walk in their shoes, knows their heart. She radiates excitement, for she is alive and interested. A creative woman has freshness, depth, audacity, and the daring to do something.

A New Project

Florence Pinnock once told of a tired, bored mother finding rejuvenation for herself. She was cleaning her son's room. On his desk was a list of many things that he had to do that weekend. At the end of the long list, he had written, "Start a new project." The mother read it and said, "So shall I."

To his wife who was having difficulty learning to carve, the artist said, "Do something with your wood, even if only to make a pile of chips." The creative woman is never bored; she does something.

Creativity means participation, eager, active, often exultant participation in life.

The creative woman thinks for herself. She who does something because it is the custom makes no choice. She who chooses a plan for herself employs all her faculties. And one idea generates another. The woman who first fashioned a bookcase using cinder blocks knew the inner glow and satisfaction of a creative act. So with the woman who thought of using wire hangers as weiner sticks for buoyant Boy Scouts. The simple act of upturning a large goblet and arranging dry flowers or figurines under the glass is doing something. As the focus of the sun causes fire, so does the focus of ideas bring life and energy and animation to the creative woman.

There is something very subtle about the creative process that defies description.

The creative woman is forever reaching out beyond the straight line of day-by-day, routine existence. She hears the bluebird just off the path, and sees the delicacy of color nuance in wispy clouds before sunrise. She enjoys the shape of muffins heating in a morning oven, and listens to the plaintive longing in her young daughter's voice. Walking creatively through each day lends added mean-

226

ing to all existence.

With Emily I would cry out to all women—live creatively; realize every minute of this precious life given you; think with imagination; feel with whole awareness; be alive to life; be vital and be the creative you.

The Straight Line Principle

Woman are naturally creative. They are God's greatest creators. Yet woman's challenge is to make this creative effort point her and all those around her towards ability to stand in the presence of God.

This life is brief and wonderful. Our creative powers as women can help us enjoy more fully life's blessings and experience more keenly the world's beauties and enhance all of living for ourselves and others.

Whatever imaginative faculties we bring into play, however, must stem from our personal preferences; they must in no way violate or disturb our principles. The principles remain the same.

One woman makes wheat muffins in the morning. Some days she prefers to use orange juice as liquid, sometimes milk, sometimes other juices, but the basic recipe remains the same.

So with the principles of living. There are many ways of being kind to a neighbor. One may be creative enough to make her favorite pastry; or observant enough to offer to share her window-washing; or perceptive enough to know when she would appreciate a quiet moment's talk. But the principle of kindness is basic and fundamental; the preferences determine the creativeness in applying the principles.

Someone has described this idea in graphic terms, thus: The straight line is the principle by which we live. The creative person may explore the fringe miracles in nature, in people, in work with all the nuances of living imaginatively, or walking with wonder and curiosity. But the straight line, the principle of good living, is there like a center to hold and sustain and strengthen.

In his poem, "Second Coming," William B. Yeats describes the falcon flying so wide and high that he loses direction:

> Turning and turning in the widening gyre
> The falcon cannot hear the falconer;
> Things fall apart; the center cannot hold.

227

In our reaching out for creatively living, we must never lose contact with the center—which is the knowledge that we are God's children enroute on the path to return to Him.

Creativity in Learned Behavior

Creativity can be developed by deliberate practice. A team of professors at the University of California experimented with workers in education, business, and industry and concluded that "originality is a form of learned behavior."

Two men working through the University of Buffalo trained groups in creative problem solving and found that through training creative ability was increased, not only to produce better quality of novel ideas but to produce greater quantities. As the creative powers were exercised they became more prolific and more refined.

Their findings show that anyone who tries to exercise his creativity or his imagination will find his ability to solve problems and to produce ideas for better daily living increased. Stretching the imagination gives the creative woman problem-solving ability. Thinking creatively, she has a choice of solutions to a situation or problem, and is trained to quickly assess possibilities. Often, premature action or judgment is thus postponed.

One young teacher walks into a room full of rowdy, noisy, fighting youngsters and says, "Sit down and shut up."

Another, taking note of their pent-up energy, crumples a sheet of paper in a wad, ties her handkerchief around it, and tosses it to one boy. Getting his attention she says, "All this energy should not go to waste. Gary, tell us_____." Then she conducts a review of the past lessons as one student tosses the ball to another with a review question.

A mother hearing her boys and the neighbor children arguing in the back yard controls her impulse to send everyone home, and instead takes out a plate of cookies, saying, "Time out, have a cookie while we arbitrate your problem."

Such creativity on the part of a woman calls for flexibility in her thinking. The highly creative woman allows her thoughts to mill about freely. There is really nothing new. The newness comes from the imaginatively gifted recombination of known elements into different arrangements. Or as Truman Madsen has said, "Creation is never totally original; it is always a combination of prior

228

realities."

Some women are ingenious in putting usual, ordinary things to work in unusual, extraordinary ways. Are you? Try this to test your flexibility.

Name all the possible uses for: a common red brick, a wire coat hanger, a rubber tire, a wooden ruler, a hammer. How creative are you? Can you think of at least 8 to 12 different uses for each one?

The creative woman breaks up old patterns and reassembles the pieces to produce something new and original. This gives her a distinctive, personal flair. It could be in the way she uses a scarf as a belt in attire, or in the manner she creates a bedside table from a large, draped storage can of wheat. The creative woman must investigate a wide variety of approaches to any problem. Fluency of thinking is a blessing to one who would be creative. Many ideas are considered before deciding on one.

Sometimes we have to think creatively within a certain boundary. We have this and this, and we would like to accomplish, or do, or have that and that. An exercise devised to test creative thinking ability within the boundaries of logic is as follows. (Progress from one word to the other using a logical sequence.)

rose ———— danger
fuzzy ———— money

(Possible answers: *rose—thorn—cut—blood—danger*; or *fuzzy—outlines—picture—expensive—money*.)

plug ———— long
end ———— face
flame ———— headache
oil ———— spring
hard ———— thirst
high ———— yellow

This type of exercise will help to find steps between the problem situation and the goal.

As a daily exercise to develop your resourcefulness, think what would happen if:

everyone were satisfied with things as they are
we also had two eyes in the back of our heads
sleep were unnecessary

229

    everyone said everything that came into his head
we never had to make decisions
all printing presses were destroyed

    Try to produce at least four to eight different consequences for each set of circumstances.

Being A Unique Individual

A most challenging area of living is to accept oneself. Many of us live lives of self-defense instead of self-discovery. We waste our powers defending the facts that we do not like to cook, that needlework gives us a headache, or that we are allergic to petunias. We should accept what we cannot do or do not like to do and go forward to discover what we can do.

Jessamyn West tells the story of the exuberant Cress Delahanty. After many adventures in her growing years, Cress with her friends visits the ice cream parlor to celebrate the end of school. When Willie asks what is the occasion for such mammoth strawberry sodas, Josephine answers, "I am going to Stanford." Bernadette says, "I am going to get married." "And what about you, Cress?" asks Willie. Cress answers, "I am alive."

Often on a morning when the sky is unbelievable pinks and creamy salmons with the sunrise promise of a new day, I say with Cress, "This is something to really celebrate, for I am alive."

To be alive is more than just to live. To be alive one must feel acutely his creative powers as a child of a Creator Father. To be alive one must be curious about his uniqueness as a self among millions of selves.

We are all individual; we are all unique in our place in the world, in the mind- and soul-strengths we brought from our spirit experience. John Stuart Mill says that each person becomes more valuable to himself, and is therefore capable of being more valuable to others, in proportion to the development of his individuality, for "...the end of man is the highest and most harmonious development of his powers to a complete and consistent whole." This is our personal challenge: to create from ourselves the special person we know we are.

Some women who try to be individual and different in dress and attitude really end up being just like others who are trying to be different. Some women who achieve a differentness because of dress or physical looks or such are quite uncomfortable being different.

There is no area in which the creative woman by use of imagination and inventiveness cannot make herself more charming and her own personal life more exciting.

Creativity in Relating to Others

In relation to others her aliveness creates an atmosphere of empathy and understanding. A creative woman is sensitive to others, responsive to their moods and perceptive of their needs.

There is a need for the creative woman to meet the new demands of the family circle, to put into perspective the world-wide brotherhood of man in this age. This takes an ability to break through her own small, personal, confining circle into everwidening circles.

Perhaps the deepest need of each of us, as one writer has said, is to overcome his separateness; to leave the prison of his aloneness. We want to love others and to show our love for others in many ways. Imagination is the key.

Donna confessed to her mother that she wanted to make friends, but when she tried to talk and be casual and gay she became tongue-tied and always said the wrong things. Her mother suggested that she say less, but look directly at each one who spoke to her and hold that person's interest with eye-to-eye contact. Soon after this Donna went to camp with her MIA group. On her return she reported with gladness her experiences of eye-to-eye listening to her friends. She said they did not know at first what she was doing, but she won many friends with her concentrated work.

Turning love into creative channels too suddenly, however, sometimes be disastrous. A mother wanting to show special love to her son sent to school with him a surprising lunch of fried chicken, pie, everything he dreamed of (without telling him). When he came home, she was eager to know, "How was lunch?"

"I didn't eat lunch today," he answered. "Somebody must have stolen mine. There was only one paper sack left when I got there and it was really great, fried chicken, pie, everything; but I knew it wasn't mine so I didn't eat lunch today."

Creating New Personal Attributes

Because of greater depths and understanding of herself and

231

others the creative woman achieves a distinctiveness that radiates from her. She has an inner poise that stems from abundant faith, from the conviction that nothing is impossible to one who believes in herself and her loving Father.

In Alma in the Book of Mormon, the Lord challenges us to "awake and arouse our faculties, even to an experiment upon his words." E. B. White in his book, "Charlotte's Web," suggests a way we can imaginatively experiment upon words. Wilbur the pig is to be killed unless his friends in the barnyard do something. Charlotte the spider finds a solution. She suggests to the rat that he bring to her any papers with printing on. From these she chooses a word and weaves it into her web in the corner of the barnyard door. Wilbur stands under and reflects the word. As Charlotte weaves humble, radiant, or divine, Wilbur demonstrates each word so well he achieves great fame and his life is spared...for a season. Attitudes play a definite role in how we think of ourselves, and consequently how we act. Like Wilbur, we can be radiant, humble, or divine as we assume that role.

Suppose you were to choose the word *courage* and assume that attitude for a day, what great things you would do. Suppose you were to decide to be believing for a whole week, myriads of little miracles would happen to you. Or if you were to choose such words as valiant, as nonjudgmental, or as compassionate, and as Wilbur did try to radiate that characteristic—what a delightfully creative person you would be.

Role of the Holy Ghost

The greatest source of help for the creative person is dependence upon the gift of the Holy Ghost and the promise that this Comforter will "bring all things to remembrance."

Parley P. Pratt tells us:

> The gift of the Holy Spirit adapts itself to all the organs or attributes. It quickens all the intellectual faculties, increases, enlarges, expands, and purifies all the natural passions and affections, and adapts them by the gift of wisdom to their lawful use. It inspires, develops, cultivates, and matures all the fine-toned sympathies, joys, tastes, kindred feelings, and affections of our nature. It inspires virtue, kindness, goodness, tenderness, gentleness and charity. It develops beauty of

person, form, and features. It tends to health, vigor, animation, and social feeling. It develops and invigorates all the faculties of the physical and intellectual man. It strengthens, invigorates, and gives tone to the nerves. In short, it is, as it were, marrow to the bone, joy to the heart, light to the eyes, music to the ears, and life to the whole being.[1]

This is being alive. To the extent that you are alive in every part of your being, you are a creative woman.

Be curious about your world.
Experiment with individual creative preferences.
Explore with imagination your thoughts, actions, feelings.
Be aware "every, every minute."
You will find yourself much more interesting than you ever thought. You will be creative.

---

[1]Parley P. Pratt, *Key to Theology*, pp. 96-97, 4th ed., quoted from p. 487, Talmage, the *Articles of Faith*, 47th ed., 1966

INTRODUCING—JACKIE NOKES

As hostess of Midday, *Jackie is in a pivoted position to accomplish a great deal of good. She, as much or more than any of the other authors, has played a major role in many civic causes of importance. She is, or recently has been: Women's Chairman and on the Board of Directors for the United Cerebral Palsy campaign, on the Board of Directors for the Utah Society for the Prevention of Blindness, the Easter Seal Society, and the Utah Suicide Prevention Organization.*

She has been on the Governor's **Committee for Employment of** *the Handicapped, a consultant for the State Hospital for Handicapped Children, the women's campaign chairman for the United Fund, and deeply involved in the Telerama for the March of Dimes.*

In 1968 she won the Freedoms Foundation Award for excellence in patriotic programs. 1971 brought an award for outstanding service for prevention of blindness, in 1972 the Utah Civic Young Men's Association presented her with Utah's "Distinguished Youth Service Award."

Andrew Grey Nokes, her husband, is a Salt Lake City attorney. He and Jackie are parents of four children. In addition to family activities, Jackie has found time for service in professional organizations and in the Church. She was the founder and president of the Utah Chapter of American Women in Radio and Television and has been the national vice president of that organization. Her skills in communication have led to various Church teaching assignments and she is presently serving as a Junior Sunday School coordinator.

One of the nice things Jackie has volunteered to do is have several of the authors of The Joy of Being a Woman *appear as guests on her show. We appreciate both her insights on the art of communication and her constant and unselfish willingness to be of service to others.* JDC & DSC

234

THE ART OF COMMUNICATION
by
Jackie Nokes

"You, Jackie Nokes, are Miss Nancy of KSL-TVs new show, *Romper Room.*"

Those words hit like a ton of bricks! Happy? No! Scared? Yes! True, I had tried out for a job on television, but only out of curiosity—and now a whole new world of adventure had opened up for me.

My education had been in the lines of Elementary Education and Dietetics, certainly not in the dramatic arts of radio and television. In fact, television was in its infancy when I was in college.

Just a few years before this auspicious occasion I had taken a speech class at U.C.L.A. in order to overcome a miserable fear of talking before an audience—a fear which made it impossible for me to give even a short talk in church. The speech class helped, for the most important points garnered from this class were:

1. Know your material
2. Outline—don't memorize
3. Remember—no one in the audience wants to be in your shoes!

There was something terribly frightening about appearing on the "tube." Would I "blow" it? Would my family be embarrassed for me? Would I forget what I was supposed to do in that half hour? Could I ad-lib a one-minute commercial and be convincing? Could I do a good job?

My first days on the air were a complete nightmare! We had no video tape in those days, so all that could be recorded was on audio tape. That first audio tape was so bad that I wanted to go and hide, but the die was cast. There was no place to hide and only one solution to my problem: IMPROVE!

Improvement came through losing self-consciousness and doing the job as it should be done. How does one improve? In most cases an individual is his own worst critic. This is fine, but criticism without guidance is deadly. Alden Richards, my director, was and

235

still is, a master in the art of constructive criticism—an art which shows a person how to overcome irritating mannerisms, word usage, etc., without making that person feel like a total failure. Without his guidance and patience, plus the good-natured teasing and encouragement of my cameramen, sound man, and floor director, my career would have been a short one indeed.

We Are What We Are Expected to Be

With so many people pulling for me and working with me, how could I let them down? There was no way.

This premise affects each one of us. All through life, we try to act as we think others want us to in nearly every situation. Take a young child, for example. We as parents communicate through language, intonation, or example what we expect a child to be and he generally reacts that way. When we show him love, he responds with love. When we are angry, he responds with anger or tantrums. When we take time with him, he is calm and wants to be helpful. Even a tiny infant responds to his mother's emotions. If a mother is upset, her baby reacts by being cross and fussy. The modern phrase, "uptight" is so descriptive, for when a parent is "uptight," so generally will the child also be.

During the teen-age years parents expect their children to do what is right. Yet parents often force their children into wrong behavior patterns by letting the young people know the parents feel they are not to be trusted. Often we learn this lesson through bitter experience.

Just Be Quiet and Listen

The greatest adventures in communication do not come only through talking, but through listening, reading, and observing.

There is something to be learned from everyone and everything with which we come in contact if we will just take the time to pay attention. Small children are the greatest attention-payers to "things." Have you ever watched a pre-schooler in the yard carefully trying to catch a grasshopper to see what makes him go? Or have you observed the wonder of a child watching a spider spin his web, or watching the bees as they dart in and out of the flowers? These little ones are paying attention to the wonders of the world. How much attention do we adults pay to such wonders?

One of my greatest adventures is the daily privilege of meeting new people who are contributing to this great world in which we live. I am blessed with the constant opportunity of meeting people who are talented in many ways, who are willing to share their knowledge and talents with the rest of the world. They are people who are involved, people who care. Who are these people? Many of them are housewives who have become involved in community projects such as caring for retarded or "special" children and adults, volunteers for various organizations such as the detention center, Central City, the local theater, etc. There are cancer specialists who tell of new developments in research and doctors who have made contributions in various fields of medicine such as organ transplants, open-heart surgery, and snake-bite vaccines. There are sociologists who work with community development and psychologists who are doing wonders with teaching the "unteachables." There are great artists, authors, actors, musicians, clowns, and dancers. The list goes on and on. The point is that each and every person with whom one comes in contact has something to offer if one will just listen.

Some of the best advice I ever received came from Mrs. Colleen Dallin, a counselor at Olympus High School in Salt Lake City. We were talking about my daughter and some of the experiences she was having as a high school student. Colleen asked if Patti and I had rapport—to which I answered yes. She then asked if I gave Patti a lot of suggestions and did a lot of talking in our special times together—again the answer was yes. Colleen's response was: "Why don't you just be quiet for a change and listen." It was after my taking heed to her suggestion that Patti and I became very close. Patti finally had an opportunity to express herself without interruption or parental judgment and because of this, was able to figure out a solution to her own problems.

Listener or Judge?

Taylor Caldwell's book, *The Listener*, could teach each one of us a lesson as to the necessity for a real listener in our lives. On the basis of a person-to-person conversation, are you a listener or a judge? Do you, through your reactions or words, show disdain toward what is being said? Often our friends, husbands, or other members of our family simply need a sounding board. Do you fill that function effectively or do you turn vital therapeutic time into a guidance and advice session? How often have you talked with a complete stranger or a casual acquaintance and poured out your heart because you knew that no judgments would be issued, no chastisements would follow? How often, within yourself, have you felt great relief for having shared with someone else your deep-set fears, worries, or joys under those circumstances? Many people seek professional help for these needs. Some fortunate ones can bare their souls to God. Some need help from every source available.

The Manner of Presentation Is Important

Scintillating repartee or boorish rhetoric? Precisely the same statement may be involved and may earn a place in either category depending on the way in which the statements are communicated. The advent of the tremendous expansion of the mass media, and particularly the electronic media, has brought this fact dramatically to light. To play on the mundane—"It ain't what you say, it's the way you say it."

Albert Spear, in his book, *Inside the Third Reich*, shows a good example of how the manner of presentation is more powerful than what is actually said. Mr. Spear describes the enthusiasm with which Hitler's speeches were received by the masses, yet on reading the speeches after they had been presented the words came out only as glittering generalities. Are we impressed by the message, or by the charisma of the individual presenting it?

During an election year particularly the art of communication via television becomes increasingly important. How many Americans today bother to read the context of a speech given by a candidate? I would venture a guess that the numbers would be minimal because these speeches are telecast and the impressions are made by the way in which such a message is presented.

Television has opened an entirely new world in the field of communication. We have instant news, dramatically presented to create instant involvement by the viewers. The validity of news coverage is sometimes questionable because of the extensive editing involved in preparing a fifteen-minute news cast. During a riot, will the news show just the dramatic or will it be candid? Count on the fact that it will be dramatic.

238

Our media has been maligned by many—yet it is the greatest potential educational tool we have today—particularly in the field of current events. I have had to wonder aloud when people will brag that they do not and will not own a television set because of the corruptible influence it might have on their children. Really! Television has played a major role in the lives of our children, not because of the hours they have spent watching (even though the national average of television viewing is approximately six hours a day), but in the horizons which have been opened to them. Consider the child who has been raised expecting to see the progress being made in the field of space exploration. Which will be the greater motivator for a young person—reading about the first space adventure or being able to see it take place, actually being a part of the experiment by the realism of television? Since I have a child who has been "turned on" to science, astronomy, space walks on television by the age of eight, my answer is obvious.

Interviewing Is an Art

Interviewing is the antithesis of listening. It is an art that requires skill and experience, for the interviewer must be able to control the emotional tone of the encounter, obtain needed information smoothly and relate to the attitudes and experiences of the person being interviewed.

What are the keys to conducting a good interview? I believe there are four important guides which can bring rich results if they are followed:

First: Have some background in the subject which will be discussed.

Second: Be interested in the interviewee as a person.

Third: Create an atmosphere of trust and credibility.

Fourth: Don't plan ahead to the next question. Follow the trend of the conversation.

We are all familiar with many of the personalities who conduct interviews and television "talk" shows. Some of these people we find provocative, some dull, some funny, and some, just plain rude.

In my opinion, three examples of polarized differences in the art of interviewing are:

Joe Pyne—known for his antagonistic, abrasive knack in

239

creating an atmosphere of total upset and frustration by putting his guests immediately on the defensive.

Johnny Carson—a master in the art of demonstrating his own histrionic talents and humor through his interview technique.

William F. Buckley—whose gift of expression and esoteric vocabulary has a proclivity to intimidate his guests unless they too have equal gifts for using a large and varied vocabulary and demonstrate a competitive make-up.

It has been said that a good interviewer is able to learn more about a person in five minutes than a friend can learn in five months.

Don't get the idea that interviewing is done only by professionals. This is not the case, for interviewing is simply the art of drawing information for the sheer interest in a subject and/or person. It is a skill needed and cultivated by every good conversationalist. Everyone needs this ability, for opportunities for its use appear constantly in casual conversations, family relationships, church assignments, and business routines. You can find out fascinating bits of information about your friends if you use these techniques sometimes in your conversations.

In a television situation most people are easy to interview, even when it might be that person's first time in front of the camera. The secret lies in putting that person at ease and getting his mind on the subject at hand, and letting him know that you, the interviewer, are interested.

In my experience I have found that those people who are the easiest to interview are those individuals who know what they are talking about. The most gracious personalities are those who have truly excelled in their fields. Some of my favorites are: Artur Rubinstein, Van Cliburn, Grant Johannesen, Maestro Maurice Abravanel, Arlene Dahl, Ronald Reagan, Johnnie Whitaker, Jimmy Dean, Ardean Watts, Raymond Burr, and Vincent Price.

If you have ever watched an interview with Jimmy Dean you could easily venture a guess as to why he would be a favorite. Although he is totally unpredictable in his words and actions, he is so honest and spontaneous that he is like a breath of spring time in an otherwise staid situation.

Then there is Victor Borge. His great joy seems to be in

240

unnerving his interviewer by reclining on whatever is handy, smoking a cigarette where no smoking is allowed, and proceeding to remain totally silent.

The most touching experience so far in my career happened a few years ago when a very talented young composer-pianist appeared on our program. This young man had been born with a malignant tumor on his optic nerve. His doctors felt that an operation would be fatal, so his parents searched for a doctor whose opinion differed. The operation was performed but the boy was left blind. He told his story without self-pity but with deep love and appreciation for all those around him. Our total program was centered around this young man as he played some of his original compositions for us. There was a short time left to "fill" so I asked him to play his favorite song. He played "Count Your Many Blessings." That was one day when our standard closing was not presented. No one in the studio could say a word after that.

Communication By Posture and Attitude

There are so many ways to communicate that when we analyze this word we realize that through everything we do—as well as the way in which we do it—we are communicating. There is an excellent book called *Body Language,* by Julian Fast, which should be a must on everyone's reading list, at least everyone who is interested in or who works with people. Don't let the cover frighten you, the information in that book is invaluable.

Is lack of communication, or misinterpreted communication, the cause of the "generation gap," or family break-ups, or adolescent problems, or unrest in our world today? Perhaps if the answer is yes we should put more emphasis in teaching this subject in our schools and churches today. We should perhaps stress in more stringent terms the art of listening, of good body language, and most particularly the art of communicating our interest and love for our fellow man. Perhaps we should stress more vehemently the art of paying attention and of caring. There is no doubt that as our quality of communication improves so also will the quality of the world in which we live.

241

INTRODUCING—LARAINE DAY

The High and the Mighty, Mr. Lucky, The Locket, Those Endearing Young Charms, Woman on Pier Thirteen, Foreign Correspondent, *and* My Son, My Son—*all are among the more than forty film credits amassed by this talented actress. You've seen her on television too, in* Dr. Kildare, Studio One, Playhouse 90, The Name of the Game, The FBI, *and on various "talk" and "game" shows. She is one of the few that Hollywood consistently points to with pride when it calls attention to its fine style and impeccable taste.*

Laraine Johnson was born in Roosevelt, Utah, but moved with her family to California when she was nine. She began the actor's craft in the Long Beach Player's Guild under the tutelage of drama coach Elias Day. Later, when it appeared there might be some marquee conflict with another actress named Johnson, she adapted the last name of the mentor for her stage name. During the course of her career she has been cast opposite such male superstars as John Wayne, Spencer Tracy, Gary Cooper, Kirk Douglas, Cary Grant, Robert Mitchum and Gregory Peck.

She and her producer-writer husband, Mike Grilikhes, are the parents of two daughters and time is taken from her busy schedule for "room mother" and car pool duties and other home tasks.

Laraine is concerned about civic responsibilities and is involved in a number of projects. For instance, she is one of a 60-woman task force of film personalities who each year produce a major stage production which annually yields over $200,000 for mentally-retarded children. She has also been a hostess and narrator for a New Zealand group, the Te Arohanui Maori Dance Company. As a member of their Board of Directors, she helped them tour Hawaii and the western United States.

Her chapter speaks pointedly concerning what she perceives to be a real need among Latter-day Saints. It gives cause for real introspection.

JDC & DSC

242

EXPANDING OUR CIRCLE OF LOVE
by
Laraine Day

First—a gift that I would like to share with you—two small
masterpieces of religious verse.[1]

Betrayal
Still as of old
Men by themselves are priced—
For thirty pieces Judas sold
Himself, not Christ.

Hester H. Cholmondeley, 19th Century

Bigot
Though you be scholarly, beware
The bigotry of doubt.
Some people take a strange delight
In blowing candles out.

Eleanor Slater, 1903-

Once upon a time there was a little orphan girl about eight
years old. She wasn't a very pretty little girl, nor very bright, and
she wasn't very amusing or charming. As a matter of fact, she
wasn't even very desirable to have around. Most people didn't like
her. And so. one day the orphanage shipped her off to a school in
the country.

She didn't fare much better there. Not only did the other
children avoid her, but even the teachers disliked her. After a
while the little girl began to disappear every afternoon for a half-
hour or so, and one of the teachers who didn't like her at all decided to follow her one day and see what kind of mischief the
little girl was up to. So when the little girl slipped out of school
one day, the teacher followed her. She saw the little girl walk
slowly to the rear of the school grounds where there was a large

---

[1] From *Masterpieces of Religious Verse.* Reprinted by permission of
Harper and Row, Publisher.

oak tree, and stand there for a while staring off into space. Then, she took something from her pocket and placed it in a fork of the branches of the oak tree. After a while, the little girl left.

When she was gone, the teacher ran quickly to the oak tree to find what the little girl had placed there. Now, thought the teacher, we'll find out what she's up to.

When she reached into the oak tree she found the little girl had left a slip of paper. On the paper she had written: "To anyone who finds this note—I Love You."

Isn't that what life is really all about?

It is what this chapter is all about, in a way; only it doesn't start "Once Upon a Time." It goes way back to the beginning, to the knowledge that "God so loved the world, that he gave his only begotten Son, that whosoever believeth in him should not perish, but have everlasting life." (Jn. 3:16)

And it goes back to his commandments, "Thou shalt love the Lord thy God with all thy heart, and with all thy soul, and with all thy mind." And to the second commandment, "Thou shalt love thy neighbour as thyself." (Mt. 22:37-39)

We Shouldn't Limit the Scope of Our Influence

I have long felt that one of the greatest weaknesses of the membership of our Church has been its habit of gathering together to the exclusion of meaningful social contact and associations with other people not of our faith.

We narrow the world down to our own individual wards and stakes. We limit our knowledge, our experience, our friendships, our understanding and tolerance and, most of all, the scope of our influence. We also deprive ourselves of the tremendous opportunity to serve the really needy and desperate people who cry in the darkness around us and stumble blindly in the brilliance of the sophisticated world, confused by its everchanging sense of values, and truth, and lost hopes.

I don't know why we should be so hesitant or afraid to put on our shining armor of faith and venture out to broader horizons to really practice what we preach: to love our neighbors, and to make Christ's influence felt.

Maybe it is because we are afraid that as individuals, we and our children will not be strong enough to keep our moral standards

244

intact and withstand the many glamorous, highly publicized temptations that await us on busy main street.

The Protected Life Deprives Us of Growth

Surely being so protected is being deprived of growth. There is no personal spiritual achievement accomplished by overcoming something that has never been a temptation or challenge.

Our isolation also deprives the rest of the world of the truth and knowledge of what and who is a Mormon.

I do not mean to ignore or minimize the many wonderful aspects of Mormon gatherings: the obvious virtues, pleasures and advantages, many of which were an important part of any achievement I have made. And I certainly do not intend to criticize anyone who devotes all his time and talents only to service to the Church. I just feel that "service to the Church" has a much broader and more meaningful definition.

In my own particular sphere of endeavor, the motion picture and television industry, why should Mormons be judged mostly by ethics and actions of prominent "Jack Mormons" who are in executive positions at the studios?

Where are the "good" Mormons? Where is their important influence in probably the greatest opinion-making media in the world?

Most of the "good" Mormons are off in their own special groups, singing together, praying together, canning together, sewing together, visiting and helping each other, but nevertheless isolating themselves.

Using Our Influence for Good

And who is being the Good Samaritan? Who is working in the black and brown and white ghettos? Who is being personally concerned about the educational opportunities and welfare of non-members?

I understand that each Stake President is responsible for every single person in his Stake area, not just the members of our Church. That is an overwhelming responsibility, and he certainly needs all the help that he can get. He does get it from some.

There are the Ettie Lee Homes for Boys, and last year there was the inspiring project undertaken by the young people in Salt

245

Lake City when they raised a great deal of money to help a minority group complete its own church.

In Los Angeles I personally know of six Mormon women who are actively working for the benefit of mentally retarded children, but I'm not aware of more than four other prominent "good" Mormons serving on the boards of many other charitable organizations for the blind, deaf, crippled or needy.

But like Will Rogers said, "All I know is what I read in the papers." Of course there must be many Latter-day Saints involved in various important community activities. Unfortunately there are not as many percentage-wise as Catholics, Jews, and Protestants. That's what concerns me deeply. We should be involved more than all of them, much more involved.

In Church publications I have read of non-member children being helped at the Children's Hospital in Salt Lake City.

I know that a few scholarships are awarded by the Church College of Hawaii to non-member Polynesians, but that is not enough for Latter-day Saints.

Great Potential for Group Service

If it is necessary to work as a Church group to keep one's faith unwavering, why not extend the scope of group activities beyond the confines of the chapel and help to meet the needs of the non-members around us who affect our lives in so many ways? So much could be accomplished for the betterment of the entire community! Elders Quorums and Relief Societies could undertake or participate in many civic projects to help all kinds of people— our neighbors outside of the Church.

We could move out and through service share the great light we have, and the marvelous truth we have, and the abundant blessings we have been given. We could truly become Latter-day Saints by letting others find the glory of God in the love and concern we feel for them as individuals.

My fellow Mormon does not need me as much as the stranger does, and I can never find the stranger if I do not go out and seek him. I can never help create or contribute anything to a great man or woman until I find the child who needs a friend with truth, understanding and honor to inspire him, as so beautifully expressed by Mamie Gene Cole in "The Child's Appeal".

The Child's Appeal

I am the Child
All the world waits for my coming.
All the earth watches with interest to see
    what I shall become.
Civilization hangs in the balance.
For what I am, the world of tomorrow will be.[2]

There, I feel, is the real obligation of a "good" Mormon: to become involved, to move out where the rest of the world can see clearly what he is—what he will share with them—what he will do with them and for them, and mostly that he cares about them.

Last year there was a large billboard in New York City which read: "I Love You! Do you Mind?" In the lower right hand corner it was signed "Jesus Christ."

If we are truly His saints, our names should be there too.

---

[2]From *Masterpieces of Religious Verse.* Reprinted by permission of Harper and Row, Publishers.

INTRODUCING—STELLA H. OAKS

Stella is a choice example of the influence for good a woman can wield in her own community. Just as this chapter was being written, she retired after twenty-four years of service with the schools of Provo, Utah. She has been a supervisor of adult education in that area ever since she came there from a teaching job in Vernal in 1948. For years she also served as director of public relations.

When Provo adapted the council-manager form of government, she was elected the only woman member of the city council. She became affectionately known as the "city mother" along with all the city fathers. Stella served as acting mayor of Provo for several months during her city council years.

Many honors have come to her. The Sertoma Club presented her "Service to Mankind" awards, the BYU Alumni Association awarded her its "Distinguished Service Award." She has been made an honorary life member of the PTA, and the Utah chapter of the American Association of University Women named her "Outstanding Woman of the Year" for 1972.

Although she was left a widow after eleven years of married life, Stella has raised three children. Dr. Dallin Oaks, who is now president of the Brigham Young University; Dr. Merrill Oaks, an eye surgeon and specialist (and husband of Jo, another author of this book); and Mrs. H. Ross Hammond, wife of a college professor.

She is now president of the Provo Senior Citizens and has been instrumental in building that program into one of the finest in the nation. She was recently released as the Relief Society president of one of the BYU stakes, which is her latest Church calling.

As we talked with Stella, several subjects were considered. But we felt, as she did, that a chapter suggesting ways that widows could best meet the challenges they faced would be most helpful. She writes with experience and with a sweet spirit. We appreciate the ideas she shares with others.   JDC & DSC

THE WIDOW'S MITE
by
Stella H. Oaks

It was two years after the numbing loss of my husband that I was brought face to face with the term *widow*. My little children stood near me as we answered the doorbell that evening preceeding our first Thanksgiving Day alone. It was a fellow high school teacher and member of our bishopric who was there with a basket of food saying, a bit shyly, "Sister Oaks, will you accept this. The Bishop wishes every widow in the ward to receive a basket of food." Inwardly I was calling on all my reserves and soon could reply, "Yes, tell the Bishop I accept, understanding the spirit in which this is sent." Before the door was hardly closed, Merrill, age five, tugged at my skirt. "Mommy, what is a widow?" There came a strengthening force into a resolution made that moment that, with the Divine help of my Heavenly Father, my little children, Dallin, Merrill, and Evelyn, should never feel they did not have a father in our home. The reality of the term widow would be minimized by making his personality felt. My husband's name would be part of our daily casual conversation, as we referred to his books, his tools, his scriptures, his deer hunting stories, his experiences, his medical advice or anything in connection with the ideals and standards for which he stood.

My spiritual muscles became stronger that Thanksgiving time. It was a turning point in resolute determination to fill a double role. And now, years later, being in my sixty-sixth year, with fourteen grandchildren—all my dear ones close about me, with each striving to live the gospel of Jesus Christ, I will endeavor to share some of the ways our Father in Heaven has gently, firmly, consistently watched over me in thirty-three years as a widow.

Though alone, I have always felt I had a husband. That sweet assurance has been distilled in my soul as I sought the further meaning of temple vows and the eternal covenant. I turn in memory again to the manifestation given to me the night of his passing. I had fasted many days and sought in the agony of my soul, the meaning to the seemingly contradictory promises given for Lloyd's life and glorious fulfillment, which I had interpreted as a need for me to have greater faith and trust. I felt sure the faith and fasting of our dear Twin Falls (Idaho) saints, his fellow highcouncilmen, and his large youthful Sunday School class would be effective in his being raised up in health. I could only entertain the idea of fulfillment here and now. I was full of guilt that I had not exercised enough faith to have him healed. I did not know how to exercise spiritual insight—how to trust the fearful unknown—how to say "Thy will be done." But when I was bowed low alone in my room, as I rose from my knees, a glorious manifestation was granted to me! I was given the assurance by the Spirit that Lloyd's mission on earth was completed, that his passing, to occur within the next hour, was right. I knew that God loved me and that this event of death was a divinely planned part of later events which would open doors to those blessings I sought for now. My task was to face straight ahead. It was years until I dared look back, except for fleeting moments.

All the anxiety of the past weeks melted away, leaving peace and quiet in my heart. The sound of a nurse's hurried footsteps coming down the hall and her call, "Come quickly, Dr. Oaks is sinking" had brought me rapidly to his side. But now I was as one reborn. I stood in reverent awe to participate in this hallowed event—death.

The Early Years

For the first several years many broken dreams came to torture me.

In the eleven brief years of our marriage we had never owned a home, but had just made a decision to buy a beautiful expansive place, large enough for the big family we anticipated, when the final illness came to my husband. Yet the children and I have since owned our own home in every community in which we have lived. The great security and blessing of having our own home has fulfilled the promise from the Lord that He will provide for the widow and the orphan who seek Him in faith.

Once, indeed, I felt helpless and doomed, doubting my ability to rear the children successfully. Fortunately, they were yet less than nine years of age at this occurrence: I went some distance to

250

call them to supper, supposedly from innocent play, only to find them involved in cards and betting with red, white and blue chips stacked on a table in the yard. In a flash of the mind, I could see them growing up to be gamblers, liars and thieves. It still remains one of the low moments of my life. I felt doomed to failure, but I remembered the scripture that spoke of "Reproving betimes with sharpness, when moved upon by the Holy Ghost" and I did this firmly. They never had further question where I stood on that issue and have respected my position which I in turn had learned from my parents in many discussions on the evils, the wasted time, and the sterile results of card playing.

How could I possibly find the means—alone—to give our children the education that together we had set as our goal? I was still settling bills, paying for Lloyd's medical school, for his new x-ray machine (just installed), the eight months of hospital care, and his medical attention in three states. A school teacher getting $3100 a year cannot possibly be expected to fulfill these dreams— yet there was the blessing I requested from the Patriarch following the funeral service. He promised that my children should have all the education that each desired. This has been fulfilled to the letter, even beyond my fondest dreams.

Learning Gratitude

But how does one find the Lord—find the way—alone? It is an uncharted course for each newly bereaved woman and, even when one is told by others or reads about "how," still one must evolve her own way of atunement. Discovering the Lord's way is life's greatest adventure, the most satisfying learning one can pursue. The course is long and lonely only until you discern and acknowledge the constant evidence of daily blessings. One can learn to discipline oneself to have a grateful heart, then live in joy on new levels of communication with Heavenly Father, for a true spiritual paradox is that we "see after we know."

Ye cannot bear all things now; nevertheless, be of good cheer, for I will lead you along. The kingdom is yours and the blessings thereof are yours, and the riches of eternity are yours.

And he who receiveth all things with thankfulness

shall be made glorious; and the things of this earth shall
be added unto him, even an hundred fold, yea, more."

(D&C 78: 18,19)

It was helpful to hear one of the general authorities, who said
in conference: "Let your first good morning prayer of gratitude be
to your Heavenly Father. . ."

Establishing Priorities

During the early years when the children were small, I was
hard pressed to know how to be with them as much as they needed
me and as I needed them. I was Dean of Girls and Speech and
Drama Director at Uintah High School in Vernal (my husband's
home town and where I had taught while he was in medical school,
two years prior to our marriage). There was much night activity
and rehearsing. Those were the days I was driven to my knees seeking extra strength, increased wisdom, expansion of my time (the
only thing I have ever coveted). As I sought specific help in each
project, the way opened—TIME seemed to stretch as my spirit expanded and so the children were not seriously denied.

I remembered the comforting words of Pearl Buck, whom I
heard speak at Columbia University, saying, "My mother loved us
with all her heart but not with all her time."

I would hold fast for certain priorities: We would have our
evening meal together at 5:30; this made piecing and nibbling unnecessary. The children ate with eager, hearty appetites and there
was this special time for conversation, planning together, and for
evening work, and story time before returning to school for play
rehearsals. One or more of the children accompanied me to this
evening activity.

During one of my busiest weeks, Merrill, at age five, was
asked to be in a special program at Primary. The teachers knew
how occupied I was with the opera and other special features at
high school, and had offered to make the outfit Merrill needed. As
they distributed the patterns and material, they told him they
would provide his costume. He promptly claimed the set of things
saying, "My mother has never let me down yet! She'll make my
costume!" And she did!

Another priority was our Saturdays together. The work was
never fully done by night but we had accomplished the making of

252

bread, major cleaning and readiness of clothing for Sunday, as well as preparations for a quick, easy meal, appropriate for the Sabbath. We walked together morning and evening to the beautiful chapel where we had the association of strong, loving, understanding, Latter-day Saints living the inspired pattern of the Church. My gratitude and feelings of love for these people are eternal. Their dear faces come before me now as I recall their goodness and example—and how they helped heal me and give me opportunity for new directions of accomplishment and satisfaction. They knew my sorrow and shared my loss as did our Twin Falls Stake friends who welcomed us back through the years for an annual summer visit for business and pleasure.

There was a day by day task of earning a living. My parents kept Evelyn until she could be in school, and though this meant we could only see her at holiday time, I have learned one can bear whatever need be borne as I prayerfully set up priorities leading toward righteous goals.

Maintaining Family Relationships

A widow's family is more than herself and children. Family strength comes from uncles, aunts, cousins as well as grandparents. Dallin and Merrill were included in many memorable activities. Uncles took them on fishing and hunting trips, providing memories for them as they reminisce.

It was while I was away 6 weeks for summer school at Columbia University—torn between the need to complete a higher degree and the desire and necessity to be with my little ones—that an encouraging event was told me in a letter. The three children were attending Junior Sunday School with their Grandma (Chasty O. Harris) in the Payson Park Ward. Since the two younger little ones seemed hesitant and shy, she remained with them for opening exercises and was astonished to hear that nine-year-old Dallin would give the two-and-a-half minute talk. He hesitated a moment, then walked up and gave a creditable incident of faith from the Old Testament. Later his Grandmother asked him why he had not told her and he replied, "Grandma, I had forgotten all about it. I was about to refuse and then I said to myself, 'Anybody who has read Hulbert's Stories of the Bible through three times ought to be able to get up and give a talk.' " So he rose to that responsibility and my heart rejoiced at his growing sense of who he was.

My husband had always said our children must be taught to work and put their own effort in what they wished to attain—life must not be made easy. Each learned to work, both alone and together on common projects, and to find satisfaction in a day's accomplishment. Being of moderate means financially became one of our greatest blessings. We sought the fulfillment of our "impossible dreams" from the Lord and He remembered us in all things in which we had learned to do His will and follow in His ways. One of the greatest growths we all had was increased ability to feel, to express love, gratitude and appreciation to one another and to the Lord.

Our daily story time together gave us delight and common incidents for conversation. We traveled far in mind and outreach, identifying with the experiences and thought of favorite characters. This love of books, good literature; the search for answers in the wisdom of great writers; accumulating and exchanging bits of philosophy, appealing incidents, thoughts and humor has continued.

Putting up hair was a good time to read some more of Scott's *Lady of the Lake*, or *Rhyme of the Ancient Mariner*, or *Hiawatha*.

Encouraging Individuality

A great challenge to every parent, but especially to a widowed mother, is to loosen the bonds of parental authority, to make way for an adolescent's progressing need of independence and individuality. A parent first faces this new demand with the oldest child. With no father a widow's sons are likely to be very independent. This admirable quality poses a dilemma: how to give direction and yet not interfere with his independence. I recall my feelings when Dallin proposed to save money, and at the same time to enjoy an exciting trip by going east to bring us back a new family car. And so it came about that the day after Dallin graduated from high school, Merrill, Evelyn and I waved goodbye at the train depot as he and his friend, Morris Jackman, were off on the car assignment. On the return trip, the boys had gained consent to extend their trip to Washington, D.C. and many historical places. I was questioned by friends for this foolish chance I was taking, but I had inner calm and peace. We had prayed together about this decision. Dallin was fully ready for a man's trust and knew how to heed the whisperings and promptings of the spirit. He was already employed as a first-class radio engineer at a Provo station, having previously studied in Vernal for the special exams on his own initiative. Then he traveled to Denver alone at 15 years of age, took all-day tests and returned with his operator's license.

Merrill never deviated from his preschool statement that he would be a doctor like his father. Every opportunity to choose his own topics in school would result in his writing on a medically related subject such as Circulation of the Blood, or entering into a debate on socialized medicine. His early decision gave him poise and great serenity. He made time during his intense medical training to be a counselor in the bishopric of their ward.

Rearing Evelyn took even more careful planning, more special blessings from the Lord to compensate for a lovely sensitive little daughter without a father, with no sister, and with a working mother and brothers engrossed in boys' interests. But the Lord knew our total family mission and had sent a rare, choice spirit to fill this difficult role. She spent many, many hours alone, but knew that I was as near as the telephone and that I would be home for our early evening meal together. Evelyn loved to do many extra house duties to surprise us. Our appreciation and love was her reward. She developed many artistic talents and was always very creative in expression and accomplishment. I had a secret worry that when she married, by engrossing herself in family interests, her singing talent would be neglected. Instead her husband encourages Evelyn in her stake music calling and personally serves as her accompanist. Evelyn has summarized the feeling and tone of our home in this way, "Self-pity was an attitude entirely foreign to our home. We never felt incomplete. True, ours was a home without a father, but we never talked about his absence, only of his presence and how he is nearby and aware of our activities, and helping us when we need him. Because of her faith, Mother didn't allow death to build a wall of separation between us and Daddy. Thus, we did not sense a deficiency in our home; on the contrary, there was even a sense of being privileged by the challenge—the mission—to carry on and grow and become all that our earthly father and our Heavenly Father would desire in us."

The boys enjoyed athletics in school, and I was pleased for them to have identification with strong masculine figures such as their coaches. For this same reason I placed the children with men teachers at school. Particular effort was made to help them identify with the good men at church. They gained much from their identification with our Bishop who was a respected BYU Professor, our home teacher who was a prominent judge, and our Stake President, a great promoter of scouting and youth. All were men of proven ideals who respected their priesthood. We took time to discuss the fine qualities of the men who were part of our lives and I can see these attributes reflected in the lives of the children. I have had men say lightly, "What is it about you widows—you seem to have the magic touch in rearing your children."

Building Memories

I sound like the rearing of my children went along with all smoothness and light. I feel constrained to share an incident which my children love to tell friends so they can see me cringe. It was time for Saturday morning breakfast which I was serving with extra push so we could accomplish a big day's work. I fried the very large eggs the family from Maesar farm had left the previous night in a small box by the back door. I commented that I had never seen such enormous eggs. At the first taste Dallin objected, then Merrill also. I believed children should eat what was placed before them, with gratitude to match the blessing on the food which they had just uttered. From the stove where I was still occupied I urged them to be happy about those "nice big eggs and get breakfast finished." When Dallin called the eggs "rotten" I was irritated at such a word about good food while people were eating. I insisted he clean up his plate. Merrill dawdled, but eventually finished. Dallin ate two bites then insisted he wasn't hungry anymore and just sat there! In a few minutes I sat down and started my egg and grudgingly agreed it didn't taste very good and released the children from finishing their last bites. Later in the day, my brother-in-law came to ask if his children had mistakenly left goose eggs he had carefully packed in a special box for setting his broody hen. He laughingly told me that no one ever eats goose eggs—they are too strong. It was with some difficulty I later confessed this to the children who seized upon it as a wonderful story to be told anytime we had visitors.

Another vivid event occurred when the boys announced at

256

breakfast that each was assigned to bring a homemade pie to the church for a bake sale. I was hastily making ready to leave for school and reproved them some for not telling me of this at least the previous night. But after some discussion, and remembering Merrill's esteem of my ability to never let them down, I arranged to leave early that afternoon and return home to hastily make each boy a pie at the promised time. When removing the first one it slipped and landed upside down on the floor (fortunately clean). I was stunned at the tragedy! In a mental turmoil I reached for the second pie and slipped on the oozing juice on the linoleum and the next pie landed beside the first. I was near to despair and then, tears and glee being in close proximity, we all began to laugh uproariously. I gave each a big spoon and spatula, and the four Oaks had all the warm homemade pie they could consume. Then we drove to the bakery and they agreed they could take pie from there and say nothing about the "homemade" requirement.

Acknowledging God's Will

When in need of encouragement I would turn again to my patriarchal blessing to discover special talents divinely granted to me. This was the key to what I should build on, expand and magnify.

I came to feel as one with all my noble ancestors—partakers of all their blessings—humbly grateful to realize that "They pray for thee at the gates of heaven." I sense their dependence and hope in me to rise to the zenith of my possibilities and to fulfill the full measure of my creation in service—to reach out beyond myself— beyond my family (who must always remain my first responsibility) —into neighborhood and community needs. I must practice in my relationships there the principles of service, understanding and love of fellowman—that others might be led to seek greater knowledge of the glorious principles of the Gospel.

Though there was plenty to do at school, at home, in church callings I caught the vision, the motivation, that "when ye are in the service of your fellow men ye are in the service of your God" and that my physical strength and spiritual vision would be increased and made equal to my daily dedication. This has transpired many times. I could give many examples of accomplishment far beyond the earthly strength of one person.

My employment grew to be a great fulfillment and satisfaction for me, for I was using fully the talents and professional training for which I had prepared myself.

We are told that faith is a gift from God! So with all my soul I desire to express gratitude for the faith that is part of me. My constant prayers are that I be worthy of the abundance of daily blessings given to me—to live that I may participate worthily in eternal progress.

I have schooled myself to endeavor to work with a willing heart even though weary. Part of our blessings are lost, I am sure, when we serve reluctantly or give service grudgingly. Life is *growing, changing, becoming.* Above all things I am grateful that the destiny of His children is the sole business and glory of God, our Father, and that He will bring us through to eternal maturity if we will learn His way. As I look back on the foolish and minute goals that I would have chosen at various times—things for which I have even earnestly prayed—I am grateful that He has taught me, led me, inclined my heart through many bitter-sweet experiences to say *Thy will be done*—to rejoice in whatever part, large or small, I may play in this great and final scene in which I am privileged to live. Over the years, I have grown in faith and confidence that the Master's promise is true:

> Seek not for riches but for wisdom; and, behold the mysteries of God shall be unfolded unto you, and then shall you be made rich. Behold, he that hath eternal life is rich.
> (D & C 11:7)

INTRODUCING—JAYNANN M. PAYNE

Did you say twelve children? Jaynann has heard that question many times and is happy to give an affirmative reply. This petite bundle of enthusiasm has talent and interests pointed in many directions, yet she feels that being a wife and mother are her most fitting accomplishments.

Jaynann graduated from the BYU with an English major and a music minor. Her background has led her to leadership positions in several literary groups. She is also the author of Beauty for Keeps *and* Inspiration from Great Women. *Public speaking gives her real satisfaction and she has spoken to hundreds of groups as a lecturer for BYU special courses and education weeks, for American Business Institute Seminars, for the U.S. Government WIN Program, and as teacher of a Personal Development course.*

One of her greatest interests has been in music, and she has worked to support musical activities in her community and state. She has spent many years on the Board of Directors of the Community Concert Association and on the Board of the Utah Valley Opera Association. She organized "Debonaires," the youth auxiliary to the Utah Valley Symphony. The city of Provo, Utah presented her with a "Special Commendation of Merit" for her community and Church service to families and youth.

In 1967 a friend entered her name in the Mrs. Utah contest. She felt that the judges would never choose a mother of such a large family but, to her surprise, she won the event and went on to become the second runner-up to Mrs. America in national competition. Her comment on the experience: "Dean deserves the credit for that honor because he has always treated me like a queen."

She enjoys her present Church position as Blazer B leader. Her life is active, but she regards her mother's role as most important; her chapter reflects this philosophy well.

JDC & DSC

BE A LIGHT SET ON A HILL
by
Jaynann M. Payne

As I walked into a charming little bookstore in Atlanta the first thing that caught my eye was a quotation painted along the top of the walls as a border:

We have been so fond of the stars, we are not afraid of the night.

Many thoughts came flooding into my mind. How desperately the world needs the gospel of Jesus Christ as a star to guide it through the night of spiritual darkness we are living in. How woman needs to be a star to light lives, to set a course to eternal life by her teachings and to reflect God's majesty by her example.

Two examples of the influence of women upon the world are unforgettable. The first is Lady MacBeth, who pandered to her own selfish lust for riches and power, and encouraged those same weaknesses in her husband until he descended from being a once-noble Lord to become a vile murderer. She caused not only a King's death, but her husband's, her own and the loss of a kingdom. Her influence was evil, degrading and fatal. It led from nobility to annihilation.

The second is that of Abraham Lincoln's mother. Lincoln was about as disadvantaged as it was possible to be in his day. Poverty haunted his home, lack of opportunity for education dashed his hopes, physical homeliness trampled his love dreams. Sorrow over the deaths of his mother, Nancy Hanks Lincoln, and his beloved Anne Rutledge, burdened his youthful heart with melancholy. And yet out of the fiery crucible of his disadvantages and disappointments, he rose, inspired, encouraged and loved by a stepmother, Sarah Johnston Lincoln. "All that I am, or ever hope to be, I owe to my angel mother." Such is the tribute Lincoln paid to this woman who had so much faith in him. His Christlike nobility has had a profound effect upon all mankind since.

Women Set the Tone of Life

A woman's influence, for good or ill, is a power we cannot ignore, nor can we escape from that responsibility. It has been so since Mother Eve ate Adam out of house and home. It shook me a bit to realize that in the Garden of Eden Eve had absolutely *nothing to do!* She had no flowers to plant, no cookies to bake, no dishes to wash, no furniture to dust or move, no cooking to do, no clothes to wash or iron! She probably was the only woman who could truthfully say: "I have absolutely nothing to wear!" And most devastating of all: no babies to cuddle! No clothes? No babies? She must have been simply bored to death!! She must have realized she was spinning her wheels, going nowhere fast. Although she was deceived by Satan, she had the courage to risk spiritual and physical death to gain a greater prize. And though she found out that mortality wasn't "instamatic" happiness, but more like blood, sweat and tears, when she found out they would be redeemed by the Son of God, she rejoiced, saying: "Were it not for our transgression we never should have had seed, and never should have known good and evil, and the joy of our redemption, and the eternal life which God giveth unto all the obedient." (Moses 5:11)

What faith and hope she must have engendered in the hearts of her children and her husband. In a whimsical story by Mark Twain, called "Adam's Diary," Father Adam writes these entries in his journal:

[After They Had Been Banished From the Garden:]

After all these years, I see that I was mistaken about Eve in the beginning. It is better to live outside the Garden with her than inside it without her. At first I thought she talked too much, but now I should be sorry to have that voice fall silent and pass out of my life. Blessed be the fruit that brought us near together and taught me to know the goodness of her heart and the sweetness of her spirit!

[On Eve's Grave:]

Wheresoever she was, there was Eden!

In the same vein of thought Elbert Hubbard said: "If it was woman who put man out of Paradise, it is still woman, and woman only, who can lead him back."

261

Women should be the keepers of good morals and the conscience of men. Today, with such publicity and emphasis placed or misplaced upon women's equality and rights, there is a tremendous opportunity for the Latter-day Saint woman to be a light set upon a hill. We are center stage and in the spotlight. We must create the kind of marriage, home and family that will not only make an impact on our society for good, but will strengthen the priesthood and Church in its great task of preaching the gospel and preparing for the advent of the Savior.

This is a day of misplaced values, of irreverence for that which is good, of inhumane actions. Day after day man's irreverence is published in two-inch caps as headlines in all news media. For instance, the recent desecration of the priceless "Pieta" sculpture of Mary, the mother of Jesus, holding the crucified Savior on her lap, illustrates how prevalent is man's irreverence for God and the artistic masterpieces created by His inspired children. In other parts of the world, terrorists murder the innocent with no sign of remorse, with no reverence for human life, or God.

It is the women and mothers of our society who must teach respect and reverence for life and all God's creations, including our earth. If we would encourage all men to honor their temporal and spiritual stewardships, then many of the world's problems like pollution, would be solved.

"Do Your Own Thing"

One evening recently my husband and I formulated the World's Version of some of the Ten Commandments, based upon what we saw or heard advocated in the current newspapers, magazines and entertainment media. They are:

WORLD'S VERSION OF THE TEN COMMANDMENTS

1. Thou shalt have no other Gods before me unless you like something else better like power, popularity, riches or fame.
2. Thou shalt not take the name of the Lord thy God in vain except when you're angry, or trying to make an impression.
3. Remember the Sabbath Day when you don't have anything better to do.
4. Honor thy father and thy mother on Mother's Day and Father's Day and when they do what you want them to.
5. Thou shalt not commit adultery except on Monday, Tuesday,

262

Wednesday, Thursday, Friday or Saturday, but never, never on a Sunday, unless you feel like you just can't resist.

6. Thou shalt not steal unless you have a really good opportunity or it's something you just can't live without.

7. Thou shalt not bear false witness unless you absolutely can't stand the person.

8. Thou shalt not covet anything you wouldn't want anyway.

Satan's counterfeit of the Lord's Commandments can be reduced to one sentence: "Do Your Own Thing!"

Alma and Abinadi, in the Book of Mormon, both make interesting comments to us about "doing our own thing." Alma said to his rebellious son, Corianton:

> And now, ye see by this that our first parents were cut off both temporally and spiritually from the presence of the Lord; and thus we see they became subjects to *follow after their own will.* (Alma 42:7)

When men "do their own thing," which is probably one of the most appropriate descriptions of our society today, they become spiritually dead.

Abinadi warns us as well as wicked King Noah of the consequences in the Book of Mormon:

> Remember that he that persists in his own carnal nature, and goes on in the ways of sin and rebellion against God, remaineth in his fallen state and the devil hath all power over him. Therefore, he is as though there was no redemption made, being an enemy to God;... (Mosiah 16:5)

Those in our society who would attempt to please others or be obedient to parents, teachers, or policemen, have fallen from favor among the so-called "educated elite." Their efforts are interpreted as hypocrisy or phoniness in our society. The norms run more to brutal honesty, candid obscene language. If you don't like the law don't obey it, and above all, "Do your own thing." Youth think parents are hypocrites because they have weaknesses and sometimes fail to live as they believe. But hypocrisy is not failing to live a perfect life, but *pretending to be something you are not.*

Perhaps a drunk is the best person to point out to his son the evils of drink. You can repent from sinning but not from hypocrisy because hypocrisy doesn't recognize that you are sinning!

All of these attitudes have selfishness as their basis. My husband and I feel that selfishness is the greatest sin in the world today because nearly every evil is based upon it. If I might paraphrase Alma: *Selfishness never was happiness.*

All about us we see disdain for the procreative powers given us by God. Gratification of the senses is enthroned as an idol worshipped by the entertainment media—the celluloid queens and political pawns. The flames of immorality lit in Hollywood and Washington have swept like a holocaust from coast to coast and back again. Even the seas are slimy with the sludge of men's selfishness.

Titles like these are in every bookstore and newsstand:

Everything You Always Wanted to Know About Sex

I knew a young girl who found out about sex. She was sixteen, beautiful, pregnant and unwed. She had refused to marry the boy who was the father of her unborn child. When she was ready to leave the hospital, this young mother had to take her beautiful baby boy from the arms of the nurse and give him to the adopting parents. It tore me apart inside as it did her. She turned to me with tears in her eyes and said: "Sister Payne, he lied to me when he said nobody would get hurt, and that because we loved each other, anything we did was alright. That's why I didn't marry him. It's all a great big lie and I don't want to live a lie."

"Oh, if only I had known five minutes before I was immoral— how I would feel five minutes after I gave my baby away!" were the heartbreaking words of another girl lost in the wilderness of lies and lust. Such are the true voices—but how many stories do you read with titles that speak truth like these?:

He Lied to Me When He Said Immorality Was Beautiful!

Abortion Is Not Only Murder—It's Hell!

If Only I Had Known Before I Took Drugs How Much Sorrow and Suffering I Would Cause My Family and Myself

A woman needs the protective assurance that a man loves her enough to marry her and provide the security of a home and an honorable name before she can ever find fulfillment in her relationships with that man.

We don't need to know more about sex, it's the knowledge of love that we lack.

Bonnard said:

> The virtuous woman flees from danger, for she trusts more to her prudence in shunning it than in her strength to overcome it.

What a challenge the Mormon woman has, to care enough to speak out against the debasing and obscene. What can we do? Write of our indignation to magazines that carry filth; make phone calls to theatres showing unfit movies; support the war against illegal drugs by writing government officials and supporting those in our community who are fighting drug abuse. Most important, we need to discuss with our children and youth the false ideas that are insidiously undermining our society on TV, in movies and periodicals. Discussing doesn't mean preaching, it means listening and enlightening.

Richard L. Evans, in a timely message from Temple Square, said:

> To be indifferent to error or to any evil is to give great comfort and encouragement to error and evil. And in such circumstances indifference is not neutrality. In such circumstances indifference is an active evil.

Nothing Down—E-E-Easy Monthly Payments

How easy it is to "get taken in" to economic bondage for tinker toy treasures...those material unnecessities that fall apart, get lost, or have no eternal value. Yet they turn into debts that enslave us economically. Someone said: "We have been so anxious to give our children what we didn't have that we have neglected to give them what we did have."

At our personal interview during the Mrs. America Pageant, one of the judges asked me: "How on earth can you afford to give a college education to your ten children?" My answer: "We can't—but they can get their education the same way my husband and I got our degrees, by working and paying their own way!" And one of my most gratifying moments recently was when our daughter, Janice, a senior in college, told me: "Mother, I'm really grateful you and Dad have given me the experience of earning my college education and paying for it myself. It hasn't been easy, but I have appreciated the opportunity to learn so much more than I would have otherwise."

Another experience that helped me put into perspective the siren call of worldly treasures was an all-expense paid trip to Hawaii that Dean and I won. There I discovered the futility of eating lobster tail for breakfast, lunch and dinner. And found that my own bed at home was much superior in comfort to the plushest hotel bed on Waikiki Beach. Further, we learned as we mingled with people dripping with diamonds and dollars that boredom, loneliness, and anxiety rode the elevators with them. So few cared to be courteous or friendly. So we spent most of our time there with our dearest friends: warm, witty and wonderful Japanese people, whose charming but unpretentious homes showed their own handiwork, and whose gracious hospitality would impress the Queen of England.

Jesus said:

Lay not up for yourselves treasures upon earth, where moth and rust doth corrupt, and where thieves break through and steal: But lay up for yourselves treasures in heaven...For where your treasure is, there will your heart be also. (Mt. 6: 19-21)

"Riches are not from an abundance of worldly goods, but from a contented mind," said Mohammed.

The fact is inescapable: The things with which we identify control us. How we visualize ourselves tends to become a reality. Our time, talents, money and efforts are given to those things which we regard as desirable.

Wives and mothers who seek careers and fulfillment primarily outside of the home, while failing to fully meet the needs of their families, run the grave risk of losing the real treasures of life. For if a woman doesn't identify herself as a mother and homemaker, how can her heart and mind be concerned with nurturing and loving her husband and children?

Mothers Belong In the Home

After a fireside at which I spoke on the home and family, a young woman introduced herself to me in this manner: "Sister Payne, I'm a nurse and I have a little two-year-old boy that drives me up the walls. I found a very nice grandmotherly woman to tend

266

him every day. She just loves Billy and he loves her and she can handle him so much better than I can. So I have gone back to work at the hospital where I feel I'm really making a meaningful contribution to mankind. I have felt good about the whole thing until I heard you talk and now I'm a bit confused. Don't you think I am doing the right thing?

I put my arm around her shoulder and as kindly as I could told her I felt she was making the biggest mistake of her life. I said:

"Friend, nobody, but NOBODY should take your place as the mother of your little boy. Good mothers are *made*, not born! And it takes a lot of hard work, self-discipline and inspiration from the Lord and the priesthood to help us love and raise our children well.

"Think of what you are missing: funny little jokes shared, the first time he counts to ten; the discovery of a mushroom in the lawn; making cookies and playing in the bread dough. Oh sure, you can pick those things up later at night when you get home, like an old re-run on TV, but it just isn't the same as being there in person is it? Think of what he's missing, not having his 'real Mommy' there to share his growing and becoming.

"I believe I have made just about every mistake in the current 'How to Raise Kids' books, but I'm not a quitter and after 24 years and 12 children I am getting more confidence and winning some of the battles with my own worst self.

"Yes, I can sympathize with your dilemma. What you are trained to do and can do well (nursing) is not what you should be doing right now. What you should be doing right now (learning to be a good mother) makes you feel like a miserable failure. It is a paradox that a woman can devote decades of her time and talents to the study of Motherhood and still not feel she has enough hours to graduate. Just don't give up. It would astound you to know just how many people are interested in you personally and want to help you succeed. Number one on the list is your Heavenly Father and following him are your husband, parents, the Prophet and President of the Church, the Relief Society, and literally thousands! With a team like that you can't lose!"

A child can understand and cooperate with your need to be gone from the home occasionally for a church responsibility or good samaritan service, but when it is every day that you are gone from him, physically, mentally and spiritually, he will begin to feel rejected, unloved, and uncared for. And rejection is the most enervating and destructive experience a human being can suffer. It withers the soul with self-doubt and dries up faith. When a mother leaves her children to work day after day, the child feels rejected and neglected. Subconsciously he feels she would rather be somewhere else with someone else, and so does her husband!

She is bound by only 24 hours in a day and limited physical and emotional energy. When the interests and pressures of a career outside the home siphon off her physical strength and emotional reserve, and deaden her interest in homemaking and mothering, you can be sure that a woman isn't going to have left over what it takes to minister to the needs and desires of her husband and children. The clock becomes the metronome and she dances to its tune. Meals prepared in 20 minutes, house clutter shoved into the nearest hiding place, and children hurried into bed. "If it's quick and easy, that's for me," say working mothers.

Women who leave their family to work outside the home to lay up material treasures will find themselves robbed of their opportunities for spiritual and cultural development, which in turn will rob their children of treasures that money cannot buy.

This challenge is one of the most fundamental problems the Latter-day Saint woman faces. If we choose a course that will weaken our homes, it will devitalize the Church and undermine the nation. The consequences have eternal significance.

Seeking Beauty, Wisdom, and Spirituality

> Women are the poetry of the world in the same sense as the stars are the poetry of heaven. Clear, light-giving, harmonious, they are the terrestrial planets that rule the destinies of mankind.
>
> Hargrave

I wish we women would put forth a little more effort to live up to the nice things men write about us. There are three spheres of influence or stewardship in which a woman operates. First, as a woman, second, as a wife, and third, as a mother. If all women, young and old, were to be aware of the importance of cultivating things of beauty and refinement such as art, music and literature, the impact upon our society would hasten the millennium. When there is so little time for us to sample all that is lovely, virtuous or praiseworthy that life's banquet offers to us, to seek out or support the sensational or debasing is wasting our stewardship.

Goethe said:

A man should hear a little music, read a little poetry, and see a fine picture every day of his life, in order that the worldly cares may not obliterate the sense of the beautiful which God has implanted in the human soul.

Cheap, shoddy things try to intrude upon our consciousness, from early until late, like a garrulous salesman stealing valuable time. But we must plan, organize and hew precious moments out of an unyielding day for the refined and aesthetic. Let's be beautiful—for keeps!

Education is desirable, but wisdom is a precious commodity. Recently, I discovered a remarkable letter written by Eliza R. Snow, when she was President of the Relief Society, to Mary Elizabeth Rollins Lightener. It outlined the responsibilities of the sisters and then closed with this superb answer to Women's Liberation:

Tell the sisters to go forth and discharge their duties in humility and faithfulness and the Spirit of God will rest upon them and they will be blest in their labors. *Let them seek for wisdom instead of power and they will have all the power they have wisdom to exercise.*

We are counseled in the 88th Section of the Doctrine and Covenants to "seek ye diligently and teach one another words of wisdom; yea, seek ye out of the best books words of wisdom; seek learning, even by study and also by faith" (verse 118).

God created woman to be a refining and noble influence on man. He gave man strong drives and ambitions that he may conquer the world and subdue all things, but those same instincts and drives can debase a man unless he is inspired and encouraged by women to conquer himself, subdue his appetites and to be tender, noble and refined. When women become crude and coarse, men do not generally have the strength to guard virtue and instigate righteousness. It is the feminine influence that draws out the virtuous and spiritual qualities in man.

269

Wheresoever She Was—There Was Eden!

What is our responsibility as wives? To settle for nothing less than an eternal marriage, for marriage was ordained of God and He said:

Therefore shall a man leave his father and his mother and shall cleave unto his wife; and they shall be one flesh. (Gen. 2:24)

And also:

Therefore, if a man marry him a wife in the world, and he marry her not by me nor by my word, and he covenant with her so long as he is in the world and she with him, their covenant and marriage are not of force when they are dead, and when they are out of the world. (D&C 132:15)

Creating an eternal marriage requires a profound commitment not only to our mate but to God. We have to want to be with our husband or wife more than anything else in the world. Any couple, no matter how deeply and sincerely in love they were when they married, can fall out of love and become dissatisfied, disenchanted and unfaithful. If they let Satan deceive them, or if they fail to keep all of the Lord's commandments, they give the adversary power over them. With God there is no coercion. If we don't want to spend eternity with our mate, we won't.

I read an interesting parable once: "In a dream I visited the Lord's vast storehouse. I said to the angel in charge:

I'm sick of the fruits of war, hatred, lust, greed, lies and blasphemy. Please give me some love, peace, honesty and godliness."

The angel turned to me smiling and said: "Oh but we don't stock fruits. We give only the seeds!"

We have the seeds for successful marriages in the gospel of Jesus Christ and the priesthood provides the benevolent help and guidance we need to nurture the seeds.

To me the most significant counsel ever given on marriage is found in Ephesians 5:22-29. The prophet Joseph Smith also quoted it in his teachings:

Wives, submit yourselves unto your own husbands, as unto the Lord.

For the husband is the head of the wife, even as Christ is

270

the head of the church: and he is the saviour of the body.

Therefore as the church is subject unto Christ, so let the wives be to their own husbands in every thing.

Husbands, love your wives, even as Christ also loved the church, and gave himself for it; ...

So ought men to love their wives as their own bodies. He that loveth his wife, loveth himself.

For no man ever yet hated his own flesh; but nourisheth and cherisheth it, even as the Lord the church: ...

For this cause shall a man leave his father and mother, and shall be joined unto his wife, and they two shall be one flesh. ...

Let every one of you in particular so love his wife even as himself; and the wife see that she reverence her husband.

Embodied here are many profound concepts. First, when we enter the eternal marriage covenant we no longer have a brother-sister relationship, here or after death. Ours is a new relationship wherein our husband is our personal representative of the Lord Jesus Christ. We are to submit ourselves unto him, *as unto the Lord*, for he is our steward and is personally responsible to the Lord for our spiritual and temporal salvation. "The husband is the head of the wife and the Savior of the body." The husband is to call forth the wife in the resurrection by the power of the priesthood.

When he is using the gifts of the priesthood righteously, a man may obtain the inspiration, wisdom and power necessary to bless (and save) his wife and family. And if the wife is rebellious and does not submit to his counsel or direction, she cheats herself of the divine counsel he has received and his help in her own stewardship and that of her children. She also denies her husband the opportunity to magnify his priesthood and use the powers of heaven to bless her.

I once heard a young husband say:

My wife is a natural-born "improver." She hates to see me doing things in my own inefficient way. She always has a better way to do things—hers!

But if it's the last thing I ever do, I am determined to make my own mistakes!

271

Bravo for that young man. Perhaps it's men who need a little liberation—from all the "natural-born improvers" in the world. "Therefore as the church is subject unto Christ, so let the wives be to their husbands in every thing."

If we women will honor the authority and direction which God gives to us through the priesthood, and submit ourselves for counsel, we and our children will be blessed with power to keep the commandments. We will know the joy of divine love and our "confidence will wax strong in the Lord." This I know for a certainty.

The second marvelous aspect of this passage in Ephesians is that the Lord didn't just ask the wives to submit to their husbands and then let the husbands become tyrants. How about this for a challenge to men? "Husbands, love your wives, *even as Christ* also *loved* the church, and *gave himself for it*; ...So ought men to love their wives as their own bodies."

The divine love and concern for women shown by the Father and his Son is manifested in this counsel: Men are to emulate the Savior's example in loving, counseling, teaching, and ministering to the needs of their wives. He only asked that they give everything they have, even their lives if necessary.

How glorious a privilege it is to live in a marriage relationship that is blessed and guided by God, and that will not be ended, but grow eternally.

Manners Are Morals

Phyllis McGinley speaks of manners as morals, and courtesy as "exercises of the body for the sake of the mind and soul." Good manners are one way of teaching virtue, for is not courtesy a demonstration of "love thy neighbor as thyself?" And in marriage as in the family relationship, "A noble man is led by women's gentle words." (Goethe)

I adore cooking because my husband and children are so generous with the thanks and praise. Dean has taught the boys to hold my chair for me and he always reminds them to thank me for every meal, even the Heidi suppers (bread, milk and cheese). They hold doors open for me and help me on with my coat. Daily I can see how going through the motions of love and respect for mother can become a genuine love and appreciation for her. It tides them over the times when they want to say: "Hey, Mom, get off my back will you, you're bugging me!" The reverse is also true. If we women encourage men and boys in the art of becoming gentlemen what miracles may be wrought.

One of the major events at the Mrs. America Pageant was the cooking and entertaining competition. We were given 2½ hours to prepare a gourmet dinner called the "Fireman's Feast" because the firemen and their wives were our guests. After surviving a few minor catastrophes (like getting a knife caught in my portable mixmaster just as I was about to be interviewed on a roving TV, and being required to make coffee, which I hadn't the faintest idea how to do), whom should I bump into but a tall handsome Negro gentleman. He asked who I was and then informed me that he was Chuck Robinson and this was his wife, Edna, and they had been assigned as our guests for dinner! My legs grew roots and I felt some portentous or foreboding thing was about to occur—like his asking why the Negroes couldn't hold the priesthood. I visualized the headlines in all the papers: "Mrs. Utah causes a riot at the Mrs. America Pageant!" But rays of sunshine broke through those black clouds a moment later when I went to serve them the extremely well-done coffee. (It had boiled for one solid hour because I didn't know how long to cook it!) Edna looked up at me and said: "No thank you, if you don't mind, Mrs. Utah, we don't drink coffee!"

"Well bless your heart!" said I, "Those are the most beautiful words I have heard today." And then we discovered that they were a Seventh-Day Adventist couple who observed the same code of health as our Word of Wisdom. She would be receiving her sociology degree from the University that next week, and was a counselor in the high school. He was a fireman and also involved in giving of his time freely to a youth program called ABC—Any Boy Can. Her wisdom and charm captivated us and his sense of humor was delightful. They were both spiritually oriented. The hour spent dining with them was over too soon. Three days later, after the final Pageant on nationwide TV, we were at the Mayor's Coronation Ball when one of the Judges came up to me and congratulated me on being 2nd runner-up. Then he said: "By the way, I'd like to know how you entertained your young couple at the

273

Fireman's Feast."

"Oh boy, I was petrified because I had never entertained a Negro couple before. But they were two of the most intelligent and charming people we have met during the whole ten days in San Diego. Why do you ask?"

Dr. Littner then said: "Well something very interesting happened after you and your husband left the stage after dinner. Out of all the 51 couples which you girls entertained in this event, your couple were the only ones who came up and thanked the judges for inviting them. They told us how much they had enjoyed being your guests. You know, we were very impressed."

The lump in my throat was enormous but I managed to say: "Don't give my any credit, Dr. Littner. They knew how to express brotherhood on a one-to-one basis—where it really counts! Never has a courteous thanks meant quite so much to me, except from my husband."

The Food of Love

In marriage we become what we ingest. Love will shrivel and die when fed upon a diet of four letter words and filth. Movies and literature like some of the Love Stories of today are a lie. A heroine who proclaims her undying love in profane, gutter language is grotesque. She turns me off. Obscene or profane language does just the opposite to love—instead of refining and uplifting us, it dehumanizes and debases that which is sensitive and God-like within us. S. Hayakawa, the president of riot-ridden San Francisco State University said:

> Courteous and reasonable words, addressed even to those with whom we are in sharp disagreement, are invitations to discourse and debate. They are an acknowledgment of the other fellows' basic humanity. Obscenities on the other hand, are a studied rejection of the other person's rationality, and therefore his humanity....The radicals' (rioters) claim that they want a more humane society while they use a kind of language that makes humane relationships impossible is the ultimate hypocrisy of the youth rebellion!

"Love means you never have to say you're sorry" is another falsehood that is sweeping the country. It denies the blessed prin-

274

ciple of repentance, and the opportunity of saying we are sorry for mistakes and ignorance. It denies that improvement is important, but purports we should be content with ourselves "as is."

Whatever is "virtuous, lovely, or of good report or praiseworthy" will feed our love and nurture our divine natures. The physical, emotional and spiritual intimacy that marriage should have will be enhanced by expressing our love with exquisite and poetic language and spiritually elevating art and music. Those examples of the fine arts which elicit from us the most pure and noble responses will inspire a love affair that the world knows nothing about. One of the significant experiences of our courtship was the reading of Elizabeth Barret Browning's love poems, "Sonnets From the Portuguese," high on a mountaintop, overlooking breathtaking Utah Valley. And we have continued to share and give expression to our innermost thoughts and feelings through the great masterpieces of art, literature and music. It is the food of love.

Suffer Little Children to Come

The first commandment given to Adam was to multiply and replenish the earth. The greatest privilege God has given us is to participate in the godly function of procreation—to create life, and to become like him. Those who don't have the desire and aren't willing to have children profane the gift of God, which is to participate in eternal creation. The perpetuation of the universe is dependent upon godly procreation.

Having children and perpetuating the family is fundamental to the whole design of earth life. To make parenthood an inferior role, or to proclaim that having more than one or two children is immoral is the basest of lies.

Well might every Latter-day Saint couple echo the words of the Savior when He said: "Suffer little children to come unto me, and forbid them not: for of such is the kingdom of God." (Lk. 18:16) How can a child know and come to the Savior if he is never given the opportunity to obtain a body and earth-life experience? The greatest purifying influence in this earth always has been the coming of the sweet and innocent spirits of new-born babes from the presence of our Heavenly Father. Take this influence away and the earth would be wasted and desolate indeed.

When my husband's grandmother, Mary Smith Ellsworth, was a young woman in Lehi, it was fashionable to have tiny waists. The young women stated that they didn't want to have a horde of children like their mothers and lose their small waists and pretty figures. They also didn't want more than one or two children so they could educate them properly. As Grandmother sat in a testimony meeting she was suddenly given the gift of tongues to interpret a message from the Lord, which stated:

I, the Lord, love the women of Zion above all other women on the earth for their willingness to bear the choice sons and daughters of God in this last dispensation, and when they have finished their missions on earth they will be thrice welcome in my Kingdom, and crowned above all other women.

The Lord has not made us wait to try Godhood. We are given the power to create life and to save it. In Moses 6:59 we read:

By reason of transgression cometh the fall, which fall bringeth death, and inasmuch as ye were born into the world by water, and blood, and the spirit, which I have made, and so ye must be born again into the kingdom of heaven, of water, and of the spirit, and be cleansed by blood, even the blood of mine Only Begotten; that he might be sanctified from all sin, and enjoy the words of eternal life in this world, and eternal life in the world to come, even immortal glory;

For by the water ye keep the commandment; by the Spirit ye are justified, and by the blood ye are sanctified.

A child enters this world through the three elements of water, blood and spirit. A mother sacrifices her blood to give life and become a savior by making mortality possible, by providing the elements of water and blood. That also is the symbolism by which we enter back into our Heavenly Father's kingdom. And the husband and father becomes a savior by conferring on his child the saving ordinances of baptism (water) and the gift of the Holy Ghost (spirit) through the priesthood. He also teaches his children the saving principles of the gospel and to accept the atonement of Christ (blood). For us to be given such honor and power as that of creation and salvation in the context just mentioned, is to partake of the divine nature of God. It is becoming like God more

276

than in any other way.

Blessed are the mothers of the earth, for they have combined the practical and the spiritual into the workable way of human life. They have darned little stockings, mended little dresses, washed little faces and have pointed little eyes to the stars and little souls to eternal things.

Stinger

The popular notion that abortion is of little concern is another of Satan's counterfeits, because to God it is the same as murder and the shedding of innocent blood. The law punishes attempted murder and the idea that life can be taken at the will of human individuals is a dangerous and evil falsehood. Abortion is an echo of Satan's plaint: "There is no God."

Motherhood lies at the foundation of happiness in the home, and of prosperity in the nation. God has laid upon men and women very sacred obligations with respect to motherhood, and they are obligations that cannot be disregarded without involving divine displeasure. To be a successful father or a successful mother is greater than to be a successful general or a successful statesman.

President Joseph F. Smith

Homemaking—The Most Noble Profession

The most important business of life goes on in the home. Eternal relationships are to be cultivated and cherished there. In the home and the family is where all the most meaningful relationships in life are fostered and tested. One of the last statements that President Joseph Fielding Smith said before he died was this:

The family is the most important organization in time or in eternity. Our purpose in life is to create for ourselves eternal family units. There is nothing that will ever come into your family life which is as important as the sealing blessings of the temple and then keeping the covenants made in connection with this order of celestial marriage.

April Conference, 1972

Brother Neal Maxwell made this statement about the home and family in a talk at Brigham Young University:

It is easy for us to love people in a faraway country be-

277

cause they make no demands on us. One really tests the principle of love when he is third in line to brush his teeth in a busy family bathroom! What I admire about the Church is its insistence that you and I face up to the principle of love where it really can be tested—in our homes!

And daily it is tested with scenes like the following that occurred in our home: My husband had previously arranged for me to have dinner ready promptly at 6 p.m. for he had an important Stake Missionary meeting to attend. I had asked my daughters to please set the table so father would be assured that dinner was ready. Just a few minutes before the appointed hour, the girls were still gabbing. When Dean walked in and saw the table wasn't set he spoke up in a gentle way: "Why isn't dinner ready?" With resignation I asked: "Dear why don't our children ever threaten to run away?" Dean rose to the occasion and replied: "You know the answer to that. They know we'd pack their bags and kiss them goodbye!" Janice walked up to us with her hands on her hips and said: "Well, if we can stand to live with you, you ought to be able to stand to live with us!" We dissolved in laughter. But her statement has caused me serious reflection since. A happy, well-adjusted family should experience more than just toleration, or being able to "stand" to live with one another.

There should be hopes and dreams verbalized, confidences shared, commitment encouraged, the windows of heaven opened, ears listening to souls, weaknesses worked on together, and above all, love—God-like, unconditional, and eternal, flowing and vitalizing and regenerating every member.

Thoughts at the Finale

It was the final night of the Mrs. America Pageant and all the contestants were on stage, beautifully gowned and breathless with anticipation. In a few moments a new Queen would be chosen and crowned. The show was being televised coast to coast and there were thousands of people in the audience.

The events of the preceding ten days of competition came rushing into my mind as we waited backstage for our entrance. There had been failures—forgetting my banner and crown, not winning the child communication event (I had the most children of anyone), breaking my mixmaster, having the only defective pan-

278

cake griddle, watching with dismay as my centerpiece fell apart just as the judges got to it. But there were successes too—winning the entertainment award, placing high in driving, finances, and child communication.

But the judges weren't even aware of my greater successes. I had been able to tell the other contestants about my Golden Gleaner pin, the youth program of the Church, our year's supply of food, bearing my testimony. But the greatest success was in being able to call on my Heavenly Father and my husband to bless and heal me when I became violently ill the evening before the Pageant.

I was standing well and happy on stage as a result of one of the greatest blessings a woman can have in her lifetime—the power of the priesthood.

As the final scenes of the Pageant were played out and I found myself still standing as one of three finalists left on stage— the possibility of my being Mrs. America, remote though it had seemed before, was now something I had to consider. I felt it would be a mistake to leave my husband and children for a year to be a money-making project for someone else. But I also wondered if the Lord had some special purpose or mission for me to fulfill. As the emcee announced "Mrs. Utah, 2nd runner-up" I was relieved and happy, as was my husband who shared my emotions and embraced me.

As they brought the robe and crown I noticed that the crown was made of imitation diamonds. The robe, though a beautiful red velvet with white trim, would be retained by the man who owned the Pageant to be used again, year after year. As Mrs. Kansas was crowned Mrs. America, I thought, she is a Queen for only a short year. How typical of the honors of men. Does the Lord give imitation diamonds and fleeting honors? No, Jaynann, you have something so much more valuable and precious than she has. You have a beautiful white robe and veil that are the only robes of a real Queen, not for a day or a year but for eternity. You don't have to give them up to someone else next year. And you have twelve precious children that are genuine jewels to adorn your crown of eternal life if you live worthily. And finally, you have a Prince standing by your side who can and does call down

279

the blessings of heaven upon you and who loves you with the kind of a love the world only dreams about.

I can never forget that Christ loved me enough to die for me and asked my husband to love me as much as He does. Our Lord and King doesn't offer us just an imitation Kingdom with transient honors—but He offers us all that He has!

I am overwhelmed by the magnitude of God's love for us. And I know that to return His love and serve Him forever is the royal road to happiness here and eternal joy hereafter.

INTRODUCING—FRANCES N. BOYDEN

Frances Boyden is no ordinary woman! She marches to a different drummer as she wends her way through life, and her interests reach out in different directions than do those of other women. She has a-chieved and accomplished much, and in a variety of endeavors.

For years she has served as chairman of the Drama Committee of the YWMIA General Board; she now has a new assignment as member of the central committee responsible for the Promised Valley Theatre *recently established by the Church. She is a past president of the Utah Pharmaceutical Association Auxiliary. From 1963-65 she served as president of the Utah Women's State Legislative Council and became intimately involved with state level politics. She's a former Governor in the Society of the Descendents of the First Voyage of the Mayflower. She's also a member of Alpha Beta Theta literary sorority and Theta Alpha Phi dramatic honorary fraternity. In addition, she's a teacher of dramatics and speech— many talents, many varying interests!*

Frances graduated with a bachelor of arts degree in speech from the University of Utah, then taught school for four years before marrying Walter Everett Boyden. Walter is now a retired pharmacist. They are the parents of two talented children.

Her teaching and communications skills have made Frances an ideal person for supervising and training others in the various Church auxiliaries. She has served as in-service trainer and leader in the Primary and MIA, on several stake boards, and as a teacher, drama director, and counselor in the MIA as well as in the other organizations.

Perhaps it is her diversified interests which lead her to identify so carefully the many roles played by today's woman. The questions she asks at the end of the chapter are well worth real consideration by everyone.

JDC & DSC

THE MANY LIVES OF WOMAN
By
Frances N. Boyden

A terrible sense of inadequacy sometimes comes over me when I ponder on the fact that I am attempting to do so many things—play so many roles—in my daily life! But most of the time I feel serene, well organized, and in charge of the situation. And I realize that *all* women are playing many roles. I see in my life the continual challenge to fill many needs. But with the challenge come problems of balance, of perspective, and of changing responsiblities.

All women have the same challenge, the same need to function in many roles. Each person marches to a different drummer, but everyone of us finds herself with a variety of roles to play simultaneously.

Analyzing Our Roles

But every woman should take a look at her roles and their relative importance. She should ask herself, "Why am I doing the things I do? Am I achieving the things I want to achieve? Am I gaining satisfaction and fulfillment from my activities?

Several years ago I attended a women's conference at the University of Utah. The group was invited to list the roles they played in life and then evaluate them. We asked ourselves why we played certain roles, pondered what our motivation was, and determined whether or not our goal was being reached. We also tried to determine what were we doing that we really didn't want, or have, to do.

We listed in order the five roles we considered most important. This exercise was like drawing a map of one's own life. Here are some of the roles we play. Specifics, of course, will have to be filled in by each individual.

Roles of Women

1. Wife

2. Mother
3. Homemaker
4. Counselor
5. Daughter
6. Friend and neighbor
7. Family member, sister, cousin, niece, etc.
8. Teacher
9. Church worker and participant
10. Wage earner
11. Civic worker
12. Political worker
13. Traveler, student
14. Social participant

The above are not necessarily listed in order of importance—they are all important. The placement of emphasis depends on the individual, and the relative importance of the various roles can even change from time to time. But we must always be aware of what we're doing, and why. Our roles must provide us with individual growth, with pleasant social relationships, and with opportunities for service to others. For instance, number six is a special category to me. Good friends are a must in a good life. And to have friends, one must truly be a friend. True friends fill an important place in one's life that nothing else can fill, and the sharing of friendship makes better people.

Every Woman is Different

I remember when I first realized that women are not all alike. My mother was beautiful, perfectly groomed, and kept an immaculate house. She was charming, full of confidence, and very popular among her associates. I remember how proud I was of her when she came to my school to visit.

Mother was so efficient that everything around the home seemed to happen easily and with little fanfare. It never occurred to me to help with the house, except dishes—because I would just "get in the way." Besides, I always had to study.

My father's sisters were slower and were somewhat less attractive. Mother referred to them tactfully as "heavy." When I was in "the awkward stage," mother's friends would often meet mother and me on the street, greet her warmly, then look at me with great sympathy and say to each other, "My, isn't it too bad she doesn't look like her mother!"

"Takes after her father's side of the family."

"Although he was a very handsome man!"

"Somehow it doesn't come off as well on a girl."

Mother would always disregard these remarks and tell her friends how smart I was—in glowing detail. And she did it so well that I believed her!

Years later, after I finished college and was newly married, I couldn't believe what was happening to my house. Things piled up all around, the furniture got dusty, and even the walls and woodwork began to look strange. Taking care of things took me all day long!

Mother's rule had always been that she didn't go out before the housework was done. When she left for a party, a movie, a PTA or church meeting, her house was always in "dying" condition. No problem. Everything was always spic and span by 10:00 a.m. or earlier.

So I tried to follow in her footsteps. But if I waited to go out until everything was done, I couldn't ever go any place—until about midnight. And then I'd think of the story about the old lady who said, "Even while you're sleepin', the dust is a-layin', and the sheets is a-wrinklin'."

My husband has always been patient and very helpful. I soon found that I had a gift for organization, so with his support and a long list of faithful and talented day workers, the house was presentable and I "got out."

Each Makes Her Own Choices

I was teaching an in-service class one evening in the ward when one of the sisters asked a question so juvenile that I couldn't believe my ears. Here was a woman who kept a lovely home, furnished it in good taste, entertained beautifully—but she obviously wasn't at all aware of intangibles.

On the other hand, I had just the day before visited with a woman whose husband was a professor, and who had her own PhD in child psychology. Her house was a shambles, and she was at a complete loss to know what to do about it. She was miserable!

I told my cousin that as I assessed the role of woman in

today's society, if I had to choose between being "school smart" and "house smart," I'd take the latter—because the "house-home" aptitude is really the most important for your family—and, of course, makes everyone happier.

My cousin said, "But you don't have to choose. You can be both!" And she was right! Every woman can make her own choices, tailored to fit herself and her family. Indeed, choosing our roles properly is one of the greatest challenges of life!

Stimulation From New Activity Is Needed

As our two children were born and began to grow, we delighted in them, we enjoyed being with them and watching them achieve and develop. But as they became older, I realized that I, as a person, needed more challenges outside the home. I was becoming homebound and needed the stimulation of outside activities. I worked in the Primary, Sunday School and Relief Society—but I always went back to MIA—and drama. I was also active in my sorority and other civic and social groups.

In the autumn of 1954, my husband purchased a beautiful old home, and we moved from our smaller house. Our daughter, Ann Marie, was entering high school that year, and Walter, Jr. was in the fourth grade.

I remember remarking to a friend that I wished time could be like it is in most of the comic strips, and that my family could forever remain at the ages we were then! But I didn't get my wish—we went right on growing up and older. However, we did have the sense to savor the happiness of those days, the togetherness of our family, and we never took these blessings for granted. In fact, I feel that one of our greatest assets has been an acute awareness of our blessings as life has moved forward. We truly have grateful hearts! There are so many little daily joys in family life to be thankful for, to say nothing of the big, overpowering ones!

Determining Skills And Identifying Weaknesses

I had been president of Walt's elementary school PTA the year before we moved and was den mother for his cub scout troop. In the latter I learned a real lesson! We're not all cut out to do all things. This fact is clearly stated in the Book of Mormon—in Moroni. We have each been given certain gifts and talents. I

285

think that the position of den mother was the greatest challenge I've ever met in my whole life! One of the tasks of life is to identify our skills and also determine our weaknesses. The most productive life is achieved when we devote our energies to areas where we have the greatest capabilities. Yet we never know if we have ability in an area until we try it and test ourselves. Part of life must be devoted to exploring new horizons and testing our skills and capacities for interest and enjoyment. Without this exploration, life becomes habitualized, and we accomplish little.

Doing Something And Being Somebody

In 1957, everything at home was under control, and our daughter was in college. She came home one day, very much out of patience, and said—"I wish Professor 'So-and-so' were a Mormon."

"Why?" I asked curiously. This was the teacher of a large performing organization.

"Well, then his wife could be president of the Relief Society, and she wouldn't have to keep coming to school and getting in everybody's hair! She's the type of lady who has to be 'doing something' and 'being somebody.' "

"Doing something" and "being somebody" are legitimate needs, and very demanding ones. But there is a time and place for such needs to be met. Happiness is found when one finds appropriate situations in which to use her abilities—situations which will allow her to contribute to the well-being of others while continuing to increase in personal growth and satisfaction.

What a marvelous organization our Church is to fill such needs! For me it has given personal growth and satisfaction and also opened the way to non-Church growth.

I was stake drama director when a neighbor who was in charge of teacher placement in our school district called and told me he could not find a teacher for a traditional drama class at the junior high school where I had taught before I was married. Would I consider going back into teaching—six periods a day, English, speech and drama? The thought frightened me. It had been twenty-three years. When I told my husband and my mother about the call, they both laughed. "It's been too long," they said. "Everything's changed. You couldn't stand it!" And my husband added, "I

286

don't want you to work. There is enough to do here at home and in the Church."

But somehow I wanted to try—especially when they laughed—and I felt I was needed at the school. The situation offered opportunity for personal fulfillment while helping to serve others. I'm very grateful that I did. Even my husband now admits that these teaching years have meant growth for all of us.

New Roles Add Perspective To Life

Meeting and guiding all the different students from various backgrounds has helped to stabilize our values and has made us recognize and evaluate the truly meaningful things in life.

My mother thought it was sort of disgraceful for me to teach when I had a perfectly wonderful husband to provide for me. Mother could have done any number of things professionally, but her generation felt that "ladies" did not work. Apparently mine did too, because some people started to treat me as if I had started to "go out in my nightgown" when I took this assignment. They were, I think, appalled! In 1957, if I had gone into interior decorating or a gift shop, it would have been socially acceptable for a married woman and a mother. But *teaching*—and just anybody's children! (The greatest riddle in life is the fact that parents consider their own children so special and superior but most others a bore, a drag, or downright offensive. And sometimes they are.)

I sincerely believe that every intelligent mother and father should be drafted into teaching—in public school—for a month or so, every once in a while. One sees one's own children in perspective, as others see them, and is filled with compassion. I really felt quite noble about going into teaching—but was soon brought down to earth with humility.

What a picture of life and people the schoolroom is—the individual differences in culture, intelligence, talents, beliefs, manners, health, financial situations, etc. A classroom of forty students in a public school is like a chart of our population. And you realize that a small percentage will have to be trained and prepared to lead and direct the others—and that skills have to be taught and attitudes shaped for happy and productive lives.

Teaching is like having a curtain raised, revealing "the real thing." Many women live in a closeted world of people just like

287

themselves and lose track of the fact that there are many and varied types of people "out there," all of whom need to be dealt with, helped, directed, recognized, appreciated—and loved. And we learn many truths from these people.

My family were cooperating very well at home. I took two years away from school and then taught three periods the next year, because I was needed for the drama class.

In 1965, I went back to a full day like an old fire-horse. I really liked my English classes also—*Romeo and Juliet, A Tale of Two Cities,* and Greek mythology.

While I was teaching three periods, one of my college professor acquaintances asked me if I were still teaching. I answered, "Only three periods." His response—"*I* wouldn't consider teaching more than *one* class a day!"

Why? I'm glad all teachers aren't like that!

I love to teach! I would like to tell everyone in the world about my last year's students. They were marvelous. So much is made of the disinterested and rebellious youth. I wish we could hear more of "kids" like "mine." Of course, we had problems—which incidentally rob one of a great deal of energy and sometimes a night's sleep—but for the most part the youth are tremendous. They are going to be all right—but wise and prepared teachers must stay in there—in that classroom—guiding, directing, listening, encouraging, and helping them to build good self images, whatever their talents and abilities may be.

That the press often judges teachers "en masse," and that some speakers, even educators, seem to delight in making teachers the springboard for tasteless jokes, is sometimes hard to take. When I come home from school, I often sit quietly in my car in our driveway, or I ride around for a while to change roles from a concerned and involved teacher to a loving and pleasant wife and mother. And fortunately, my family is still proud of me.

Maturing Years Provide Opportunity For Church And Civic Roles

As we increase in years, we gain the maturity and ability to function effectively in new roles. Often they are positions of leadership. The challenges are great, but the satisfaction and opportunity for enjoyment in our roles are also multiplied. Many of the struggles and difficulties of earlier years have been overcome by this period. In overcoming them we have grown in stature and wisdom. This can be the most rewarding time of our lives in many ways.

In the fall of 1961, I was called to the drama committee of the General Board of the MIA. This work has been a real challenge and a great joy. I'm now looking forward to working and teaching in the Church in the beautiful, newly-restored "Promised Valley Theatre."

In 1963 I became the president of the Womens' Legislative Council of the State of Utah. I have always enjoyed politics, and I wish everyone could attend this type of council. Women who participate become conversant with current legislative issues and hear our governmental problems both pro and con from the experts. They learn why lawmaking isn't as simple as it seems to "armchair generals." Nothing is black or white, all good or all bad. I have learned much from many wonderful people.

I have had the privilege the past three years of serving on the advisory committee to the Utah Technical College at Salt Lake City. My sights have been raised any my understanding of people enlarged by this experience. I am impressed with the good accomplished at this college and the caliber of the faculty and student body. This new role has given me a chance to serve and also influenced my entire philosophy concerning education and the way our youth should plan their futures. I have become more aware that parents and educators both used to stress far too much the importance of an academic college education for all young people. The youth whose talents and aptitudes did not conform to this end were inadvertently made to feel inferior. Pictures of college graduates in caps and gowns were posted in many schools with a caption concerning the stiff competition ahead. This pressure discouraged many young people and even made some of them anxious, nervous and afraid.

The fact is that academic college isn't for everyone—and why should it be? The Lord gave us different talents and aptitudes, and these should be developed in each person according to that which has been given. Students are now sent proudly to technical college— and they should always have been.

Some of our young people still haven't learned this important lesson, however. Just several years ago the president of the Utah

Home Builder's Association gathered a group of young people together and offered to pay them to learn the skills involved in home building. These were young people who needed training and whose aptitudes pointed in this direction. But the president did not have one "taker." The consensus of opinion among the young people seemed to be, "You're nothing if you do this kind of labor, even if you work like a dog! If we're going to be nothing, we'd just as soon do nothing also." The pay he offered for this work didn't seem to mean a thing.

All Family Members Fill Several Roles

My family has not been idle while I have pursued my many interests. Each of them has also had many projects and we all have helped each other. This mutual help and cooperation is vital as we each pursue our personal goals. Ann Marie builds ships, shows her poodles, and has many other hobbies besides her work as an advertising executive. She writes, produces, and directs commercials, plays and movies. Walter just finished his master's thesis in musical theatre at the "U" and will continue for a doctorate at BYU. He sings in at least one sacrament meeting every Sunday, does many shows and revues, and is a member of the Tabernacle Choir. Dad, at present, is all wound up in Kiwanis for which he is the Utah-Idaho Lieutenant Governor, besides his profession and Church work. Life is full and busy—and wonderful for all of us. Each and every talent comes from our Heavenly Father—and every person should confidently develop his own to the fullest. Each of us needs to follow his own talents and aptitudes with dignity and pride! Success in achievement makes for true happiness, and there are many different types of work to be done in our society.

But right now, I'm going to take a look at this article, list the activities I've mentioned—and re-evaluate my life, asking myself— "*Why* am I doing these things? Am I doing what I really *want* to do? Am I doing what I *should* do? And are these activities *best* for me—and for everyone else?" Won't you join me?

290

INTRODUCING—LENORE ROMNEY

"Wife, mother, lover of the Gospel of Jesus Christ, concerned citizen"—this was Lenore's response to our biographical questionnaire asking for a concise identifying phrase. It describes her well.

But that is not all, and this page will not nearly suffice for us to list all the accomplishments of Lenore LaFount Romney. Here is a woman held in such high esteem that she's been the recipient of no less than six honorary doctorates! Religious Heritage of America named her "Churchwoman of the Year" for 1972. The National Conference of Christians and Jews awarded her its silver medallion for "Inspiring Leadership in Raising Children of Good Will." She received the Hadassah Woman Zionist Organization of America Award.

She is the Vice Chairman of the Executive Committee for the National Center for Voluntary Action. She has been a national director of the YWCA and American Field Services and was National Chairman of the National Conference of Christians and Jews in 1970-71.

During the interval that her husband, George, was Governor of Michigan, she campaigned for constitutional reform, an improved school system, and worked for the Human Resource Council. In 1970 she was a candidate for the United States Senate, and relates that the experience "gave me new insights into the bruising aspects of running for political office, and a need for greater citizen participation, involvement and willingness to become informed."

Lenore has served in many ward and stake capacities in the Church and written that "an opportunity to participate in Church programs has shaped my life significantly—studying, teaching, listening and discussing spiritual aspects of living..." She frequently speaks to LDS youth groups as well as on panels at universities.

We were thrilled that she made time to respond to those who seek to redefine women's roles. She champions the cause of virtue and we applaud her words. JDC & DSC

291

ARE WE LIBERATED?
by
Lenore Romney

The singing in our land that Walt Whitman wrote about in his poem, "I Hear America Singing," has changed to shouting. Today we hear America shouting—many groups, blacks, youth, women—shouting for "liberation." Some of the most strident voices are those of women. They complain that they are suffering from an identity crisis related to a role that is stereotyped, dull, unfulfilling, and inferior to that of a man's. Most educators and psychologists tell us that there is no question but that women today are suffering from a sense of not belonging, or apathy, or being meaningless. It is this meaninglessness that has made women libbers out of so many as they search for something to make them feel important.

The Need To Reach Personal Potentials

Unfortunately, young women are constantly barraged with propaganda to the effect that they cannot be fulfilled in today's society unless they have careers outside of the home. Typical of the current attitudes are the ones expressed by Betty Friedan in *The Feminine Mystique* and by Lucy Komisar in her article, "The New Feminism." Mrs. Friedan, after making a thorough study of young married women, reported that the general response was "I feel empty, incomplete, as if I don't exist." Many reported that they waited all day for their husbands to come to make them feel alive. Lucy Komisar, after her interviews with many married women, quotes one of them as saying, "I felt so trapped when my baby was born. I wanted to leave my husband and the child." Miss Komisar concludes that "women have been forced to accept an inferior role in society. We have come to believe in our own inferiority." The words "trapped" and "inferior' come up time and again in depicting young women's feelings about themselves and their role as wives and mothers. This position has become so prevalent that many young mothers who are happy in their motherhood think they need to apologize for this "unnatural" attitude.

It is healthy and natural for each person to want to feel relevant and pertinent. After all, life is the most magnificent of gifts, and it deserves the best searching and the best living. One of the most eminent psychologists of our day, the late Dr. Abraham Maslow, had some interesting conclusions in this regard. He contended that all mankind strives for self-actualization, creativity, and productivity. Man tries to realize his potentialities and become fully human, everything that a person can become. He taught that capacities clamor to be used—that each person wants to be able to contribute effectively. To do this, each person needs self-esteem and the respect and approval she receives from others. These are love needs which are as important to emotional health as are the physical needs of food, shelter, and clothing. Thus when women do not feel that they are contributing, that they do not have the respect and esteem of others, they become frustrated.

LDS Women Can Define The Essence Of Womanhood

It seems to me that we, as Latter-day Saint women, have a unique opportunity to make a marvelous contribution by defining the essence of womanhood and the fantastic way women can contribute to this age. I believe that unless the women in our country understand their role and take an active part in preventing and solving the social, human, and moral problems all around us, America will go down the drain. This may sound dramatic, but when we see the attack that is currently being made on the three most fundamental institutions in our land: the home, the church, and the government, it is obvious that we must realistically evaluate our role and help other women understand what a great calling or "vocation" is theirs.

But first each woman must be secure in her identity. All about us are cries of "who am I?"—the core of the so-called identity crisis. Unless we know who we are, we do not know what our function is in society nor how we fit into the whole. More importantly, we lack self-esteem and become depressed. The situation in our country today is similar to that described in the Old Testament when it was recorded that there was darkness throughout the land. The Israelites, however, had light in their dwellings! They had light because they were consecrated to the Lord their God and knew

293

that His imprint was upon them. We, too, can have light in our dwellings, knowing that the imprint of our Creator is upon us and that we are literally his daughters. We know that the center of all knowledge rests on that fact and that as a daughter of the Almighty, each woman can inherit His kingdom and be a partaker of all that He has, now and forever. Thus her worth is innate, assured, and she has no "hang-ups" as far as identity is concerned. She is liberated or free to perfect herself and thus become eligible to inherit all that is in the earth.

Just as her worth is innate, so is her equality before God. The scriptures tell us that every soul that is born into this world has the light of Christ in him and that the gospel, with its magnificent blessings, "is for all mankind alike." The scriptures also make it clear that "it was not good for man to be alone,"—that it was his mate that completed him and made it possible for the earth to realize the full measure of its creation.

How can a woman believe her role is inferior to that of any man on earth? She knows the incomparable opportunity that is available to her in the home. Raising a family is not a simple task. One filled with boredom or ennui will never realize it, for it is the most demanding—and rewarding—of life's opportunities.

Dr. Mary Coleman, an eminent and thorough scholar and scientist, has said that it takes more intelligence, skill, and character to run a home and raise a family successfully than it does to run a giant corporation such has General Motors.

How much we have to give to this generation! How desperately our youth need to know of the happiness that results from knowing, understanding, loving, and obeying God! Certainly no Latter-day Saint woman can wonder about her role or her ability to make a magnificent contribution at this crucial period in our history!

Opportunities Exist in Each Stage of Life

There is more than identity, innate equality and the acceptance of the magnitude of her traditional role that needs to be understood by those who are concerned about enhancing the self-image of women. In each stage of her life, as a teenager, a wife, a mother, and a citizen, she has the opportunity and privilege of making unique contributions to our society. According to the

294

way she measures up, the quality of our homes—the core of our society—is importantly determined.

There are those who discount private morality—they are all about us—yet they are the very ones who scream to high heaven about public morality. It is impossible to have public morality without personal integrity and high personal moral conduct. The future of our nation rests upon the personal strength of each individual.

The Importance of Values To The Teenage Woman

In this context, let us contemplate the role of womankind in our world first considering the teenage girl and the importance of her values and standards. In large measure, she is the one who determines the moral behavior of the dating period which in turn lays the foundation for marriage. Many boys will accept any intimacy that girls will permit, and press for ever-more familiarity. This was dramatically pointed up in a documented report which showed the promiscuity of most young boys in Sweden. When asked the reason for their blatant promiscuous behavior, the boys listed permissiveness in the home, mothers and fathers both working (thus little supervision being provided) and the accessibility of automobiles. But they noted that the most important reason of all was the complete lack of standards or morals of the girls!

And what about girls in our own country? I was indignant to hear a so-called "expert" on the Today Show say that sex was a way of life for the teenager and that he would not hesitate to give "the pill" to his teenage daughter. Many mothers in the suburbs have told me that they do not know whether to give the pill to their teenage daughters. These mothers do not know what constitutes acceptable behavior among dating teenagers, and are confused by current literature, movies and the prevailing acceptance of "liberalized" sex standards.

After listening to them and to the "expert" on the Today Show, I thought of my youth. I know I could not have been fulfilled in my womanhood had I not been taught definite standards by my parents. What would I have done had my father said as did the Today Show guest that he would not hesitate to endorse experimental sex and the pill for his teenage daughter? When I think of a statement like that going out across the nation inviting whatever for his teenager, I cannot but weep for the child, and for others whose parents might be influenced by this "expert." That same "authority" stated that although sex was a fact of life for unmarried youths, that babies should not be. He did not state that every privilege has great responsibilities, and that whether babies result or not the responsibilities are still there. He forgot to tell his listeners that sex has great emotional repercussions, that it is one of the most powerful and magnificent forces on earth. Would we be liberating our children by permitting them to experiment with dynamite? Yet there are innumerable "experts" such as Dr. Albert Ellis who lectures around the country, primarily on college campuses, preaching that "pre-marital sex is very good. It helps young people decide who they want for a marriage partner..." and "If a person doesn't wish to be faithful or thinks he cannot be faithful, I don't see why he would have to promise fidelity at the time of marriage..." If it took premarital sex to help young people decide whom they wanted to marry, then Marilyn Monroe's marriage should have been the happiest. Instead, she committed suicide.

I resent with all my heart the fact that some so-called "experts" have become the authorities for moral conduct and living. These are the ones who would tear up the eternal verities by the roots and substitute the opinions of men. As Latter-day Saint women, we have been taught to honor the precepts of Divine authority. Einstein, famous as the most eminent of scientists, wrote that in former decades the precepts of the Bible and its teachings were accepted by believer and infidel alike as the basic concepts for living. We know we cannot substitute man's opinions for God's laws. Man's standards change from month to month and year to year. They are no more stable than quicksand. Our whole structure of living, our whole value system, is based on Supreme Authority. We are not overwhelmed by an avalanche of changing mores nor by those who say that we need to be liberated from outmoded values. We know God's commandments are the same as they have always been and that we have never been excused from obeying them.

When Job was pressed with advice from men who challenged God's word, it is recorded that the Voice from the whirlwind answered them thus: "Wilt thou also disannul my judgment...that

296

thou mayest be righteous?..." (Job 40:8) In Jude we read: "Re-member...how that they told you there should be mockers...who should walk after their own ungodly lusts. These be they who separate themselves, sensual, having not the Spirit." (Jude 18-19)

Let us honor psychologists and sociologists for their scientific knowledge and the contribution that they make in their respective fields, but let us remind them that man has never been given the authority to abdicate the moral laws—to disannul His judgment that they "may be righteous."

Experimental or free sex is condoned by many who call them-selves members of the liberation movement. Liberation from what? Fidelity, keeping one's promises to one's dearest one? Liberation from home, family, knowing and loving God? From true discipline and self-mastery? From happiness and full development?

Each girl needs to know that she can epitomize the idealism of romance and womanhood and that without such qualities much of the loveliness of life is lost. Through her, her sweetheart can experience the thrill of awakening to the beauty of courtship and of love. Self-discipline, self-mastery and self-control become accept-able while anticipating fulfillment of the most personal relation-ship on earth. It is inconsistent for a generation of young people seeking identity to depersonalize the most intimate of all rela-tionships and make anonymous and trivial that which is uniquely the core of each person's personality and being.

I discussed their own ideas about "liberation" with hippies in Haight-Ashbury Park. The alienated youths attacked my generation for taking barbituates, alcohol, tobacco, sleeping pills, and tran-quilizers while criticizing them for drug addiction. My husband and I were able to gain their confidence by assuring them that we abstained from all drug stimulants or depressants.

Their charge of hypocrisy was at the base of their attitude about sex also. Unfaithfulness in marriage and hypocritical atti-tudes concerning premarital sex had made them willing to abandon the marriage covenant completely. But what about their happiness and that of their partners? I thought of the teenagers I had visited within homes for wayward girls. These young girls wept as they told me their former sweethearts were having affairs with other girls—and that their own babes were up for adoption. How they

297

longed for stability in their personal relationships and they asked, "Why didn't someone tell us how miserable we would be?"

Dr. Alexander Lowen, who has observed the emotional reaction of young women in a profoundly penetrating way, wrote, "If a woman has a series of lovers or husbands, she is like a child who has a series of parents. Such a child knows the meaninglessness of limited love. Lacking the secure feelings that she will be loved forever, the child searches instead for ways to please, impress or manipulate others. Similarly, the woman with a number of men in her life fails to develop a sense of herself as a sexual object. One man, one love, one enduring commitment—these are the ideal circumstances for the full development of woman's sexual nature."

Natalie Shainess, a psychiatrist, lecturer at the Columbia College of Physicians and Surgeons, and a member of the faculty of the William Alanson White Institute, wrote similarly in her article in *Mademoiselle*, July, 1972. She observed that a woman cannot be fulfilled without absolute trust in her partner. "For a woman, trust is essential. Absolute trust requires knowledge of one's mate."

The Wife's Role

We are already into the next step in our consideration of the role of womankind in our world: that of wife.

Eric Fromm in his "Art of Loving" writes that "Love is not blind, but knowledgeable. In love, one knows the other more deeply than does anyone else; one sees more deeply into him. One becomes acquainted with his inner rhythm and tastes, with his potentialities, even with his dream of himself."

This true knowledge of and love for one another is the foundation for eternal marriage—together with a longing to help the other become fulfilled in every way. One longs to see the other develop all of his talents to become everything that he or she is capable of becoming. This is the essence of love. But this does not come about automatically. To give of oneself without reservation, not asking whether the other is equally sharing in each chore, requires a mate who is sensitive and understanding. This results in respect and love for each other, understanding and appreciation for each one's contributions, and affectionate consideration with no thought about whether one is giving too much.

298

I believe that a large part of the current dissatisfaction with woman's role can be attributed to the casualness of sexual relationships that are temporary in nature. Naturally, the woman is filled with insecurity and is distrustful, becoming self-centered and apprehensive. In such a situation, rigid rules for the performance of each partner can be understood. The confusion is easy to understand after viewing such TV shows as one on national television recently. The panelists were supposed to be marriage experts—yet one of them stated that the sex act was "a little different from a handshake, but not much!" And no one challenged him—not one of the experts! Here we are dealing with the ultimate, and he treated it as trivial and inconsequential—to be shared by many.

The depth and quality of each personal relationship is the most important thing of all. If each partner really cares about the other and is committed to making that relationship a beautiful one forever, he will do whatever he can to make life a greater blessing for his mate.

I still remember my husband saying to me, as a bride, "If you treat your wife like a flower, she will give you perfume all of your life." I also remember vividly an incident that resulted in one of the greatest lessons of my life. We had been married only a few weeks when I became moody one morning over some misunderstanding. When my husband returned home from work, I was still in a bad mood. He became very serious as he said, "You can't be in a mood, because I depend upon you for my happiness." That statement hit me like a bolt. Good grief, if he depended upon me for the greatest thing of all, happiness, he was going to get it! What a fantastically important role—to be able to bring happiness to the one you love most.

During World War II, a Japanese couple was released from the internment camp to live with us temporarily. Each morning, the wife would say to me, "I no chose Joe, my mother chose Joe," and Joe would look so dejected. I thought of American girls. We have always had the opportunity to choose our mates, but after making our choice, many then seem set upon destroying their poor husbands through criticism, hagging, belittling and ridicule. I believe this is the antithesis of liberation. Our freedom to choose our mates should carry with it the responsibility of building them up, increasing their self-respect, and bringing them happiness.

Like women, men need to develop all of their talents and to enlarge their capacities for happiness and fulfillment. A wife plays a vital part in her husband's development of his self-esteem and self-image. The way she feels about him and his priesthood and whether she encourages him in all good deeds and pursuits are important factors in the way he feels about his callings and responsibilities. What is life unless manhood is excellent? Who wants to live with an ignoble character, an unfaithful partner, or one who feels inferior and without joy in living? What kind of a society will we have if men are belittled and debased?

Each woman is free to make a heaven of her home, to create an atmosphere where those who live there can become all that they are capable of becoming. To be able to do this, she must have faith, wisdom, know herself, be self-actualized, and be in partnership with her Creator.

One might ask, "What about her happiness?" Certainly it is realized in the fulfillment of each member of the family and in being capable enough and loving enough to be able to respond to the needs of her mate and children. This takes true liberation, for she must have freed herself from selfish considerations and developed herself so that she has the skills, capacities, abilities, and attitude to bring out the aliveness and completeness of her husband and children.

How abused are those "libbers" who never know the joy of being committed to make their mates happy the rest of their lives. They do not know the satisfaction that comes from "forsaking all others," keeping alive the romance of one alone, and always having the assurance that she is first in the life of the most important person in the world for her. *That* is true liberation of mind, heart, and spirit.

Dr. Calderwood, a nationally known marriage counselor, when asked about marriage as a base for family life, said that marriage had failed and therefore new modes of living should be explored. Marriage failed? It is not marriage that has failed, but the men and women involved, those who for various reasons have not understood the true meaning of the union of a man and his wife. Of course it will fail if it is a casual, permissive experiment, if in the name of liberation, it is demeaned and considered inconsequential as a base for family life.

Natalie Shainess writes that "What is happening today is that more men and women are engaging frantically in what I call pseudosex. It's not real for either of them, and involves all kinds of indirect modes of expression instead of the authentic..."

The celebrated women's lib is fighting for equality for women. But too often the equality means descending to the level of the lowest man. What good is equality if we all become equally rotten? It is only as we insist that it is desirable to lift and ennoble all human beings, bringing out the finest in each, that equality has meaning.

Instead, we hear many libbers demanding sexual "freedom," the pill, and abortion. The rhetoric is that each woman is mistress of her own body. It is because she is mistress of her own body, and soul, that she can determine who her mate will be, the time and the place of their union, and the consequences of their mating.

Our bodies are magnificent gifts of God. The scriptures tell us that our bodies are the temples of God and that His spirit dwells within them. Why debase that which is holy and deny our magnificent stewardship?

How tragic for our youth that freedom is mistaken for licentiousness. We read in Corinthians: "Now the Lord is that Spirit: and where the Spirit of the Lord is, there is liberty." (2 Cor. 3:17) Paul writes that man is not without the woman in the Lord and woman is not without the man in the Lord. For total fulfillment, the Lord must be included. Are we free, are we liberated, do we have the Spirit of the Lord to direct us? There cannot be the ultimate in marriage without including the Lord.

Why should there be the current "hang-up" about a marriage certificate? One is supposed to be liberated when she doesn't have to depend upon a "scrap of paper" to determine the legality. But if the Lord has been taken into the partnership, the couple longs for the marriage altar where they can pledge their troth before God and all the witnesses. They want to dignify the relationship in every possible way, to shout to the world their choice and their promise. They realize the grandeur of marriage lies in the commitment of two people to make each other happy the rest of their lives. The stronger the vows, the stricter the requirements, the greater the partnership with God. We have the opportunity to pledge before God in His holy temple to live His laws so that this relationship can be ours throughout eternity! It is inconceivable that such a magnificent opportunity for life and forever would not involve great discipline and absolute commitment. Such a relationship requires all the judgment, understanding, guidance, love and total commitment that one has.

The woman's role in a temple marriage is one of full partnership. She is to fulfill her sweetheart's manhood—and her womanhood is to be fulfilled by him. Exaltation, the ultimate goal, is impossible for either man or woman without the other.

I stated earlier that private morals do affect public morality. It is unrealistic to believe that in the name of liberation we are free to "do our own thing." No one is an island. Whatever each person does affects not only her own life, but that of her family, her friends, her community, church, and eventually her nation. Women always have been the basic source of self-esteem for the nation. Their warmth, understanding, sensitivity, and tact have "lubricated the rise of man and nations." Therefore, it is vital that we understand the essential role we, as women, have.

This was illustrated in a conversation I had recently with a General in the United States Army who had returned recently from Vietnam. As a career officer, he had observed the conduct and morale of enlisted men since the beginning of World War II: The life of a soldier on the battlefield is essentially demoralizing. His body is encrusted with sweat and grime, his rations unappetizing, the language of his companions often rough and obscene. His strength at times is driven almost beyond endurance, he suffers with inactivity and boredom at other times. Always the possibility of instant death or being maimed is upon his consciousness. The general observed that the GI's at such times needed something outside themselves to give them the courage and hope that would sustain them. In former decades, he noted, this had been provided by their sweethearts and wives at home through their letters, their faith in them, their fidelity and goodness. But recently, he observed, things had changed. They no longer believed in the goodness and fidelity of their sweethearts or wives. Therefore, the soldiers

302

sink deeper and deeper into moral quagmire. Do we understand, as sweethearts and wives, the power we have to either enrich life or to debase mankind?

Those who engage in fornication and adultery are called "swingers" today and we are told that their conduct is acceptable because it is so prevalent. Is prevalence the criteria? There is more murder and rape than ever before. Does that make those crimes less reprehensible or are we just sicker? What really is at stake is the quality of life in America and her future as a great force for good in the world.

Because the term "quality of life" is discussed in so many contexts today—denoting population-control, ecology, and pollution of our air, land and water—I think the definition given by Neil Armstrong is clarifying. When he was asked whether technology improves the quality of life in America, he replied: "Technology doesn't improve the quality of life; it improves the quality of things. Things can improve the convenience of living, the experience of living (TV, spaceships, etc.) and even the duration of living (vitamins, X-ray). Things can also degrade the environment of our living and reverse the fact of our living (guns and bombs). Improving the things that surround living can be achieved by the application of knowledge. Improving the quality of life, however, requires the application of wisdom."

It is in the application of wisdom that I believe we as Latter-day Saint women can make an impact for good in today's society. We are liberated completely to do the job. We are fortified not only with ancient revelation, but with modern revelation as well. How we use that freedom and knowledge becomes the crucial test. Many experts in our society are turning to science and the opinions of men instead of applying the injunction of the holy scriptures where wisdom is to be found.

Man's happiness and the glorification of the human race is at stake. Those who believe infidelity brings "liberation" and happiness should read the famous Cuber report on marriage. The Cubers made an intensive study of upper middle class married couples, those who were considered successful people. The Cubers reported that three-fourths of the marriages were regarded as merely "utilitarian" by the marriage partners who were interviewed. This was defined as marriage without deep commitment to one another, marriages which more frequently than not included other partners, and were therefore hypocritical. Such couples reported that they were unfulfilled, apathetic, despondent, and without joy. They looked forward to escape from their marriage relationship—they remained together only for utilitarian purposes. One of the typical unfaithful partners was quoted as saying, "When I think of us and the numb way we sort of stagger through the weekly routine, I could scream."

One-fourth of the couples studied had "total" marriages. The contrast between their marriages and those of the utilitarian group was dramatic. The Cubers noted, "The vital and total marriage brings exciting mutuality of feeling to the partners." Said one husband with a vital marriage, "The things we do together aren't fun intrinsically. The ecstasy comes from being together in the doing." Another husband said, "My wife and I are really pretty square—and we like it this way. I doubt that either of us could live any other way—that means respect for the God-given rules, but they don't seem like rules. They've stood us in good stead for over 30 years now, and we aren't fixing to thumb our noses at so bountiful a blessing."

The study further reported that "Affection and love remain warm and powerful in these marriages...sex, too, seems to remain deeply satisfying and profoundly exciting. The total marriage is the mutual sharing of a vital marriage extended into practically every area of life: leisure, homelife, career, problems, day to day accomplishments and almost all thoughts and moods. The devitalized or passive marriage, with its relative freedom and individualism seems to the partners of a total marriage, hardly like a marriage at all."

After depicting adultery, divorce and promiscuity among the upper middle class as prevalent in utilitarian marriages, but not in the total marriages, the report concluded on this note: "Thus we can make the decision to emulate the unfaithful or reject them on a more rational basis than has been possible before."

One life is all we have. Isn't it worth any discipline, and any effort to experience a "total" marriage? Regardless of what some libbers would have us believe, there is no fulfillment or joy unless things are right within the core of an individual, the core of a marriage.

If you include God at the marriage altar and thereafter—if your life becomes an overflowing of your love, your talents, your strength and your aliveness, you will find true liberation: freedom to develop all that is within you while at the same time, filling the cup of your mate.

God has said that "man is that he might have joy." Such a magnificent blessing is predicated upon law. We can't replace God's laws for man's—we cannot annul His judgments and still reap His blessings. True liberation is attained when our knowledge is in order and this requires the application of wisdom.

If men pull up eternal verities by the roots they have only the philosophies of men. In Romans 1:24-25 we read; "Wherefore God also gave them up to uncleanness through the lusts of their own hearts, to dishonor their own bodies between themselves: who changed the truth of God into a lie, and worshipped and served the creature more than the Creator..."

With life as complicated as it is today, and things about us in such turmoil, with the roar of changing mores in our ears, it is imperative that we have "hitching posts," sound moorings, for ourselves and for our children. Our period has been described in the scriptures, where we are told that men will be "lovers of their own flesh, disobedient to parents, breakers of treaties, despising dignities that they know not of." (see 2 Tim. 3:2-3) With all of this upon us, life is more challenging and frustrating in many areas than even before, but it can be more magnificently rewarding. This is possible because in our age each one of us can stand out like a light upon a hill—a beacon light. Each one of us can make a significant contribution to our generation as wives and mothers by preserving and intensifying the light that is in our dwellings!

Woman's Role as a Mother

Of course, children are the ultimate fulfillment of love in a fruitful marriage. Woman's role as a mother has been glorified universally in other generations, but today the importance of rearing her own children is being questioned and denigrated. It seems incredible, but some libbers have even said that they resent having uteruses! Resent their own miraculous ability to conceive and bear

305

offspring! And many believe that their own personal development is impaired if they are required to stay at home to raise their babies.

Personal development and a self-esteem are very important. In fact, they are vital if a woman is to be able to realize the full measure of her creation and thus rear her children successfully. Her role as a mother gives her the fantastic opportunity not only to educate and motivate her children, but also to determine the whole atmosphere of living for those dearest and most important to her. The qualities and background necessary do not come automatically, but because women train for their professions and careers, and erroneously believe that motherhood requires no special skills or training, they misunderstand its creative demands.

I remember how impressed I was by a speech given by Adam S. Bennion at a Devotional when I was in high school. He began by speaking to the girls directly, telling us how important our appearance was. He said that it was our "duty" to be as lovely as possible physically and that our appearance had an immeasurable affect on society as a whole. Then he stressed how important it was for each of us to fill ourselves to the brim with knowledge, and he voiced the same thought that was recently enunciated by the Dean of Women at Smith College: "When you educate a man, you educate a person, but when you educate a woman, you educate a family." He said the doors to every discipline were open to us if we would but knock—the doors to religion, science, literature, music, biography, history—all were there for our enrichment.

He projected us into our motherhood and made it obvious to us that for the most demanding role of all, we should be complete individuals, secure in our own personality development, our knowledge, and our self-esteem which would intensify with the aura of learning.

Then I thought of my own mother. Even household tasks were made productive and pleasant because of her own capacities and her love of learning. She reviewed new words for her vocabulary while she was ironing and read Shakespeare to us while we did the dishes. Oh, we grumbled, but we learned to love Shakespeare. She sang joyously while she polished or scrubbed floors, baked pies and kneaded bread, and her four daughters automatically sang with her as we helped. Her love of life was contagious.

Today it is even easier to create beauty while doing mundane chores. There is the stereo with grand opera, symphonies, and drama; there are tapes made from powerful experiences of past presidents of our Church, as well as of our current Church leaders and their magnificent testimonies; there are abundant reproductions of art masterpieces in book form to be opened on our tables. In innumerable ways, there are opportunities to expand and enlarge the experience of living with beauty.

I know a young mother who plays the violin magnificently. Before putting her baby daughter to bed each evening, she played her favorite concerto for her. This she has done from the day she brought her babe home from the hospital. Now at age three, the little girl goes into raptures when she hears that music. Wherever she is, when she hears any classical music, she crouches down beside the stereo in ecstasy. She has been awakened to beauty that will enrich her throughout her life.

The atmosphere in a home is absorbed by osmosis from the time a child is born. Associations and mental pictures are part of the warp and woof of the final pattern for one's personality.

We hear mothers say that they do not wish to give their children their own set of values. They want the children to determine for themselves what they believe and how they wish to live. This is impossible because a vacuum left by the mother only leaves the child open to what she sees on television, at school, or on the street. Someone will be teaching your child—why abdicate?

Maybe the reason so many are talking about the dull and unfulfilling role of being a mother is because they have abdicated their responsibilities. Educators have found that children are most unruly when they do not know how to cope. Maybe women today have become incapable in their own minds of dealing with the complexities of being a wife and mother and thus demonstrate against their role. Maybe because motherhood is so demanding they "give up" rather than admit their incapabilities. Maybe that is why they are screaming about liberation. They want to be free from a task they feel incapable of fulfilling.

Educators report that they have to spend at least 50 percent of their time on discipline problems. This was unheard of in earlier periods. Now windows are broken and school buildings

307

defaced to such an extent that often the authorities don't even try to find the culprits! The job, they say, is too large. They, too, have given up.

Moral conduct and sex education are left up to the schools. Good grief, are men and women in the schools better prepared to teach your children than the men and women who are their parents in their homes? Some religious sects show lewd films in Sunday School to twelve year olds to "prepare" them for something. Why? What good will this do children—or anyone else? Their misguided concept is that if one knows enough about technical terms and techniques he will know how to relate in a meaningful way to life's experiences and relationships!

But if the mother believes it is more important for her to be out of the home than in it and her child has no direction there, who is responsible? The government? And who is the government? Often those in governmental jobs are the very ones who are escaping their responsibilities at home by getting jobs elsewhere.

In many instances, "liberation" means the right to turn over to some agency or anyone the responsibilities that are rightfully hers. And who suffers? All of us—because our children are left without direction, values, discipline, and nourishment.

Wherever I travel in the world, the one question that is universally asked is, "How are the children in America turning out? Can you still produce leaves, flowers and fruit? Do you have the roots you had in other generations to do this? Or are you now a cut-flower civilization living on past accomplishments and past values and principles?

We, as Latter-day Saint women know our vocation—know that the blessing given Abraham is ours. Our seed is indeed to be a blessing to all mankind. We are liberated for the greatest of all tasks.

We now have documented proof that the first five years of a child's life determine in large measure his personality, intellectual, and emotional capabilities. It has also been established that the babe learns much faster and to a greater degree from his mother than from anyone else. Thus we, as mothers, are free to shape the future of our civilization! What other role is more powerful or important? Yet we are told by many that this, our opportunity to glorify God by teaching and guiding His children, should be doled out to others so that we may be "free" to become fulfilled. As American mothers, we don't realize the freedom that is ours to enlarge our calling.

Consider the women in Red China who are supposedly liberated. Not only are they free to shovel the snow and clean the streets, but they are obliged to do so as reported by Barbara Walters after her visit there with President Nixon. She also reported that the Red Chinese mothers have to place their babes soon after they are born in nurseries or Day Care Centers so that they may be free to work at tasks assigned by the government. Can you imagine their longing to be able to rear their own babes? Let us, as American women, not be duped into believing that "liberation" means turning over to others the most important and wonderful of all responsibilities. This is our message as Latter-day Saint mothers.

Of course, I know it is necessary for some mothers who have small children to work outside their homes and that Day Care Centers are necessary for them. But let us understand their problem, not glorify it.

We can help other mothers understand how erroneous it is to believe that they must entrust their toddlers to others who are regarded as experts in child-care. We can help them understand how necessary it is for us to be experts ourselves—to be specialists in the truth so that all the child absorbs will be beneficial. Always the important principle to keep before us is that the babe has greater rapport with his own mother than with anyone else on earth and can learn and absorb much more at home with his own mother than with the most learned experts.

Although a mother doesn't "create" the child, she has an opportunity to nourish the seeds within him so that they may grow to true greatness. What mother would knowingly relinquish this opportunity in order to accept a position where she could help shape policy in a financial enterprise?

I do not want to imply that there are no heartaches or frustrations in rearing a family. I know that meeting the problems as they arise day by day takes tremendous inner stamina, love, faith, intellectual and emotional resources as well as patience and resolution. These, together with the demands of daily living, require

309

character and discipline beyond that of any other career on earth.

To bring to one's own babe the affirmation of God—that is the greatest privilege of all! To see in him the imprint of God and to know that you can help him to quicken to the divinity within him—that is the greatest blessing!

Robert Raynolds writes in *The Choice to Love* that each person is born into three rivers of life; one is represented by the biological chain of being, another is the increasing heritage of practical information, and a third is the spiritual river of life. The spiritual river is the warm and radiant flowing of love. He writes, "What we love in one another is not the fierce drive to biological survival and is not the cool accumulation of science; what we love in one another is the presence of God, manifest in whole trust. The first and most profound devotion of a woman's life is to listen to God, and then she may humbly tell her children and her children's children what she has heard."

This my mother did for me—she listened to God and she prayed with me in a way that made me know of her devotion to and dependence upon Him. Her every prayer was ended with the words, "Little girls, love one another." We were four sisters and, as we were growing up, we quarreled and pulled hair like other youngsters, but ingrained within us was her prayer for love. Its strength has always been beyond calculation, the love mother pryaed for was universal as well as personal in scope. We know now it was meant that we were to love all little girls and big ones, girls and boys, men and women, all of God's children.

Who would question the fact that there is no satisfaction greater than having good sons and daughters? I remember how I quietly wept as I read a letter from my son who was on a mission in which he wrote, "I always knew I loved my family and friends, but now at last I have learned that I love everyone." And, again, "I know that I want to devote my life to righteousness."

We must let others know how joyous it is to be a mother!

Accepting Responsibilities in the Community

Finally, we should consider our role as citizens of this great land. Earlier I referred to the critical condition prevailing in our country, with our gravest problems relating to the social, human, and moral issues. The need for the involvement of LDS women in a meaningful way has never been more vital. We urgently need the voices of those who can refute the philosophy that is tearing us apart: that there is no such thing as unchanging, universal concepts of goodness and justice—that these values are all fluctuating and inconstant.

Unfortunately, at a time when women can and must make an important contribution as citizens, some women's groups are in the ludicrous and untenable position of feeling that they must hit men head-on to prove their adequacy and equality. Thus they become small facsimiles of men instead of magnificent figures of women. Some even feel that by being profane and boisterous they prove equality. It was sad to hear a prominent woman politician state publicly that she could use four-letter words as effectively as any man. What good does that do her or anyone else? Again, it is only when equality means lifting and ennobling society that it has relevance.

I regret the fact that equal wages for equal work was not granted as a principle of fairness decades ago—it is a shame that women are having to use their talents and energies for that battle now when their strengths should be concentrated on ways to increase justice, ensure liberty, equality of opportunity, brotherhood and quality of life as national goals.

We all recognize the need for both fathers and mothers in the home. In our nation, our collective home, it should be obvious that both men and women with all their talents and insights are needed.

For instance, I believe had there been more women in Congress the present welfare act would never have been approved. Women know why fathers and husbands should not be equated with a meal ticket and that children are left spiritually and emotionally disinherited if there is no father in the home. Yet present welfare regulations actually encourage men to leave their families because a woman receives greater welfare benefits if the father is not in the home. The regulations concerning benefits for ADC mothers often encourage illegitimacy.

It was because of my overwhelming concern in the social areas that I became a candidate for the United States Senate in 1970. Although I was unsuccessful, I hope that my efforts helped many women become more convinced that their understanding and active participation as citizens is imperative. It gave me great

311

strength to have my husband and children support me actively and enthusiastically. It was inspirational that when I sought counsel and advice from some of the magnificent leaders of our Church, I was encouraged to seek political office, encouraged to try to communicate the need for integrity and private and public moral accountability to underlie the current issues.

As Latter-day Saint women, we recognize the fact that we cannot leave the great problems of our day to those who do not understand, as we also recognize that America is not just another country, but that it has a profound destiny. We have a life-and-death stake in the government of our country and in preserving our constitution.

The late Rabbi Morris Adler wrote,

> Only once in several centuries is a nation singled out by history to serve as a decisive factor in lifting all mankind to a new level of understanding, of policy, or act. . . When a nation finds itself in so severely challenging and critical position it cannot improvise. . . It is ours to find the guidance and determination we need. We must rediscover that which is truest and best in the American dream and thus bring to the surface that which is truest and best in ourselves.

This is the core of our citizenship.

In conclusion, I believe that we as Latter-day Saint women would all agree with Dr. Daniel Moyniham of Harvard University, who said that the crisis of our time is not political, it is in essence religious. If our democracy is to be stable, we must realize that government cannot provide values or meaning of life—government cannot cope with the crisis in values which is sweeping the western world.

We are living at a time when women are free to be educated in the finest universities in the land, free to use the ballot and to be accepted in the halls of science and government. But if women do not understand their role in undergirding the nation with the eternal principles, with a philosophy of life and a framework of values to live by—values that are dependent upon divine authority and not the changing philosophies of men—then the world will never forgive us. It will not be remembered how many women held various posts, but how our children turn out. Whether they are a blessing

312

or a cursing to all mankind will be forever to our glory or to our shame.

The greatest meaning in life is to be summoned by God; that is the supreme dignity of an individual. We know that the supreme joy is to answer that summons, to have the courage to harness all of one's energies even to the last breath of one's life, to answer the appeal of God. As teenagers, wives, mothers, and concerned citizens, our true liberation is to answer the summons and to promote truth, goodness, and beauty with abiding love.

With the challenge of such enormous magnitude, we dare not make a weak response—a great challenge will receive a magnificent response, because we can do no less—and that is the joy of being a Latter-day Saint woman.

INTRODUCING—LEONE W. DOXEY

When we read Leone's chapter, we were so touched by it we commented, "This one is extra special—we'll save it for last." It carries a particularly sweet flavor and conveys the feeling of love which emanates from her.

Duane first met Leone several years ago when he was asked to teach a year-long course to a woman's group to which she belonged. Even at that time he was impressed with her comments as she responded to questions and statements in the group's discussions. She is precise, accurate, has a good knowledge of the gospel, and accomplishes the projects she undertakes.

She is the wife of Graham H. Doxey, now deceased, who was the manager of Zion Securities Corporation, the real estate control for the Church. They are the parents of four children, all of whom are married and have children of their own. In 1943, Graham was called to preside over the East Central States Mission and Leone assisted him in that assignment.

A call came to her in 1953 to serve on the Primary General Board. A few months later she was called to be Second Counselor to President LaVern W. Parmley. In April, 1962, Leone was set apart as First Counselor in the General Presidency of the Primary Association, which position she held until October, 1969. In these years she was influential in shaping the training and the lives of many thousands of the youth of the Church. During this period she was privileged to visit most of the stakes and missions within the Church: the British Isles, Europe, South America, New Zealand, Australia, Tahiti, Hawaii, Central America, Canada, Japan, Hong Kong, Thailand, and throughout the United States. Her husband accompanied her on all the long trips for the Primary.

Among her many talents, Leone is a poet—the verses found in her chapter are materials she herself wrote. We feel she radiates so very well the many joys of being a woman and appreciate her testimony that "the best is yet to come."   JDC & DSC

314

THE BEST IS YET TO COME
by
Leone W. Doxey

To eighteen grandchildren and two little great-grandsons I am "Grandma." To twelve other grandchildren, I am "Bunkin." Confusing? Not at all. Fifteen years ago at Halloween time we had a pumpkin, a jack-o-lantern, placed on top of a stepladder that was draped in a white sheet in our front entrance way. David, eighteen months old, evidently was impressed with the word "pumpkin" for he started calling me "Bunkin" and I am still Bunkin to him and his younger brothers and sisters and to five of their cousins. The children in our other families already were calling me "Grandma" and so they and their younger brothers and sisters have always called me "Grandma."

What's in a name? Sometimes name calling can make a greater difference in family relationships. How wonderful it is when our sons-in-law and our daughters-in-law affectionately call us "Mom" or something else as endearing instead of waiting until their first child is born and then call us "Grandma" forever after. How soul-satisfying it is when our own sons and daughters lovingly continue to call us "Mother" instead of "Grandma."

Shakespeare said, "What's in a name? That which we call a rose by any other name would smell as sweet." So it should be with us as mothers and grandmothers. We need to be sweet no matter what title is given to us. Of course, it is easier to be sweet when the title pleases us.

The Gift and Responsibility of Influence

As grandmothers we need to be sweet and kind in every situation. That is not always easy! It takes self-control and supreme effort to refrain from taking over when we know the answers and we think the voice of experience should be heard. Sometimes we are put to the test in our own homes and sometimes in the homes of our loved ones. I do mean loved ones because the same situation in the homes of friends or acquaintances does not bother us be-

315

cause we have no responsibility there. In the homes of loved ones we are responsible for some of the feelings and attitudes of our grandchildren. Whether we realize it or not, we bear the gift and responsibility of influence.

As grandmothers we need to accept each child as he or she is. Each is precious to us and to lose one through rejection would be tragic. We may not approve of some of the actions of grandchildren but each child needs to know that he is loved and that we accept him. We cannot change another person. The only person we can change is our own self. However, in our changing, others may be motivated to change.

Ever since I read *Spiritual Roots of Human Relations,* by Stephen R. Covey, I have been putting this to the test. I have found it to be true in my own experiences. For instance, when I was invited to dinner one Sunday, sitting at the table, one of our young grandchildren told her mother she needed a spoon and asked her to get one for her. My reaction was one of judgment, thinking "You lazy child;" one of criticism, "You ought to get the spoon yourself;" one of accusation, "You let your mother wait on you you should wait on her. She has so much to do you should be ashamed of yourself." None of these expressions would have helped. They would only have done harm. Irrespective of the validity of my first reactions, if expressed they would have been received as being unkind. To maximize this influence for good, grandmothers must always be kind.

I experienced another valuable lesson that day. At that moment I kept silent, but I fear my attitude radiated resentment and the child could feel it. Children, as well as adults, are sensitive to attitudes and can detect true feelings. I knew I had to change my attitude before she would change hers. I tried hard to pay more attention to her, to be more tolerant, to give her more consideration, to try to know her better, to understand her feelings and moods. It was worth the effort for it resulted in better communication between us. No one can fight kindness.

Teaching Grandchildren

The youngest child in each of our families seems to demand and get more attention. This can be annoying and frustrating. When I visit in their homes, these youngest ones seem to command

316

the center of the stage and to monopolize the conversation. They prevent any conversation that is not to their liking by interrupting constantly. I know it is not my place to correct them but it is my responsibility to help them when I have an opportunity.

I have the opportunity as a grandmother to be a teacher and I must be ready to teach when the time and circumstance seems right. I must take every advantage to teach with kindness whether it be in their homes or in mine. There are ways I can help them to appreciate and be considerate of others in their family relationships.

Grandmothers can teach and provide fun by telling their grand-children what they did when they were younger. A grandmother can recall some lovely thing each child has done, something praise-worthy the children have accomplished. Children never tire of hearing stories, especially about themselves. Children love to hear about family traditions and relationships. Any day can be Grandmothers Day if she has a mind to make it so. Her teaching can be meaningful and effective. Storytelling is an excellent way of teaching.

Listening Attentively

What a joy it is for us grandmothers to have our teenagers come to talk with us. In order to bridge the generation gap (a gap of two generations) I know I must give my full time and my rapt attention. I must forget myself momentarily and give myself completely. I must listen attentively and not be waiting to get my own words in. I must just listen. When I let our teen-agers do the talking and I encourage them to continue with their ideas and opinions, I have a better understanding of their feeling. There are times when I disagree and am even frightened by some of their values; their words and ideas are sometimes unreasonable and unacceptable to me. But I must not panic, no matter how serious the problem is. I try desperately not to accuse or criticize but just let them talk it out. They know me by my heart without me saying anything. They know what I think and what I believe. They also know of my love for them for I take every occasion to tell them individually.

I realize that sometimes they are talking only to relieve pent-up emotions, but other times I realize they are confused and bewildered—they are asking for direction. Only when I have allowed them to express themselves without my upbraiding, denouncing, or rejecting them or their views are they able to listen to me. Most

317

often they already know how I feel on a subject and of my point of view. It is at the time that specific advice is needed that I pray fervently for wisdom, inspiration and guidance. I pray that they may know that I accept them even though I may not accept some of their thoughts and actions. I pray that I will radiate the glorious gospel of Christ and I reverently ask that they may have the Lord's Spirit. I try to flood my heart full of understanding and love for them even though they may have done wrong in the situation. I know that the Lord's Spirit comes only through love, and it is only through His Spirit that our communication can be effective and problems can be solved.

Giving Love

People need love. Grandmothers certainly have this need. They need love and there is only one way for them to get it. They must first give love. Even grandmothers cannot say to the stove, "Give me warmth and I will give you wood."

You may think you've given enough love away
It's time to store for your own rainy day
That others, in turn, should give love to you.
It's the only right and fair thing to do.

But you can't store love—it withers and dies,
It's not like food stored by the provident and wise.
Perishable love must be given away,
Only shared does it multiply day after day.

Love can grow and replenish its own seeds.
Love is basically what everyone needs
And only when we give and give and give
Will we know love throughout the days we live.

Avoiding Self-pity

My children and grandchildren are busy, sometimes so busy I could feel left out and neglected. But I cannot afford to feel sorry for myself. Self-pity is a luxury no one can afford, especially grandmothers. I realize that when the children or grandchildren might have included me and did not, that it was not intentional nor deliberate. Sometimes they cannot even find me. I have a busy life, too, and I am humbly grateful for it—I know that an idle mind is the devil's workshop. A grandmother who lives in the past, preoccupied with the obsession that there is no future for her, can make life unpleasant for herself and for all who are nearby.

When my husband passed away nearly three years ago, it was difficult for me to force myself to go out with people. It was easier to stay at home. It was not as lonely at home as it was to be in groups with friends with whom we had associated together. I am thankful for a kind, wise friend who said to me, "You can stay home and feel sorry for yourself and your friends will feel sorry for you. But your friends will let you stay at home and feel sorry for yourself if that is what you want to do." Of course, that was not what I wanted to do and I found that each time I made myself go out it became easier and less lonely.

The worst part of my self-pity was that I lost that marvelous peace, the comfort that seemed to envelop and sustain me. Whenever I felt sorry for myself and questioned, "Why?" or wished for life as it had been, the Lord could not bless me. I had to start recalling the blessings of the gospel I knew were mine. When my heart was filled with gratitude, then that peace "which passeth all understanding" returned to me. I had to forget myself and lose my life in service to the Lord in order to find life. The Savior has said, "For whosoever will save his life shall lose it: and whosoever will lose his life for my sake shall find it." (Mt. 16:25)

Maintaining Cheerfulness

Grandmothers need friends as well as family. Therefore, as grandmothers we need to be cheerful and pleasant—that is a must. No one wants to be near a person who reflects sadness and gloom.

"How are you?" is the greeting you hear everywhere
As people seem anxious about your welfare.
"Just fine," is the answer expected from you
Although it may be far, very far, from true.
They don't want to hear that you feel ill today.
They hope your response will be happy and gay.

So forget your pains and conceal any ache
You can say, "I'm fine, thank you," for their own sake.
Everyone needs cheer and joy along life's highway;
You can help another with your bright "Good day."

319

Adjusting to New Family Relationships

We resist change because we usually like things the way they are. Any change in the family, especially a marriage, requires adjustment.

We did not want to push our children out of the nest—we enjoyed them there. But when they were ready to leave we gave serious consideration to what our roles and theirs would be. They had to try their own wings, soar on their own. They had to make their own decisions.

We would stand on the sidelines and cheer.
(But never, never interfere.)

Our home would be open—the welcome mat out.
(When they failed to come, we'd not pout.)

There were in-laws now with whom we had to share.
(We'd let them decide what was fair.)

There were holidays, only part of which we might claim.
We accepted all this—but—our heart-strings tugged
Just the same.

The answer we found was to get close to the members of the families that were also our children's families now. The more we associated with them the better our understanding was and our appreciation for them. We found it became easy and natural to love and enjoy each one.

Meeting Responsibilities

Being a grandmother came to me only a few short years after I had resigned myself to the fact that there would be no more babies of my own. I still longed for another child, so becoming a grandmother was an exciting and glorious experience. At last there was a baby, a baby to cuddle, to hold, and to cherish—our very own grandchild—a beautiful little granddaughter, Becky Leone. It was wonderful but not quite the same as having a baby of my own. A grandmother is something like a "mother once removed;" just as there is a relationship referred to as "first cousin once removed." Our daughter had her own ideas about baby care—new ideas, a generation newer than mine. That baby did very well and we were proud of her and her parents.

320

When little Becky was two years old, her family moved about two hundred fifty miles away and we missed them. We kept in touch. We called and we visited them and they visited us. However, we never invited our daughter to visit without her husband. "What God hath joined together, let no man put asunder." Our daughter and her husband were now "one flesh" and we wanted to do all in our power to help keep it that way.

As our other children were married and we were blessed with more grandchildren, our children sometimes asked us for suggestions and advice, which we freely gave. Our advice was not always used, and that is as it should be. We had had the opportunity to teach and rear our own children as we thought best. Now these young parents were entitled to that same privilege.

Through the years, our children have come to welcome our counsel, our concern and our love, especially our love. We tried to show love in every way we could. We made it a point to be present at all significant occasions.

We have been privileged to be present when our grandsons have been ordained to the Aaronic Priesthood and when they have been advanced in that priesthood. It was our joy to go to the Temple with Becky, our first grandchild, when she received her endowments and was married to a worthy holder of the Melchizedek Priesthood.

I am grateful for these rich, spiritual experiences I shared with my husband. Now he is no longer here to share them with me, except in spirit; but I know he still does share these experiences for I feel him close.

A widow must do double duty, so I continue to make every effort possible to be where I know the head of our family would want me to be. I have attended the blessing of another grandchild and the blessings of each of our little great-grandsons. I attended the three meetings in which our grandchildren were honored before leaving on their missions and the meetings when our granddaughter spoke upon her return from her mission field. I hope to attend and hear the reports of her brothers when they return from their missions. As these young people have gone to the Temple to receive their endowments, I have been privileged to be with them in that holy house, rejoicing with their parents.

321

I try to get to every Court of Honor when our grandsons are being advanced in Scouting: five of them are Eagle Scouts. It is a thrill to attend the grandchildren's advancements from Junior High School, graduations from High School, and their college commencments.

Bringing Presents

Whenever my husband and I returned from a trip, our grandchildren, especially the young ones, looked forward to receiving presents. That was not too hard on us as grandparents when there were just a few grandchildren, but as the number increased we found it difficult to shop for so many and too time consuming. So instead of a gift for each child we brought gifts to keep in our home which all the grandchildren could share. Instead of a little trinket for each child that might have become broken, lost or forgotten, the value and the fun of the shared gifts have lasted through many years and traditions have been established.

There are wooden puzzles, quite a few. After we found out how much the children liked them, we added a new puzzle each trip. There are animals to play with, farm animals in one set and zoo animals in another. There are games for the older children, which the cousins enjoy together. There are cars and trucks for boys and dolls for girls. One special doll with a wardrobe of lovely clothes is reserved for the girls to play with when they are eight years old, after they have been baptized.

Our grandchildren have enjoyed their library in our home. We had some special bookshelves reserved for books they could choose, take to their own homes, read, and then return to the "library." In that way we could afford to provide more books, good literature, for more children to read.

The children have found that taking turns with cousins reading the same books is fun. There are discussions and more interest is generated when others are sharing and participating in the same experiences, real or fiction.

Happy children are a joy to have around. I like them to feel free and comfortable in our home. There are some rules and restrictions which they must keep but there are accidents which happen anyway. When this happens I want the one who is responsible for it to own up to it, not run away and hide or deny it. If a

322

child breaks something I prize, and this has happened, I want that child to come to me and tell me how it happened. We will both be sorry about the accident but I will love him or her just the same. I will be proud that he is honest and brave. His courage and demonstration of fine character are more important to me than any treasured vase or figurine could ever be and I want to be sure every grandchild realizes this. There is nothing as precious as he or she is.

Experiencing Faith

When my husband became ill he had excruciating headaches. He said he had never experienced such pain. It was unbearable. The doctors told me it would get worse, it could not get better. They gave him powerful drugs which did very little to relieve the agony. Our sons administered to their father, which was comforting but still his suffering continued. On Father's Day all the children and grandchildren came to call but he was in bed and, although he was delighted to see them, he was too ill to enjoy them. Our children decided they would fast the next day, which they did. Our children, our grandchildren and our extended families through marriage all fasted.

Our children and grandchildren came to our home at six-thirty the next evening and we assembled in our living room for prayer. Our eldest son, Graham W., took charge. He called on his next younger brother, David, to offer prayer. Their father came and knelt with us. We knelt around a low round table in the center of the room and the circle extended into rings of many circles. David said that he had not thought beforehand of saying the words he did but as we were praying he was impressed to pray that the headache would leave his father's head immediately. At the close of the prayer his father arose from his knees and told all assembled that they had been part of a miracle. He said that as David prayed that it was as if something was peeled from his head, as one might peel an orange. The headache was gone. From that time on he never again had a headache. He was not made well; he passed away five months later. But during that time he had no ache or pain. We all will be eternally grateful that he was so kindly blessed that he could be comfortable and enjoy the visits of family and friends.

That evening the families had all planned to go to their own homes to break their fast. No one left. We continued to sit in the

323

living room, some of the children on the floor. First one person and then another expressed gratitude for the answer to our prayer—for that miracle. Each one told of some other spiritual experience that was sacred to him or to her. It was the most inspiring and glorious testimony meeting I ever hope to attend. To hear the three generations of our eternal family acknowledge their blessings and affirm their testimonies brought heaven very close.

If only each one of us will be able to endure to the end! As a grandmother, I am conscious of the fact that the forces of evil are so strong and determined it takes constant vigilance and effort to withstand the power and the subtle ways of the Destroyer.

Reaping Rewards

When Mary Lou calls and says, "Mom, are you too busy or could you take Lisa to her dancing lesson? I can't start the car," that really "pleasures" me. Little Sister begs to come along too and I get to visit with little sister, Lisa and the friend we pick up who is in the same class. It thrills me that Mary Lou calls me to help instead of a neighbor or someone else. It is rewarding to feel needed and to be able to help.

When I see Scott trudging along up the hill weighed down with his newspaper bag it is rewarding to see his eyes light up when I stop and to see his broad grin when I ask if I might help. He climbs in my car and I fold newspapers on the front seat. He runs back and forth with the papers as we drive around his route. We get close to each other in our communication.

There is a cedar chest that fits under our stairs in an area that is just right for a playhouse. The chest is one I used before I was married, my hope chest. I will have more to say about that cedar box. Now, it is filled with clothes little girls like to dress up in, out-of-style party dresses and such. It is rewarding to see a group of young cousins having fun trailing up and down the stairs in their pinned-to-fit finery.

When one little girl comes alone, it is fun for both of us when she invites me to play house with her.

Jewell and Roger have five darling little girls. When I visit in their home, the girls clamor to go home with me. Each one contends that it is her turn to "sleep over" with Bunkin.

My youngest great-grandson rewarded me with one of the

324

most touching compliments I have ever received. I was sitting by him at the dinner table. He is not quite two. Jennifer looked over at him and asked, "Who is that next to you, Stevie?" He put his arms around my neck and said, "Fwiend."

Grandmothers have special joys! Jim, our thirteen year old, rode over on his bicycle the other day. As he was ready to leave, I told him how glad I was to have him come. He smiled and said, "It's sure fun coming over."

Jim's mother, Joanne, has written the words and music to a song that is rewarding for any grandparent, anywhere:

Born of Goodly Parents

We, being born of goodly parents, and taught in ways of
    righteousness

Give gratitude for loving parents, whose goodly name we
    do possess.

For toil and care o'er us as children, for thoughtful watch
    o'er us as youth—

For silent guide in our decisions, for leading us in ways
    of truth.

Life has been blessed by goodly parents, to them we owe
    a debt that's due—

To guide and teach our own dear children, that we may
    be goodly parents, too.

Hope Chest

As I consider my old "Hope Chest," there may be a lesson that would be helpful. I remember my enthusiasm in preparing for marriage when I was a young girl waiting for my missionary.

As I acquired linens and special things for my future responsibilities, I put them in my cedar chest with great hope and faith and wonder. In the more recent days, as I once again look forward to a reunion with my beloved companion, I see this hope chest, now the plaything for my grandchildren. I reflect on the days long past, days which had been the object of my hope. Our life was ever so much better than I had imagined in my fondest dreams.

During these years of marriage I have been storing a new hope chest. Not a cedar box. But deep in my soul are treasures which are

325

the object of all my days and eternal future. The words "for time and all eternity"—the sealing of our posterity under the covenant.

Looking to the Future

For close work I look through the lower part of my bifocals. I see life close up. That magnifying part of my glasses tells me I am not as young as I used to be, the years are taking their toll.

When I lift my eyes I see through clear glass. I see distance, mountains and green pastures, the future. It takes a long range view to recognize that the best is yet to come.

The Lord has told us what the glorious prospects are if we will focus our attention and direct our vision, as we should. He has said:

> If your eye be single to my glory, your whole bodies
> shall be filled with light, and there shall be no darkness in
> you; and that body which is filled with light comprehendeth
> all things.   (D. & C. 88:67)

The challenge is to rid ourselves of darkness and become so filled with light we can comprehend where we came from, why we are here, and where we are going. The Saviour defined the way when he said: Seek ye first the kingdom of God, and his righteousness; and all these things shall be added unto you. (Mt. 6:33)

If we will serve the Lord first, that which will be for our good will be added unto us. The Lord knows what is best for us, for our children and for their children.

What comforting assurance it must have been to the Savior's disciples when he said, "These things I have spoken unto you, that in me ye might have peace. In the world ye shall have tribulation: but be of good cheer: I have overcome the world."

Because our Redeemer overcame the world, we have the assurance that we can have peace. No matter what adversity or affliction may come to us, or how old, or what enfeeblement may result in mortality, life ahead is a glorious prospect. The best is yet to come.

> Eye hath not seen, nor ear heard, neither have
> entered into the heart of man, the things which God
> hath prepared for them that love him.
>   (I Cor. 2:9)